Shakespeare's Guide to Hope, Life, and Learning

Shakespeare's GUIDE TO HOPE, LIFE, & LEARNING

LISA DICKSON
SHANNON MURRAY
JESSICA RIDDELL

UNIVERSITY OF TORONTO PRESS
Toronto Buffalo London

© University of Toronto Press 2023
Toronto Buff alo London
utorontopress.com

ISBN 978-1-4875-7052-1 (cloth)   ISBN 978-1-4875-7053-8 (EPUB)
ISBN 978-1-4875-7051-4 (paper)   ISBN 978-1-4875-7054-5 (PDF)

Library and Archives Canada Cataloguing in Publication

Title: Shakespeare's guide to hope, life, and learning / Lisa Dickson, Shannon Murray, and Jessica Riddell.
Other titles: Guide to hope, life, and learning.
Names: Dickson, Lisa, author. | Murray, Shannon, 1961–, author. | Riddell, Jessica, author.
Description: All authors have made contributions to each chapter and collectively written the Prologue and the Epilogue. | Includes bibliographical references and index.
Identifiers: Canadiana (print) 20220396051 | Canadiana (ebook) 20220396167 | ISBN 9781487570521 (cloth) | ISBN 9781487570514 (paper) | ISBN 9781487570538 (EPUB) | ISBN 9781487570545 (PDF)
Subjects: LCSH: Shakespeare, William, 1564–1616. King Lear. | LCSH: Shakespeare, William, 1564–1616. Hamlet. | LCSH: Shakespeare, William, 1564–1616. As You Like It. | LCSH: Shakespeare, William, 1564–1616. Henry V. | LCSH: Hope in literature. | LCSH: Life in literature. | LCSH: Learning and scholarship in literature.
Classification: LCC PR2976 .D53 2023 | DDC 822.3/3–dc23

We welcome comments and suggestions regarding any aspect of our publications – please feel free to contact us at news@utorontopress.com or visit us at utorontopress.com.

Every effort has been made to contact copyright holders; in the event of an error or omission, please notify the publisher.

We wish to acknowledge the land on which the University of Toronto Press operates. This land is the traditional territory of the Wendat, the Anishinaabeg, the Haudenosaunee, the Métis, and the Mississaugas of the Credit First Nation.

University of Toronto Press acknowledges the financial support of the Government of Canada and the Ontario Arts Council, an agency of the Government of Ontario, for its publishing activities.

Funded by the   Financé par le
Government   gouvernement
of Canada   du Canada

ONTARIO ARTS COUNCIL
CONSEIL DES ARTS DE L'ONTARIO
an Ontario government agency
un organisme du gouvernement de l'Ontario

To our students

Contents

Illustrations

All illustrations by Lisa Dickson

Acknowledgments

There are many people who have conspired to make this book possible.

Thank you to the 3M National Teaching Fellowship for putting us on a bus on that fateful day in Vancouver and for introducing us to a vibrant and supportive learning community. The Stephen A. Jarislowsky Foundation and the Stephen A. Jarislowsky Chair in Undergraduate Teaching Excellence made it possible for the three of us to connect in person in the following years as we worked to weave this text together; the Jarislowsky Foundation also provided funding for mentorship and student collaboration, and it has been a staunch supporter of the alignment between research and teaching in the humanities and in higher education across Canada and around the world. Heartfelt thanks to the Stratford Festival in Ontario, Canada, and all of the creatives there who welcome us, inspire us, educate us, and share our love of Shakespeare and the joyful, transformative power of theater. And deep thanks and gratitude to Natalie Fingerhut, our unbelievably patient editor at the University of Toronto Press, who not only took a chance on this wyrd project but urged us to go even further to find our voices and speak our hearts.

This project would not have been possible without the thoughtful contributions of our many student collaborators. Thank you to Kelsey Barendregt, Sally Cunningham, Conor Dever, Solomon Goudsward, and Rose Henbest for joining us in conversation and graciously allowing us to bring their words into our book. Very special thanks to our indispensable Wyrd Apprentice, Cécilia Alain, who, as our river guide and research assistant, navigated us around the snags and shoals of the technology, kept us organized, and helped to bring our website and podcast to the world, all with unwavering enthusiasm, proficiency, and good humor. This entire process would have been so much more difficult without her. We'd like to thank the Social Sciences and Humanities Research Council of Canada (SSHRC) for providing the funding for Cécilia's position. We'd like to thank Bishop's University and the Senate Research Committee for a publication grant and the University of Northern British Columbia for a publication grant.

Shannon: Thank you to the friend of my life, Gerald Wandio. I am so grateful for your patient ear and sharp eye through this project.

Jessica: My deepest gratitude goes to Team Riddell-Burns for creating a world in technicolor: my fiercely loyal and steadfast husband Rob Burns, my wickedly sharp and delightful daughter Sophie, my eternally joyful and generous son Henry, my (very Shakespearean!) twin brother – who was my first friend and favorite theater buddy – and to my parents, whose unconditional love and limitless belief in me made this all possible.

Lisa: Thank you to my partner and one true thing, Kevin Hutchings. And to Brent Carver for those three beats of breath that changed my life in Stratford, Ontario, in 1986.

Prologue: Shakespeare, the Classroom, and Critical Hope

The three of us came to Shakespeare via different paths, on different continents, in different decades. Our academic trajectories differ, as do our institutional contexts and our research portfolios. We are at different ages and stages of life, and we have young children, adult children, and no children. We live on opposite sides of the country in different communities. What we share in common – at the fundamental level of our souls – is the belief that Shakespeare's plays unlock a space for us to explore the world and navigate its complexities and that the conversations we have in classrooms with students have the capacity to build empathy in a world that is fraught and disorienting and troublesome. We are propelled forward by hope – particularly by a theoretical framework of critical hope – with an increasing sense of urgency in a new global reality where truth and justice are embattled, where peoples' ideological positions are entrenched, where unexamined opinions overpower nuanced arguments, and where divisiveness dictates the rules of engagement. While this book is not overtly political, we do not operate in a vacuum above or outside of our current political, social, or economic climate. Shakespeare was embedded in his own social and historical context and was at times shockingly political in both maintaining and overturning the status quo. The classroom should not be removed from lived experience, either: the convergence of Shakespeare and the twenty-first-century classroom encourages us to explore the strange and familiar, the alienating and the kindred, the political tensions and social concerns as diverse lenses we put on and take off, as a way to see and to move forward into the future, into the realm of the possible.

This is no ordinary project, but we do not have an ordinary set of texts, nor an ordinary approach to learning as a fundamental part of what makes us human.

- Why does Shakespeare matter in the twenty-first century?
- Why does the undergraduate classroom matter in higher education?
- Why do critical hope and critical empathy matter in the academy and in the world?

These are fundamental questions in our book and the resounding response we wish to proclaim, standing on top of our desks and shouting through the lines on the page is: THIS MATTERS.

This matters more now than ever.

This matters more to us than any other project we have undertaken.

We will navigate – with you and one another, with the chorus of students that animate our thoughts and our imaginative spaces – four Shakespearean plays: *King Lear*, *As You Like It, Henry V*, and *Hamlet*. We explore a diversity of genres – tragedy, history, and comedy – and approach these plays from different angles with distinct perspectives. Each of us writes from our own lived experience, taking as our starting point the following writing prompt: What is the most wonderful thing about teaching this play in our classrooms? Together, we are searching for an authentic voice that has hitherto been elusive to us in our own disciplinary language and in the language of teaching and learning. It is the voice of critical hope. It is the quest for critical empathy. It is the desire for critical love.

In the following essays, we seek out a space that is rigorous and playful, generative and curious. We use our voices to rage and howl, to laugh and inspire, to urge and to caution. But above all else we use a polyvocal structure that takes as a central premise that generating new knowledge happens through conversations between and amongst people who occupy multiple perspectives and, moreover, that we enrich our understanding of ourselves and the world when we make spaces for togetherness in our difference. In our mutual inquiry, we do not seek out an ideal or unified reading of these plays; rather, we aspire to create a rich dialogue as a means to probe some of life's most daunting questions, facilitated by and enriched through Shakespeare's plays.

The process of writing this book has demanded that each of us learn and unlearn things about ourselves, our discipline, and our classrooms. While we explore these transformations in depth in our Epilogue, it is worth mentioning that this collaboration has shaped our identities in ways we will be excavating for years to come. Early on in our project we started to refer to one another affectionately as the wyrd sisters, a reference to the three witches in *Macbeth*. What started off as playful – we address emails to one another as "dear wyrdos" – is an act of naming that illuminates our position within the academy and in the classroom. In *Macbeth*, the wyrd sisters occupy the margins and haunt the fens of Scotland. These women are called "witches" in the stage directions and "weird sisters" in the text. The "weird sisters" moniker originates from "wyrd," the Anglo-Saxon word for fate, and in *Macbeth* the wyrd sisters appear at unexpected moments with prophetic utterances that can be interpreted in many different ways. Macbeth's failure to engage in a close reading of their words, which contain truths that are troublesome and complex, leads him down a path of (self-)destruction. In a delightfully subversive reading of the role of the witches, Terry Eagleton states:

To any unprejudiced reader – which would seem to exclude Shakespeare himself, his contemporary audiences and almost all literary critics – it is surely clear that positive value in *Macbeth* lies with the three witches. The witches are the heroines of the piece, however little the play itself recognizes the fact, and however much the critics may have set out to defame them. (2)

In Eagleton's assessment, the wyrd sisters are disruptors of traditional hierarchies and offer an alternative model to the masculine, warring factions at the center of the play. In writing a book like this, we are occupying the margins of both our discipline and in the scholarship of teaching and learning. Instead of making proclamations, we embrace complexity. Instead of prophecy, we look for critical hope. Instead of equivocation, we signal a way forward through critical empathy. We roam freely at the edges of accepted, bounded disciplines and yet we hope that – just as in Shakespeare – the margins inform the center in reciprocal and fruitful ways that generate renewal and change.

In the spirit of upending traditional categories, we have eschewed an introduction in favor of a prologue to frame our project, a *dramatis personae* that introduces the authors via our individual journeys to Shakespeare. We've then added five acts, each of which describes a theoretical way of seeing that we use to animate our discussion of the plays: What do we mean by hope? Empathy? The critical? Why Shakespeare? And, finally, why this book? And why does it matter?

Dramatis Personae: How Did We Get Here?

Lisa Dickson – How Did I Get Here?

I wish I could, like Rebecca Solnit, say that I got here in a bewildering way, by getting lost and finding enlightenment in that experience. In a way, I can almost wish that I got here like Jessica did, through byways and U-turns and transformations. But this is not the case. I can tell you almost to the minute when I became a Shakespearean, and after that, excepting a brief detour into a lackluster love affair with Canadian Moping Poetry, it was pretty much a straight shot to being a professor of things Shakespearean.

It was the spring of 1986, Mississauga, Ontario. My twelfth grade English class was herded onto a bus and sent off to the Stratford Festival to watch *Hamlet* on the mainstage. I was enthusiastic, not because I was a good English student (I was) or because I'd really enjoyed *Hamlet* when we studied it in class (I did), but because of The Boy. The Boy was Older and Utterly Indifferent to me. The Boy was, therefore, the Most Important Thing in my world, and he was going on the bus, and might sit near me, and might say hi to me while we were waiting for ice cream at the festival. He might notice what I was wearing (I have no idea what I was wearing, but it was probably corduroy culottes, which explains the Indifference, I suppose). He might ask me a question about *Hamlet* and I could tell him things about *Hamlet* and after that we would most likely get married because *Hamlet* opened the door to the magical world inside my head, and he would see that and be impressed and someday when I was a doctor and saving people from the dark magic inside their heads he would tell people how it had all begun at *Hamlet* in 1986, this life we had together. (I don't know what he was to be doing in this life. I never really did figure out what he liked or cared about beyond Being Indifferent which, at the age of seventeen, looks so much like Being Deep. I expect he would have become something Deep, like a stock broker – which must be Deep because who knew what stock brokers did, anyway? – or a marine biologist – which was, obviously, very Deep. I was a card. I was. so. funny. Which The Boy would have known if he hadn't been so busy Being Indifferent to the magic in my head.)

Because the universe was in cahoots with my plans for me and The Boy. Because the universe was in cahoots, or because I have magical powers to build it in my image, the random shuffling of theater seat assignments resulted in a miracle: I was seated beside The Boy. I would be seated beside The Boy in the dark for *four hours*. I sat beside him in the weird not-quite-bright-enough-to-read-your-program light peculiar to pre-show theaters and waited to turn the key on the magic in my head and whisk him off to Our Future.

Then the lights went out and *Hamlet* began.

Now, in my memory, in a weird sort of Mobius strip where effects become causes, I remember my experience of the play out of order. In Act 2 of the play, Hamlet comes up with the plan to catch the conscience of Claudius by way of The Mousetrap and lays out it in a brilliant speech about melancholy and fear of satanic influence, powerlessness, and shame: "O what a rogue and peasant slave am I!" (2.2.535). Then, in Act 3, after The Mousetrap has been sprung, comes the Closet Scene in which Hamlet murders Polonius and confronts his mother for the sin of stooping from the Hyperion King Hamlet, who is mooning ghostily in the flies, to Claudius the satyr, who is off somewhere plotting to ship Hamlet to England, where he can be someone else's problem. But in my mind, they happen in reverse, the Closet Scene first and then the "rogue and peasant slave."

I'm sitting in the dark next to The Boy. The nerve endings of my entire left side have been on high alert since my corduroy culottes hit the seat in anticipation of The Boy's attempt to share my armrest, at which point we would touch, which was basically like having sex right there. Witness this dream universe sheering off on its parallel path and in it we are married and I'm a doctor and he's Deep and we probably have a safety deposit box and an Osterizer blender and other things grown-ups have. But that universe, attractive as it might have been, is, by this moment, gone. In my universe, Hamlet, played by Brent Carver (when I heard in 2020 that Brent Carver had died, I cried for three days, and you will see why), is turning his mother's eyes into her *very soul*, where his sense of betrayal and grief twist like knotted ropes around the once-gentle heart and he can barely speak to her. In that universe, I'm sitting, literally, on the edge of my seat. I'm gripping the back of the seat in front of me. I can *feel* the ropes tightening in my own flesh and, like Hamlet, like Gertrude, I can't *breathe* until Gertrude, exhausted, terrified of herself as much as of Hamlet, says, "What shall I do?" (3.4.182) and in that moment, from the seat to my left I hear: "*ssssnnnnoooorrrreeeee-gggggpphhh.*" With the stiff-necked, dread-full slowness of a heroine in a horror film, I turn away from drama – metaphysical, filial, political – where Hamlet's *whole being* is hanging by a twisted rope knotted in his heart and look at The Boy, who is slouched down in his theater seat *snoring*.

The Boy I love *is snoring through the Closet Scene.*

It's really no wonder that I don't remember his name.

I know I was born queer, but Team Boys took quite the body-blow that day, let me tell you.

It would be tidy to say that I abandoned Team Boys that minute and took up Team Shakespeare. But, to be fair to The Boy, the jig was already up way back in Act 2. In this bildungsroman of a Shakespearean, it seems that the earlier experience of Hamlet's "rogue and peasant slave" speech is rather a culmination than a precursor of this Closet Scene experience, because of the way it is burned into my mind with the colors and momentum of a phoenix rising, as though out of disappointment in Boykind was born a Shakesscholar. But really, The Boy (now, just the boy) has nothing to do with it. The boy is an incidental character who is only in the story to demonstrate the depth of the tectonic shifts that happened in Act 2, Scene 2. Only Shakespeare could have unseated the boy from my affections, I thought, because I was seventeen and first love is THE ONLY TRUE THING, TRUER THAN ANYTHING and so what if I didn't know if he wanted to be a marine biologist or if he liked … anything really? My horror at his snoring through the Closet Scene is only an index of how far apart we were when the plates of my world shifted.

In Act 2, Scene 2, Hamlet sighs: "Now I am alone" (534). He's been playing the madcap. He's been lying to everyone, bobbing and weaving like Ali and he is sick of himself. In this speech, Hamlet is reproaching himself for his inability to act on the passions inside him. Alone on the blank proscenium stage, Hamlet stands in Brent Carver's body, exhausted, terrified of himself as much as of any ghostly visitation or devil, twists and twists the ropes around his heart and his fists are knotted and he demands to know why he is "pigeon-liver'd," why "ere this" he has not "fatted all the region kites / With this slave's offal" (564–7) and the words are explosive and constricting at the same time, all those "b"s and those "s"s and "ch"s making his jaws ache, spitting and raging in clenched-teeth shout-whispers in a court where the walls have ears and he can't ever just *speak*: "Bloody, bawdy villain! / Remorseless, treacherous, lecherous, kindless villain! / O *VENGEANCE!*" (567–70).[1] And he throws up his arms to the heavens and it's as if he's launched his own damn heart, a heart on fire, a fireball up into the vaulted space of the theater and *I can see it*. I can see it arcing upward, trailing sparks, a dark-hearted comet that rises and rises, all through the beats of the missing feet in the pentameter of the line, and it reaches the limits of its energy and is poised at the fingertips of gravity for a breath, for another breath, and then it plummets:

Why, what an ass am I.

And we *laugh*. We laugh because, after all that, Hamlet still has this *humor*, this self-reflexive sense of irony, bitter though it is. We can almost see who he was, "Th' expectancy and rose of the fair state," this man we never got to meet and whose loss we mourn so deeply. And I'm sitting in my seat, having caught in my hands this stone that was a comet, and the speech and the play move on, and I'm still there in the beating of the missing feet of the pentameter, enraptured by what Shakespeare did with *silence*, enthralled by *what isn't there*, by the space that Shakespeare made for us to see something wondrous. And I know, in that *beat, beat, beat* as the fireball rises and pauses and falls, that this is where I have to live. This is where I have to spend the rest of my life.

The boy never had a chance.

Shannon Murray – How I Got Here: The Origin Story

I was sixteen: a last-minute student ticket at the Old Vic Theatre in London to see *Hamlet*, a pound fifty in those days for the best seats left in the house, in this case, the center of the second row. For about three-and-a-half hours, I sat stunned. It was not my first play or even my first Shakespeare, but I had never experienced anything like this. I certainly didn't understand every word, but I *got* it. Hamlet was forced to live a life he didn't choose, first by his mother and then by his dead father. What teenager hasn't felt that? But it was the greatness of the man that punched me in the chest: his whole humanness. The great Shakespearean actor Derek Jacobi made me understand the greatness of the character and of the play. I felt viscerally what mattered in these lives and in those words, and at the curtain, I couldn't understand how anyone could stop clapping. I left stunned and heartbroken: transformed.

Years later, after starting each Shakespeare class with that story, I decided to write to thank Sir Derek – and he wrote me a thank-you card back! My office now contains a little *Hamlet*/Jacobi shrine, complete with that card, my ticket and playbill, and a Derek

Jacobi action figure (from his *Doctor Who* appearance). It reminds me of the difference theater and Shakespeare can make in a young person's life.

So here's my problem. How, as a classroom instructor, can I compete with that? *You want to get Shakespeare?* I hear myself saying. Find a really good production when you're young enough to be shaken by it. My classroom isn't the same. I can bring in productions, of course – bless YouTube for giving us access to some amazing stuff – but I can't take them to see a first-class production in 1977. My consolation is that many of my students have no access to that kind of performance, so what they need is a framework for seeing what I saw forty years ago, and if possible a thirst to see or read more; I want to issue an invitation they won't be able to refuse, so that if a production does come up, or if they visit Stratford or London or New York, they know that Shakespeare belongs to them.

Jessica Riddell – How Did I Get Here?

I can pinpoint the moment I felt awakened to the possibilities of doing something differently, occupying another perspective, of seeing things from a different angle.

It was on my first day of my fresh start.

The year before I had bombed out of McGill University in spectacular fashion after two years of wandering aimlessly, partying prodigiously, and angsting at an existential level as only a nineteen-year-old can do. I jumped off the train that was hurtling dangerously toward a precipice and spent a year coming face to face with my own hitherto unacknowledged privilege, paying off my spiritual and financial debts, and participating in my own metaphysical form of self-flagellation. This journey of self-awakening took me through the smoky nights of the Halifax bar industry, the streets of Haight-Ashbury, and the AIDS orphanages of Soweto. After a year of witnessing despair and hope commingle, of observing the beauty and horror writ large in others' lives, and the growing compulsion to do something meaningful, I emerged from my own self-prescribed wilderness and went back to university with the utterly un-nuanced goal of saving the world.

I had failed spectacularly, publicly, shamefully in my first attempt at achieving an undergraduate education. My transcript was littered with D's and F's and a whole host of incompletes; and yet, there was tiny glimmer of hope in the transcript of shame: an A in Introduction to English Literature. (I also had an A– in "Space, Time, and Matter" for a paper I wrote on the physics of playing pool, but the class average was an A, so that offered very little consolation.) I had chosen to major in Anthropology at McGill largely because my roommate chose that major and it sounded "science-y" enough to provide a professional alibi when anyone asked me what I was going to do with my life (at the time I held the vague opinion that all the social sciences would sound quite respectable to parents and family friends, despite W.H. Auden's commandment, "Thou shalt not [...] commit / A social science" [stanza 27]).

Somehow in the midst of my disorientation at McGill, I had the wherewithal to take Introduction to English Lit as an elective. Despite being largely uninspired by the 600-person auditorium, the faceless and nameless TAs administering reading quizzes and shuffling attendance sheets, and the lecturer on stage extolling the virtues of Susanna Moodie, I managed to get an A. I have no idea why or how: I presumably skipped the same number of classes, suffered the same hangovers, and gave as many fucks (zero) as I had about my other classes, but there was something resilient about my love for literature that buoyed me up despite my own efforts at self-sabotage.

When I decided to go back to university, I identified law school as the fastest track to saving the world. In my (incredibly naïve) estimation, I would specialize in reproductive rights and lobby the United Nations to provide better access to health care and education for women and children in developing nations. I had seen things in southern Africa that I couldn't unsee – systemic injustices and racial inequalities and violations of basic human rights – and I saw higher education as my best chance for effecting positive change. I knew I needed straight As if I could hope to recover from my two ignominious years in Montreal: I chose English for the purely mercenary reason that if I could get an A when I was checked out, I could get As if I actually showed up.

That's when, on the first day of my fresh start, I was launched out of my self and into a new way of being.

Sitting in a small, nondescript classroom on the first day of term, my stomach was in my throat: I was anxious to begin, to start the journey to redemption, but also to get this part of life over with and fast forward to the "good part" (which was still largely undefined in my imagination, but it did include a purpose and a salary). In the middle of my reverie of mixed feelings, Dr. Janet Hill breezed into the room, unceremoniously plunked down her books, turned around and said, "Right. Who's going to be my Desdemona?" I don't remember whether I raised my hand or she called upon me, but she gestured for me to come to the front of the class, asked me to lie down on the floor, and proceeded to recite Othello's "put out the light" speech where he murders his beloved wife. As I lay on the cold linoleum floor, I looked up at this middle-aged British woman who had transformed into Othello by speaking his words. At the end of the speech, Dr. Hill wiped the tears from her face and I rose a new person, transformed, baptized, exhilarated (and very dusty).

I fell in love with Shakespeare at that moment. It wasn't that I saw myself in Desdemona or Othello, or because I had any experience with jealousy or complicated love affairs, but because this scene felt bigger than me, combining beauty and horror into art that transcended the everyday dramas that had hitherto animated my life. As I lay on the floor looking up at the class, at my professor, I felt my plans shift under the seismic forces of Shakespeare. But I see more clearly now that it wasn't just Shakespeare that caused this shift; it was my experience of Shakespeare in the classroom under the guidance of a professor who loved her craft.

On my first day of my fresh start I was asked to engage in critical empathy. I didn't have the *words for it* then (in fact, the concept "critical empathy" is a very recent seismic shift in my thinking), but I knew the *feeling of it*: I was asked to occupy someone else's perspective, see from a different angle, look through someone else's eyes. It wasn't an out-of-body experience as much as it was an embodying experience, the realization that I could be better, more insightful, more attuned to grapple with complexity if I could harness my imaginative capacities to understand other people's experiences across time and space and identity. That day, when I left that classroom, my relationship to the world – and my place within it – had irrevocably changed.

I am still in touch with Dr. Hill, who is retired but teaching classes that interest her. A few years ago I sent her a thank-you note accompanied by an article I wrote that was inspired by her mentorship, and she sent back this response:

Sent: October 15, 2017 1:34 PM

To: Jessica Riddell

My dear Jess,

How lovely to hear from you! Reading your message, I'm deeply touched, even a little teary. Thank you so much for telling me how I helped you, though I'm very aware of how much is owed to your own courage, determination and talent.

I often think of that September sixteen years ago when I found a rather sad young woman in my class who, in spite of being new to Saint Mary's, and to me and my methods, generously, and impressively, became the dying Desdemona for the class. It was the beginning of a marvellous learning-teaching partnership that I valued very much all through your time as my student; and value still, because, while I may have been helping you, you certainly helped to strengthen and refine my vision of what it is good, and – to steal your word – authentic in teaching.

I so enjoyed your article. I'm very glad to have read your commitment "to engage and struggle in the trenches and the plains, the classrooms, and the playing fields." I think you will always follow that vision.

My love and thanks,

Janet (Hill)

On my first day of my fresh start I found what would, unbeknownst to me at the time, become my guiding purpose, the compass where during the most disorienting times I can find a path to purpose and clarity: it is not merely Shakespeare, but

Shakespeare-in-conversation with my mentors as guides, students as collaborators, friends as truth tellers.

Our Book in Five Short Acts

Act I: Hope

Hope is a turning to the unknown with the willingness to love, not without risk, not without critical judgment, but with an acceptance of the unknowability of the future and the willingness to believe and therefore to "be-love." John D. Caputo says: "This is the mood grammarians call *modus irrealis*, not because it is unreal but because it would like to be real, what we would like or love to believe (from *lieben*), where to believe is literally to be-love" (*Insistence of God* 54–5). Hopefulness is sometimes dismissed as Pollyanna-ish naiveté, as if hope makes us unable to face reality. Well, to quote Elmer P. Dowd, "I've wrestled with reality for three decades, and I'm happy to state I finally won out over it" (*Harvey*). Hope helps us see the world as it could be, as well as how it is. Philip Sidney, in his *Defense of Poesy* (1579), argues that poetry creates a golden world that is better than the world within which we live, and this golden world allows us to dream of a space that is possible beyond the constraints and perceived limitations of our everyday lives.

Hope, therefore, embraces complexity, and all the discomfort and disorientation that this approach entails, in an attempt to move toward a truth that is more inclusive, more nuanced, and richer for the struggle. Hope demands we believe that there *are* answers and truths, but they are found in the dynamic interplay between context and evidence and theory. Since these conditions are always changing, the answers must also always evolve.

As an act that takes place in an always-changing, never-static context, hope is transformational. It is the act of leaping from conviction into action with the understanding that what we do and what we make will inevitably change us, so that our convictions will be tested and transformed. Hope is experiential, a *becoming*, an act of resisting reification, that freezing, deadening power of definitiveness. It is the opposite of being done. It is being doing.

Hope requires that we become comfortable with the difficulty of *knowing* in order to move forward, into the future, into the unknown. Hope is fueled by values of integrity, of ethical and moral responsibility, of citizenship and engagement. In other words: "the hopeful challenging the actual in the name of the possible" (Shor 3).

An academic vocation is among the most hopeful. We go into teaching and scholarly work because we believe, even if we haven't articulated it to ourselves fully, that development, improvement, and transformation are all possible when we are engaged in nurturing an insatiable intellectual curiosity in ourselves and in young people. Exercising the hope muscle keeps us on that optimistic course, even when we might see plenty of evidence that things don't work or don't work as quickly as we would like. Students are at the center of a definition of hope, not just as individuals but also as a philosophical impetus. Learners and learning are not metaphors for hope, but, rather, hope embodied, hope on the move, hope as an agent, a method of acting, and a way of seeing. Transformational, messy, complex, always in motion, hope is inseparable from learning. In the classroom, we are always caught up in the momentum of becoming. "We never are what we are," John D. Caputo writes. "Something different is always possible" (*More Radical Hermeneutics* 35). Every participant in the learning endeavor has tacitly announced: "I am willing to be different in five minutes, or thirteen weeks or four years from what I am now." This is a tremendous act of courage.

Teaching is an exercise in hope: you must live in a world where you cannot see the impact you might have in some distant future you might never access – and do it anyway. In *The Courage to Teach*, Parker Palmer talks about a certain model of courage that asks us to stand in front of the classroom and bare our souls, to claim the courage to examine the soul in order to share ourselves with others. In this way, teaching and learning are one and the same: to be a hopeful member of a learning community, one that encompasses us all and in which we play many parts, is to embrace the transformational potential of putting one's being on the line. Learning is embodied hope. It happens *in time*. It happens *in bodies*. Each act of learning is unique and can never be reproduced on a factory line. It cannot be abstracted from the bodies and the lives of learners who embody it, any more than a verb can function grammatically without an agent. Hope is a verb.

Act II: Empathy

The practice of empathy is the most important reason to read, especially to read great literature, old literature, literature that makes us uncomfortable, and literature from cultures and experiences unlike our own. Even more than the other liberal arts, which all teach us about how other people think and live and feel in one way or another, imaginative literature insists that we occupy other people's spaces, live in their heads, experience their lives, and think with them as well as about them. If empathy is the practice of fellow feeling, literature gives us the chance to know compassion for more varieties of human experience than we could ever possibly encounter in real life.

"Hope," Brazilian educator and philosopher Paulo Freire tells us, "is rooted in men's incompletion, from which they move out in a constant search – a search which can be carried out only in communion with others" (*Oppressed* 91). Empathy is predicated on hope. If hope is the willingness to believe and to "be-love," if hope is a verb, something that we do when we turn to the unknown, then empathy is the act of relationship that is grounded in a sort of radical unknowing, an un-possessing openness to the Other. It is an act of hospitality, of friendship. Like hope, friendship is not something you *have* but is something you *do*. Empathy as friendship does not mean that I become the Other, or that I make the Other and their experience mine. "I cannot call the friend 'mine,' like something I have," John D. Caputo says (*More Radical Hermeneutics* 61). Rather, it is a sort of love that respects the unknowability of the Other.

The highest form of love, says Evelyn Fox Keller (American physicist, feminist, and author), is "love that allows for intimacy without the annihilation of difference" (qtd. in Palmer, *Courage to Teach* 57). Empathy is a way of doing relationships, making "community with the unknowable other" (55), that recognizes our "common strangeness" in which "we concede that we do not know each other, and that, because of this, we can only speak *to* each other, not *about* each other" (Caputo, *More Radical Hermeneutics* 60). This kind of thinking, thinking about other humans as truly and separately human, is against generalization. We like what J.V. Cunningham said about why we should read early literature: not in any ordinary way to learn about ourselves – although to do that honestly would be something – but to imagine what it would be like to think differently than we do (7).

Michel Foucault reminds us of the importance of looking through different lenses: "There are times in life when the question of knowing if one can think differently than one thinks, and perceive differently than one sees, is absolutely necessary if one is to go on looking and reflecting at all" (8). This is an exhortation to embrace empathy, with its focus on sharing rather than telling, and the responsibility we have to identify and challenge our deep-rooted assumptions in order to grow as intellectuals and as human beings. There is an inherent humility that governs this process of empathy but also an inherent confidence to see through someone else's eyes and occupy someone else's perspective and not have one's worldview collapse under the pressure of scrutiny.

Like hope, empathy puts the self at risk, for to meet the Other in conversation is to open the self to transformation. To stand *with* the Other, to look at the world from the Other's perspective, is to reorient the self in the known world, to see it anew. That's why we balk at the ugly word "relatable," as it tends to be used for characters and stories: it is implicitly a term of praise, as if the best thing one could say about a work of art is that it relates in some way to our own experience. But to constantly read about characteristics and experiences that mirror our own is to engage in a repetitive act of narcissism. It is reading-as-selfie. One of our most dear hopes for a literary education is that it can make us better – specifically because, done well, it makes us see, understand, empathize with, and ultimately love our fellow humans, no matter how strange and different from us – no matter how un-relatable – they are.

Relatable has an ugly sibling named "relevance." When we ask how this text or concept or character is relevant, we engage in an act of historical navel-gazing without critical reflection on how looking through a different lens changes our own contemporary perspective. Empathy across historical and geographical boundaries – to see through the early modern lens of gender or sexuality or governance – can help move us from what we already know into the realm of things we do not yet know. And yet, in our exploration of the strange and unfamiliar, we risk instrumentalizing the Other as a convenient canvas for projecting our self-actualization (see Said, *Orientalism*). The more attuned we are to moments where *we* are the Other, where *we* are interlopers, and where we can never fully grasp the lived experience of the Other, the more we enlarge our capacities for empathy. Empathy isn't intuitive. And it certainly isn't easy. But we believe that empathy is a capacity that can be developed and expanded with thought and reflection. It doesn't have to be perfect, but it has to be attempted.

For learners to have the confidence to occupy the perspective of the Other, and inhabit two worlds simultaneously without losing their sense of self, or their sense of the independence of the Other, they need to go through a process of self-determination: discomfort, alienation, humility, reflection. Otherwise, empathy-building exercises run the risk of collapsing the divisions between self and Other, which can lead to a level of cognitive dissonance that is uncontainable or to the erasure of selfhood. If hope requires that we always understand that "[w]e never are what we are; something different is always possible" (Caputo, *More Radical Hermeneutics* 35), then we must also bring that transformational commitment into our acts of friendship, including those we have with ourselves; we must always be willing not just to meet others on their own terms but to *be* an Other. If we are to be "moved to be taught," we must always be willing to be changed and must move forward with the recognition that what we find when we step into that space of potential, where the Other awaits us, is something that will challenge our most cherished truths.

Thus, empathy is, in some ways, an act undertaken by the brokenhearted, as Parker Palmer says: "These are the broken-hearted people whose hearts have been broken open instead of broken apart" (Naropa University Address). To become a learner is to embrace empathy, to risk being broken open in order to let the Other in.

Act III: The Critical

Every time we walk into a classroom, we implicitly ask ourselves: *What is the purpose of education – to teach ourselves to accept the world as it is or to risk the brokenheartedness necessary to the creation of an alternative future?* To accept the latter is to commit to empathy and to risk being broken open, to hope. But sheer empathy without the work of understanding – and without action – is as vain as hope without practice. It is otherwise just the hollow "thoughts and prayers" launched through social media at any suffering in the world, without a real attempt to know it or to address it. It is the "critical" in critical empathy or critical hope that makes them worthwhile approaches to university teaching. What makes hope and empathy healthy, able to withstand the slings and arrows, is the element of critical thought. If all we do is blindly hope, hope without reflection, thought, or action, then how easily can that hope be destroyed? It is flimsy, like a bubble popped at the first rough wind. Hope needs to be carefully interrogated, questioned, tested, and even doubted in order to be a strong, stout hope. If the strengthening of hope comes through asking some version of *What is my evidence for hope here?*, the critical path to empathy requires that we do the work of understanding first, of coming as close as we can to understanding the Other – impossible though that may be – in order to forge a strong bond of compassion.

The addition of "critical" builds in an element of resilience for these "soft" concepts to boldly go forth into the world and to withstand the cynicism that might dismiss hope and love and empathy as less valuable than the steely flint of truth and knowledge. Indeed, compassion doesn't have to be a fluffy bunny. One can have empathy – and an understanding of the Other's reality – and not admire it or support it or agree with it. Compassion isn't about boosting at all costs no matter what. We remind students that they can't ethically disagree with someone's position until they understand that position. The same goes for agreeing. So empathy is not just about singing kumbaya. That's where the critical rubber hits the road. A strong bond of compassion is hard work.

As Freire says, "Just to hope is to hope in vain." Hope, he writes, "demands anchoring in practice." He defines critical hope as the "need for truth as an ethical quality of the struggle" (*Pedagogy of Hope* 2–3). In other words, critical hope is located in the practice of navigating our complex and imperfect world. In higher education we identify, wrestle with, and embrace complexity with our students and one another. The creator of Brain Pickings, Maria Popova, illuminates the role of hope in learning when she observes: "Critical thinking without hope is cynicism. Hope without critical thinking is naiveté" (para. 2). The purpose of critical empathy and critical hope is not to determine what the future must be, but to bring to bear on that process of making the tools we have that help us to face the unknown with resilience and an awareness of the complexity of experience.

Adopting a critical approach means knowing that there is no singular truth or right answer. The forward momentum of critical hope, and the acknowledgment of our situatedness that is critical empathy, mean that interpretation is always present, even in ostensibly "fixed" spheres (formulas, facts, etc.). The fundamental premise that empathy demands respect for the difference of the Other means recognizing that in our sublunary world no singular perspective can be universal, and this recognition in turn necessitates dialogue as the means of this forging / foraging for the future. As Freire argues, "no one can say a true word alone – nor can she say it *for* another in a prescriptive act which robs them of their words" (*Oppressed* 88). If we go into the future at all, we go together. This is a messy process, one that goes in circles, crams up against logjam contradictions and the impasses of incommensurate worldviews, waits for the tide to turn and tries again. If we truly commit to empathy, we cannot dictate where we will end up, for we cannot expect the Other to conform to us. We must always be willing to be broken open. Our relationship with each other and with the future is unruly. Critical empathy means working hard in the midst of all that messiness. Critical hope is the momentum that impels us forward.

These two concepts – empathy and hope – are critical in the other sense as well: they are essential, vital, urgent, if we are to avoid catastrophe. Far from being a groundless nihilism or a relativistic acceptance that "whatever shall be, shall be," critical empathy demands a profound commitment to ethics, for the future we make together comes into being by way of the choices we make together. Those choices are predicated on our ability to see, to name, to assess, to synthesize, to extrapolate from the world as it is. In order to embrace "thinking which perceives reality as a process, as transformation rather than as a static entity" (Freire, *Oppressed* 92) – that is, in order to hope – we must, as Ira Shor argues, employ a method of proceeding that "connects subjectivity to history while relating personal context to social context" (180). Critical empathy enjoins us to engage our full selves, our cognitive and affective and experiential capacities. "Critical," therefore, is a strategic prefix in a compound sentence to frame affective concepts that have traditionally been demoted in academia: empathy, hope, love, kindness, wisdom. The commitment to the "critical" in critical hope and empathy demands that we be awake, flexible, feeling – all those virtues that the Classical philosophers identified as essential to the "good life," in which we all become philosophers: "the very model of living well, knowledge linked with action (ethics and politics) and passion (*philia, eros*) and a sensibility finely attuned to life's joys" (Caputo, *Truth* 271). We grapple hope to our educational work with lashings of faith, a secular faith that sees the invisible goal in the mind's eye. Empathy is our angle of entry; hope is our trajectory; the critical is what keeps us from foundering in choppy seas.

Act IV: Why Shakespeare?

"O for a muse of fire" (*Henry V*, Prologue, 1). Shakespeare explores the processes of soul building. His worlds unfold with us in them, both as spectators and as active participants. The Chorus exhorts the spectators to harness their imaginations at the start of *Henry V*: "Can this cock-pit hold / The vasty fields of France? Or may we cram / Within this wooden O the very casques / That did affright the air at Agincourt?" (Prologue, 11–14). Begging the audience to compensate for the actors' "imperfections" by employing their own "imaginary forces," the Chorus emphasizes the need for the spectators to take an active part in fulfilling the illusion. What the Chorus also points out, although more obliquely, is that the "history" we are about to see is partly theatrical illusion and partly individual fabrication: in other words, the Chorus effectively undermines the possibility that "history" is anything like an objective account of factual events. This sly irony gets to the heart of complexity and troublesome knowledge that Shakespeare invites us to discover again and again.

Shakespeare engages in the habit of making what is in the sources simple into something complex; the multiplicity of voices and perspectives he presents insists on a complex judgment. To some extent, all drama has the potential to do this and much of Renaissance literature has this inspired critical hopefulness about what humans are and can achieve, even when they mess it up. Like music and dance, drama unfolds *in time* and *in bodies* and, while a play can be restaged, it can never be reiterated exactly. Each performance is unique and embedded in the circumstances and materiality of its making, and every encounter with the plays engages us wholly: cognitively, affectively, somatically, and experientially. Shakespeare gives us an entry into talking fruitfully about empathy and hope. But empathy and hope are also ways to understand Shakespeare better. The most perfect model of critical empathy is Hamlet's friend Horatio, one who "in suff'ring all […] suffers nothing" (3.2.64). As an observer (but a thinking, doubting, and questioning one), Horatio embodies the critically empathetic reader. And in Hamlet himself we get a great expression of critical hope, though more on the critical than the hope side in this example: "What a piece of work is a man" (2.2.299).

Structurally and conceptually, Shakespeare's works are sites where critical hope and empathy emerge into the collective cultural consciousness. This emergence is not smooth or uncontentious. Shakespeare's works have achieved wide currency because they were borne outward to the world on a wave of imperialist energy that, in seeking to turn all the world into England, opened the English consciousness and Shakespeare's plays to powerful reimaginings and rescriptings. We choose Shakespeare because of his currency in global relations and because the history of that relationship is one of intense and messy negotiation and dialogic encounters with a wide and various range of others across terrains of nationality, ethnicity, class, gender, and all the kinds of difference in which lived experience is embedded.

It is from Shakespeare's engagement with difference that critical empathy emerges. The very form of the plays, which subject big questions of governance and virtue and the character of humanity to scrutiny from multiple perspectives, high and low, "foreign" and "domestic," ensures that no single point of view is presented without comment and qualification. Necessarily polyvocal, the plays are written for spaces, like the "wooden O" of the Globe Theatre, that reinforce that this multiplicity of perspectives presented in the daylight performance on the bare stage demands more than mere observation, but rather the active, imaginative participation of the audience in the construction of the world.

Act V: What Kind of Book Is This, Anyway?

This is not a "how to teach Shakespeare" book. Nor is it a manual on best practices for teaching Shakespeare. There are plenty of excellent examples out there.[2] Because we are committed to the joyful multiplicity of the Shakespearean theater, we reflect that polyvocality in the structure of the book: for the four plays we chose, each of us presents an individual reading that captures a perspective on teaching, on hope, and on empathy. What you will see in the following pages is a series of discussions – with monologic chapters and dialogic margins – where we carry on conversations with each other and with our literary, theoretical, cultural, and artistic guides and fellow travelers. Less concerned with lesson plans and products, we decided instead at the outset of the project to explore some open-ended questions: *Why teach?* and then, *Why teach Shakespeare?* and finally, *How do we locate and create spaces for hope in the classroom and beyond?*

This book makes the case for the classroom experience as a rich site for producing new knowledge and attempts to challenge the typical disciplinary division of "real" research from its less-valued cousin, "just" teaching. We take up the challenge of "just" teaching to ask: What does it mean to create a *critically hopeful* classroom? How do Shakespeare's theater and his plays invite us to look through new lenses? How can the *critically hopeful classroom* generate fresh insights into the cultural, historical, and critical importance of the plays and our own contexts? What does it look like to practice *critical empathy*, the ability to occupy, appreciate, and responsibly interrogate the perspectives of others?

In exploring the *joy* of teaching and experiencing Shakespeare, we advocate for a critical hope that arises from pedagogical-scholarly practice grounded in and motivated by our experience in forging critically hopeful classrooms. The book is informed by the need for learners and scholars to live "undivided lives" (Palmer, *Courage to Teach*) and to have faith "in the creation of a world in which it will be easier to love" (Freire, *Oppressed* 40).

CRITICAL HOPE, CRITICAL EMPATHY, CRITICAL LOVE

So, orderly to end where we begun: Critical hope, empathy and love are all *orientations* toward the world, *beliefs* about the world, and *ways of moving and acting* in the world.

Critical hope is an *orientation toward the future*, a *belief* in our capacity as human beings to know and to transform ourselves and our world. It is a commitment to be *moved* in the Sidneyan sense toward ethical *action* grounded in love, empathy, and an acceptance of difference, difficulty, and complexity.

Critical empathy is a hospitable *orientation toward the Other*, a *belief* in our capacity as human beings to value, engage with, and respect the autonomy and legitimacy of diverse perspectives. It is a commitment to embrace the riskiness of being "broken open" to transformation in dialogue and to take *actions* that foster and enable relationship in diversity.

Critical love is an *orientation toward the work of being and learning in a complex world*, a *belief* (to "believe" is to "be-love") that we can and must be better and do better to and for one another. Fundamentally, it is a belief that *we matter*, as a species, as a community and an ecology, as creators and teachers and learners. It is a commitment to the messy, complex, never-ending work of hope and empathy and to the *actions* that enable the growth and transformation of ourselves and the world.

In building the collection of essays and conversations that follow, we wanted to "show our work" of orienting ourselves toward the future, toward others, and toward a particular vocation. In this book, we explore our beliefs about the world and ask how our practice would be different if we – not only we wyrdos, but we collectively – were to make those beliefs about hope, empathy, and love the *starting point* for our thinking, our design, and our undivided lives. What could we enable if we could orient ourselves around that center of value? What would be possible if we were to risk being broken open?

NOTES

1 In the Oxford edition of the play, the line "O, vengeance!" does not appear, but many other versions of the text, such as the one featured on *Open Source Shakespeare*, present this line.
2 Examples of books that focus either on teaching or learning Shakespeare include Katherine Armstrong and Graham Atkin's *Studying Shakespeare: A Practical Introduction*, Rex Gibson's *Teaching Shakespeare: A Handbook for Teachers*, Laurie E. Maguire's *Studying Shakespeare: A Guide to the Plays*, and, more recently, Ayanna Thompson and Laura Turchi's *Teaching Shakespeare with Purpose: A Student-Centred Approach*.

PART ONE

King Lear

Keep Falling, Alice: Rabbit Holes, Monkey Wrenches, and Critical Love in *King Lear*

Jessica Riddell

As people, we are attuned to the changing seasons and rhythms of the year – the promise of spring, the fecundity of summer, the crispness of fall, and the icy blasts of winter – that are familiar and anticipated but also fresh and surprising, as if we've forgotten from one cycle to the next and must relearn the ebbs and flows anew.

As educators, we graft different narratives onto seasons and months: fall displaces spring as the season of fresh starts with the advent of a new school year. We are greeted in September with smiling fresh faces, witness our students blossoming (or struggling to thrive) in October, watch these once shiny faces pale under the weight of November, and (hopefully) sigh with relief when they regain a healthy robustness once term ends and the festive season arrives. For professors, December marks a period of frantic writing, marking, research, and course planning (with a few well-earned naps and holiday cheer) before a new cycle begins in January. Despite time's passage, there is nothing inevitable about our experiences from one year to the next, and we are always in the process of re-making and re-forming. This is why, for me anyway, I can revisit the same texts with the joy and anticipation of connecting with an old friend: we pick up where we left off, learn fresh and surprising things in familiar, time-worn places, and are progressively enriched with every encounter.

For the past ten years, as regular as the seasons, November is indelibly marked by my annual communing with *King Lear*. In a play obsessed with human relationships to Nature and the passage of time, the metaphor of seasons is particularly apt. Indeed, there is something very November-y about King Lear's stage of life: he explains his retirement from the public sphere as one

Shannon: Beautiful! And no matter how we talk to our students about it, contemporary North American life shields us from what Duke Senior calls the "seasons' difference." That is a gain, of course, but also a loss.

Shannon: Yes! Which is why I like to say "Happy New Year!" at three different moments in the academic calendar: September 1, January 1, and May 1!

Lisa: Yes! We are always starting over. It's one of the special privileges I think we get in our cyclic ways as educators, this sense that it's always possible to begin again, to do the old thing in new ways. I was ruminating in Shannon's essay about the weight of choices that I sense that students feel – as Cordelia does – and the feeling that all of the future presses down on a single moment. How can we communicate to our students this other way of this way of being that begins anew every time but that also brings all that came before with it?

Shannon: A sad tale's best for winter.

framed by his desire to "unburthen'd crawl toward death" (1.1.40). Lear's declaration to "shake all cares and business from our age" (1.1.38) often rings falsely – sometimes even comically – in performance, but it never fails to elicit a pang of sympathy from our class as we so desperately crawl toward the end of term, staving off the flu, buckling under the burden of mounting deadlines, and feeling rather sorry for ourselves. The play gives us a language to explore those feelings of existential exhaustion but also the space to pause and gently laugh at ourselves through Lear. After all, the seasons turn, deadlines pass, and the festive cheer of the holiday season soon erases the harsh sting of November. Unless you are Lear. We watch him play out his final season on stage. He is denied festive renewal not because he's old and dying (he's full of vigor once he *gets mad* and *goes mad*) but because he realizes too late that when he banishes his beloved truth tellers – Cordelia, Kent, and the Fool – he cuts himself off from critical love, which is a vital life source in the world of this play.

There is a dash of pathetic fallacy when we encounter *King Lear* as the days grow shorter, the air gets colder, and the world is cast in muted shades of brown and gray. Lear believes the storm is an external manifestation of the tempest in his mind: his descent into madness wouldn't be nearly as effective if Lear bellowed at Nature to "let fall / your horrible pleasure" on a bright sunny day (3.2.18–19). We enter a bleak play-world that mirrors northern climates in November: cold, rainy, and windy. Our communing with *King Lear*, however, must be carefully managed: too much darkness threatens to overwhelm even the most sturdy of souls, but, conversely, an approach that focuses too much attention on the "moral of the story" threatens to return the play to its fairy-tale roots and erase the differences and convergences the play so poignantly explores. We must keep the "critical" in delicate balance with the "love" if we are to fully appreciate the complexity of *King Lear*.

The rhythm of the university course within which we explore *King Lear* also frames our encounters with the play in crucial ways. In a first-year, mandatory survey course (unimaginatively titled "Introduction to British Literature to 1660"), I meet students on the first day of their undergraduate careers and together we race through 1,000 years of literature in thirteen weeks, moving swiftly from the world of heroic warriors in *Beowulf* through the bawdy Middle Ages via Chaucer, exploring formations of selfhood in the early modern period, and ending our journey where it all began (at least, according to Milton's *Paradise Lost*), when Adam and Eve are kicked out of the Garden for tasting from the Tree of the Knowledge of Good and Evil. Indeed,

Shannon: Though he never loses that love, even when he banishes it. Bless them all for their stubborn love even when he doesn't deserve it! We can all hope to be loved better than we deserve.

Jessica: His textbook case of pathetic fallacy rests on the assumption that there is no other perspective but his – which is an act of erasure of the Other.

Jessica: Lear asks the Fool, "Art cold? / I am cold myself" (68–69) and the Fool responds with a song: "with hey, ho, the wind and the rain, / Must make content with his fortunes fit, / Though the rain it raineth every day" (75–77).

Lisa: I love that the Fool's response to inclemency is music, art. I'm finding more and more resonances with Milton's "Lycidas" these days, where he comes to the conclusion that the consolation for mortality is the poetic yoking of disparate things through analogy and metaphor: "So sinks the daystar in the ocean bed / ... / So Lycidas sunk low, but mounted high" (168–72). When all else fails the mourning poet, it is the shepherd's "warbling Doric lay" (189) that carries him from melancholic sunset toward "fresh woods, and pastures new" (193).

the course is devoted to confronting the complexities of knowledge, of wrapping our heads around the impossibility of a singular answer or indivisible truth, and of the pilgrimage we undertake as we grapple with how deeply unsettling these realizations can be. My students are usually fresh out of high school or CEGEP (Collège d'enseignement général et professionnel) when we undertake our journey in September, so they must unlearn (or at least challenge) their impulse to seek out "right answers" or identify "correct" interpretations. It is no wonder they often feel disoriented in this new world of shades and layers and margins.

The course functions in some ways like the apple from the Tree of the Knowledge of Good and Evil: once you taste *knowledge*, your eyes are opened to what was hitherto invisible: what you have seen cannot be unseen, and you are kicked out of the metaphorical garden of complacency to navigate a world of perilous landscapes and challenging conditions where "right" and "wrong" are not easily demarcated. But just as Milton highlights *felix culpa* (the Fortunate Fall) in *Paradise Lost*, the transformation from ignorance to knowledge makes us richer for the struggle. The "critical" – added in combination to "thinking" (critical thinking) or "love" (critical love) or "hope" (critical hope) or "empathy" (critical empathy) – is made possible only at the moment we eat the apple. To extend the metaphor into our classroom, the concept of "critical" is born the moment when we recognize that facts are not fixed, that truth is elusive, that knowledge is produced *in the act of embracing complexity*.

King Lear is the penultimate text in this survey course: after nine weeks of analyzing, debating, and playing with epics and fabliau, satires and romances, sonnets and rhyme royal, we encounter the three-dimensional space of the playhouse where meaning is created through dialogue and other forms of embodied meaning (gesture, costume, setting, etc.). There is no poet persona or narrator to guide (or misguide) us. Instead, the world is created in real time over the course of roughly three hours through exchanges amongst the players onstage. We are spectators, witnesses, and sometimes participants in this ephemeral space produced by spoken words and animated by the force of our imaginative energies. The first step in our interpretive quest toward embracing complexity is acknowledging that meaning is created through multiple and often competing perspectives. However, in this play there are no comfortable places where we can rest with the knowledge that a character is purely good or truly authentic or fully whole. The ground shifts under us as situations arise and scenarios unfold, and we find moments of critical empathy for characters we are supposed to loathe, and deep frustration with characters we feel we should love and cannot.

Lisa: But there's a sort of undertow here, in the Fortunate Fall in that it's very hard when you're up to your neck in it to see the "fortunate" bits. "Struggle," for Adam and Eve, from their position up to their necks in it, is a punishment for transgression, and so much of the literature of our period grapples with the tension between the "fortune" of knowledge and the penalty of struggle. The idea of critical hope, I think, puts the "fortunate" back in the equation and begins to recast the "fall," the idea of struggle, in a new way that can, *hopefully* ☺, shed its association with punishment. Can we model critical hope in such a way as to help students to see that their struggles are not a bug but a feature, not a punishment but the means, not lamentable but the joyful, exuberantly messy DOING OF THE THING?!

Lisa: Dear Jessica: you make me shout a lot. ☺

Lear is a case in point: he is not a nice man or a particularly good king. And he's a really terrible father. When Goneril and Regan debrief the disastrous family gathering they've just witnessed at the end of the first scene, they are understandably shaken: they played along with their father's carefully orchestrated and (terribly unfair) love test only to watch their younger sister throw a monkey wrench into what would have otherwise been a relatively straightforward retirement party. Instead of receiving their dowries and heading off to their respective estates, they must witness their dysfunctional family implode as Lear banishes Cordelia and then Kent in short order.

In the aftermath of what might qualify as the worst family party in Shakespeare's canon, the two sisters discuss how their father has always been "rash" with "imperfections of a long-engraffed condition" (1.1.292, 294) that has made him unpredictable, short-tempered, and irritable. Perhaps most damning, Regan observes: "he hath ever but slenderly known himself" (1.1.290–1). If Lear has never known himself, which is a precondition for knowing others, then he does not have the capacity for empathy. In fact, empathy would be much too risky for Lear: he cannot imagine what someone else is feeling or thinking or experiencing because he himself leads an unexamined life. If he acknowledges the legitimacy of someone else's perspective, he must also acknowledge that their views might be different from his own, a realization that would destabilize his belief that he alone controls the production of meaning. Indeed, when he finally looks inward, his mind cracks under the pressure of scrutiny and he cries: "Go to, they are not men o'their words: they told me I was everything"; "'tis a lie, I am not ague-proof" (4.6.103–4).

Lear's love test is designed to ensure that everyone stays on script: the "how much do you love me?" game isn't about unconditional love or unwavering loyalty (he has that already with Cordelia and Kent), but rather a carefully stage-managed performance in which every member of his court affirms Lear's version of selfhood: all king, all powerful – in short, "everything." He fails to realize that performance always involves risk – of disruption, deviation, alteration, or addition. When Cordelia responds with "nothing" to his question – when she strays off script with her poorly timed and terribly inconvenient expression of critical love – his sense of self and his place in the world are exposed as a regulatory fiction.

Jessica: We could have a top ten worst parties in Shakespeare's canon:

1. King Lear's love test
2. Leontes calling Hermione a whore in WT
3. Titus's cannibalistic dinner party in *Titus Andronicus*
4. Macbeth's banquet when Banquo appears
5. Hamlet's funeral / wedding feast
6. Cassio getting drunk as a fart and getting fired in *Othello*
7. The bachelor party for Claudio in *Much Ado about Nothing*

Top ten best parties:

1. *Henry IV* part 1 – Cheapside
2. *Henry IV* part 2 – Cheapside
3. Wedding banquet masque in *The Tempest*
4. Anything in *Antony and Cleopatra*
5. The feast in the Forest of Arden in AYLI

Shannon: Great lists. Also for worst party list, the Harpy takes away the feast in *Tempest* and Petruchio shows up late and leaves early to his own wedding. Or Iago and Cassio go drinking in *Othello*. (This is a fun game, with way more bad parties than good.)

Shannon: I agree, and I agree with what you say next about his mind cracking when he tries empathy for the first time in the storm – as if empathy is a muscle he has never used before and so injures the first time he tries to stretch it. I do want to put in a high five for Lear for trying here at all, though. His care for the Fool and his shock when he sees Poor Tom and laments what human life is at its core are real moments of empathy, and I think I find it MORE remarkable that an unreflective narcissist come to it. It leads him to berate himself: "I have ta'en too little care of this." Yes, too little, too late maybe, but it gives me hope that the minor monsters of the world can learn and change.

Jessica: I know I am awfully hard on Lear – and he does have these little glimmers of empathy. But then he backslides and disappoints me all over again. His realization that he has not protected the "houseless heads and unfed sides" and the "looped and windowed raggedness" of his subjects (3.4.31) is staggering – and yet he enters the hovel and goes right back to "hey, here is a crazy man who is a perfect external mirror for my own internal debasement." One step forward, two steps backwards.

What is so interesting about Lear's identity crisis is that Regan and Goneril see all this before the rest of us do. At the end of 1.1, the two older sisters compare notes on Lear's onstage meltdown with remarkable insight. His violent outbursts do not take the sisters entirely by surprise; after all, they have a long history with a father who is "rash" and "unruly" and full of "imperfections." However, the magnitude of his reaction and the targets of his rage – his favorite daughter and trusted advisor – are deeply unsettling. Regan and Goneril worry that "if our father carry authority with such disposition as he bears, this last surrender of his will but offend us" (1.1.300–3). In other words, Cordelia has just introduced a level of complexity that challenges his already superficial sense of self, his frame of mind (angry, unpredictable); this, compounded with his retirement (the "last surrender"), puts the sisters at tremendous risk. In this brief exchange we are aligned with Goneril and Regan in their shock and anxiety. We don't yet know that they will commit heinous acts and destroy one another for the love of a bastard, but their subsequent behaviors are framed at the outset of the play as defensive maneuvers precipitated by their father, who has consistently shown them he is more kin than kind. They've been mistreated and abused, and our knowledge of their perspective, compounded with their ability to exercise critical empathy, throws a monkey wrench into any easy categorization of "good guys" and "bad guys" in this play.

I often refer to monkey wrenches and rabbit holes in our classroom adventures. Both of these animal-inspired expressions signal moments where the script is disrupted in some way. The late nineteenth-century origins of the expression "to throw a monkey wrench into the works" describes a large wrench thrown into an industrial machine to disrupt or suspend its operations, sometimes as an act of industrial sabotage. While we might think about a monkey wrench as a kind of situation, I use the expression in the classroom to indicate the subversion of an otherwise neat and tidy argument with the introduction of an alternate perspective or a contradictory piece of information. If the classroom is a space for embracing complexities, we must encourage monkey wrenches of various shapes and sizes to disrupt the large, weighty machine of known knowledge in order to move toward a richer, more nuanced space that liberates us from "right answers" or "correct" interpretations. Just as Cordelia throws a monkey wrench into her father's plans, Regan and Goneril throw one at us if we dare go looking for a moral compass. For those searching for the neat and tidy version of

Shannon: Which makes it such a tough play! I think I don't want to go all the way with you here about the mistreatment and abuse. I would have to pile a lot more onto his behavior and to his preference for Cordelia to see him as an abusive parent: to them, anyway. And were they on trial, I think I'd be reluctant to accept the bad childhood defense for the blinding of Gloucester.

Lisa: The best monkey wrenches are thrown by students, who sometimes ask questions we haven't considered or offer up experiences that radically reorient our perspectives. Sometimes they do it just like Cordelia does, by saying "nothing." Then we go a little mad and either have to examine ourselves, our authority, our plans, or refuse and lose the promise of the moment.

> **Shannon:** Love that idea – so true. That's why improv is as much a pedagogical skill as class planning. Chatting about *Dream* in class last week, one of my students asked whether comedy generally (and corrective comedy in particular) erodes empathy. If we laugh at someone, do we separate ourselves from that person? Damn, son. Class derailed in a much better direction than the more bloodless one about metafiction that I had planned.
> **Jessica:** Ooooh. I like that! Let's have *that* conversation!

Shannon: For me, they throw a monkey wrench into my intellectual compass especially, if you'll pardon the mixed metaphor. They are correct, damn it, and perceptive. I don't see them being good. They would totally be sorted into Slytherin.

> **Jessica:** That is how Shakespeare messes with us: they can be right, and perceptive and NOT NICE PEOPLE. They are totally Slytherin. But that makes Cordelia a Hufflepuff.

Shakespeare, monkey wrenches are at best annoying and at worst deeply threatening. A curiosity-driven classroom demands that we wield monkey wrenches but also be confident to grapple with them using a combination of confidence and humility that is not for the faint of heart. Indeed, *King Lear* invites onto the stage a number of hearts that crack under the pressure of such exertion.

If the monkey wrench is disruptive, the rabbit hole is divergent. An unanticipated distraction in Lewis Carroll's *Alice's Adventures in Wonderland* transports Alice to a different realm where she views the world through strange and unfamiliar lenses. When she finally pops out of the rabbit hole, she is at a different spot from where she began and her concept of the world is irrevocably altered. This is a wonderful metaphor for what we hope to do in our classrooms: we go down rabbit holes together in order to look through different lenses and see things from different perspectives, only to pop out of a text or a classroom transformed. Both rabbit holes and monkey wrenches are metaphors for learning that embrace complexity as a starting point; while the monkey wrench can be unsettling and potentially destructive, the rabbit hole offers a warren of creative associations that are potentially generative. Both have their place in the classroom and both play a significant role in *King Lear*.

Kathryn Schulz, writing for *The New Yorker*, identifies three major kinds of rabbit holes in the context of our new digital reality: iterative, exhaustive, and associative. She uses the example of a flannel shirt. Perhaps you are sitting at your computer and you decide you want to buy a flannel shirt. An *iterative* rabbit hole would mean you looked at 245 versions of the shirt to make your decision. An *exhaustive* rabbit hole requires you to become an expert on the origins of the flannel shirt, while the *associative* would take you from flannel shirts to racehorses in a loosely connected chain of ideas or concepts (para. 6). If we were to swap flannel shirts for Shakespeare, a favorite iterative rabbit hole is the Shakespeare Concordance, an open-source digital tool that allows you to look up every use of any word in Shakespeare's canon. For example, if you were to look up the word "nothing" in *King Lear*, you would find there are twenty-nine uses distributed amongst a broad range of characters. Cordelia sets off the chain reaction whereby "nothing" pops up in many places and in the mouths of many. Lear is especially haunted by the word and uses it four times in Act 3 – immediately before he goes mad (*Open Source Shakespeare*). An exhaustive rabbit hole, in contrast, might follow the etymology of the word "nothing" in early modern England as a word that sounded almost exactly the same as "noting," which meant to observe, perceive, or even to mark something as important. This definitional doubling has the potential to radically change our understanding of Cordelia's initial utterance. Is there a possibility she might have just been signaling her role as observer rather than voicing her resistance to the love test? An in-depth study of the origin of the word, its multiple meanings, and how the word "nothing" operates in its many contexts urges us to embrace complexity as part of the aesthetic and philosophical meaning of the play rather than as a pesky loose end that resists resolution.

My favorite rabbit hole in the classroom is the associative one, whereby we weave together connections like daisies along a chain of meaning that is different every performance. In our search for critical empathy in *King Lear*, we often find ourselves moving from a discussion about whether or not we like the characters on stage to how closely aligned we are with them at various moments as the play unfolds. The challenge in the classroom is to imagine – through discussion and simulation – the three-dimensional space of the play in performance, whereby we occupy a position of dynamic simultaneity as spectators and as scholars. One way to do this is to identify moments where we are encouraged to inhabit others' perspectives through dialogue or stagecraft. We might then look to the Renaissance thrust stage as a way of understanding how space can change the relationship between spectator and spectacle. My favorite term used for the sixteenth-century audience is "under-standers" because the people with the cheapest tickets stood in the play-yard and were eye level to the stage. These "stinkards" were bled on, spit upon, jostled, and had a more intimate – one might even say more empathetic – relationship to the drama unfolding onstage. Play-houses were rowdy, raucous places animated by a sideshow of

Lisa: "My legs understand me": my punster partner's favorite Shakespearean pun.

Shannon: "My legs understand me better, sir, than I understand what you mean when you tell me to try my legs," says Viola to Feste in *Twelfth Night* (3.1).

vendors hawking hazelnuts, sex workers drumming up clients, and apprentices heckling one another and the actors. The players onstage had to compete for the attention of the masses with a compelling performance shouted above the din (and we think classroom management is a challenge!). An associative rabbit hole might start with a discussion of space and move into a discussion of the smells and sounds of the early modern playhouse and then into a discussion of the social microcosm of the Globe.

Associative rabbit holes often have potential to lead to associative learning. In our discussion of the love text in 1.1, for example, we sometimes find ourselves theorizing the difference between *asides* (an actor speaks lines to themselves or to the audience while other actors are onstage but cannot hear them) and *soliloquies* (spoken by an actor who is alone onstage) as an access point into a conversation about how we represent interiority – or as Cordelia exclaims, "I cannot heave / My heart into my mouth" (1.1.90–1). In other words, how can we translate our thoughts, feelings, or impressions into language in any way that makes sense to others? This concept – that you can never fully access anyone else's soul (or heart or mind) – is a point made by Iago when Othello demands: "I'll know thy thoughts." Iago retorts: "You cannot, if my heart were in your hand, / Nor shall not, whilst 'tis in my custody" (3.3.167–9). When Iago tells Othello he will never know how Iago feels, our inability to *know* someone else's interiority is framed as deeply unsettling since it implies there might be Iagos in our midst who, unbeknownst to us, harbor what Samuel Taylor Coleridge called in a note scratched

Jessica: This famous phrase originates from Samuel Taylor Coleridge when he was preparing a lecture in 1818 on *Othello*: "the motive-hunting of motiveless Malignity – how awful!" (*Lectures 1808–1819: On Literature*, 315).

Lisa: But thinkers like Iris Marion Young, who coined the phrase "asymmetrical reciprocity" (38), posit this opacity as the grounding *condition* of empathy; since we cannot know each other directly, we must *engage* with each other through dialogue. It might be that Othello and Lear share a lack of skill for or commitment to "asymmetrical reciprocity." Lear certainly does resist it, as you've argued, by insisting in the opening scene that the only self worth knowing and voice that should be heard are his own.

> **Shannon:** This strikes me as an essential thing for us to wrestle with: we can't know each other, but we can listen, engage, and imagine. Is there a link here somewhere to playing, acting, theater? Shakespeare's central metaphor of the theater explores the way an actor or anyone can embody another's experience: imitate it, represent it (and fool others). Pre-method acting as it is, it seems to me to emphasize noting and then imitating: a focus on what is external, viewable. So, suit the action to the word, the word to the action. Another rabbit hole, perhaps.

Jessica: Tom of Bedlam is an external manifestation of Lear's fragmenting interiority. Edgar gives us a clue of what this might look like when he transforms: "To take the basest and most poorest shape / That ever penury, in contempt of man, / Brought near to beast. / My face I'll grime with filth, / Blanket my loins, elf all my hair in knots, / And with presented nakedness outface / The winds and persecutions of the skies / Of Bedlam beggars, who, with roaring voices, / Strike in their numbed and mortified bare arms / Pins, wooden pricks, nails, sprigs of rosemary" (2.3.7–16).

> **Lisa:** I think it's kind of fascinating that Edgar's assumption of a false identity is done by way of getting naked, whereas Lear's discovering of a true identity is done by way of getting naked. Two different philosophies of the self at work there: Lear may be more Rousseauvian, stripping away the encrustations of "culture" to reveal the naked human essence; Edgar may be Hobbesian, since his identity as a "sane" subject depends on those very trappings of culture. If it is true that Lear "(mis)identifies" with Tom, maybe it's because Edgar's notion of culture is not "dreamt of in his philosophy."
>
> **Shannon:** It's my favorite moment on the stage in this play, and it works so much better visually than on the page. Lear points to Tom to say that he is "the thing itself," that this before them is what you get when you strip people down, take away all the artifices of culture. And he's right, but he also doesn't know how right he is, because he thinks he's pointing to a mad beggar, but we know it's a good if maligned sane person.

in his copy of *Othello* a "motiveless malignity." However, when Cordelia uses a similar anatomical metaphor – this time the heart is in the mouth rather than in the hand – we grieve alongside Cordelia that her father will never be able to see her version of authentic (critical) love; instead, he is fooled by the empty words of her less sincere sisters. Just as Iago blocks us from the experience of empathy, Cordelia invites it – and they both use the metaphor of their heart to do so.

While Cordelia throws monkey wrenches, Lear's madness is a rabbit hole. He knows he is susceptible to falling down this hole, and as early as 1.5, he exclaims: "O! let me not be mad, not mad, sweet heaven; / Keep me in temper; I would not be mad!" (41–2). Despite his incapacity for empathy, Lear becomes increasingly self-reflective. In 2.4, he cries: "No, I'll not weep: / I have full cause of weeping, […] but this heart / Shall break into a hundred thousand flaws / Or ere I'll weep. O fool! I shall go mad" (280–4). Lear struggles against the ever-present threat of madness. In 3.4, he frets: "O that way madness lies! let me shun that; / No more of that" (21–2).

The turning point is Lear's encounter with Tom of Bedlam, whom he sees as an external manifestation of himself. He believes Tom has gone mad because he has "give[n] all to [his] two daughters" (3.4.48). Despite Tom of Bedlam's alternate explanation of his madness (a dissolute life of whoring and drinking and gambling), Lear refuses to acknowledge any pathology other than his own. Running counter to empathy, Lear projects his interiority onto the external world on countless occasions, starting first with his motivation for staging the love test, then reflected in his belief that the storm reflects his own turmoil, and then again with his (mis)identification with Tom of Bedlam.

When his ability to handle complexity reaches its limitations, Lear's madness provides him with a new lens through which to see the world. He swaps his royal crown for a crown of wildflowers and speaks with astonishing lucidity about the world around him. Madness provides him with liberation not from complexity but rather from the constraints of "right answers" or "correct" interpretations. Madness offers

Lear festive renewal, a chance to swap his November-y world for one of regeneration *if* he can recognize critical love and develop a capacity for empathy. However, Lear wastes his opportunity and spends his time dreaming up ways to indict his daughters, launching into misogynistic rants, and pardoning Gloucester for adultery. Even when Cordelia's troops arrive to rescue him, Lear runs away skipping. When he is finally reunited with Cordelia, he cannot fathom how she could continue to love him because critical love – just like critical empathy – is beyond his grasp:

> If you have poison for me, I will drink it.
> I know you do not love me; for your sisters
> Have, as I do remember, done me wrong:
> You have some cause; they have not. (4.7.72–5)

Lear gives Cordelia permission to hate him because he recognizes that he has given her every reason to do so: rejection and banishment certainly, but more importantly his failure to truly *see* her as she really is, a devoted child and loyal subject. And yet he hasn't learned the most important lesson of the play, which is the ability to know all the reasons why the ones we love are imperfect and nevertheless we love them fiercely, flaws and all.

While monkey wrenches and rabbit holes create or enhance complexity, critical love deals with the effects of it. Critical love embraces complexity – of another person or an institution or a nation – that understands flaws not as an unfortunate effect but as an essential condition of experiencing love. Think about Shakespeare's greatest pairings: Beatrice and Benedick, Portia and Bassanio, Viola and Cesario, Rosalind and Orlando, Antony and Cleopatra. These lovers eventually see one another in the light of day with all their weaknesses and shortcomings exposed. They have been disabused of romantic fogs, been inoculated against love potions, and have eschewed cliched Petrarchan conceits and the naiveté of youth; instead, they love *because* of rather than *despite* their beloved's imperfections, embracing flaws *and* poor behavior. Forging critical love is an act that refuses to erase difference or overlook qualities that are inconvenient or troubling. In Shakespeare's works, however, some of the most powerful moments of critical love are not romantic (probably because *eros* often blocks the "critical" part of critical love). In *King Lear*, Cordelia and Kent practice critical love for Lear even though Lear might not have the capacity to recognize their devotion, loyalty, and self-sacrifice. Cordelia and Kent know Lear has "imperfections of a long-engraffed condition" (1.1.294) just as Goneril and Regan do, but what they choose to do with this knowledge couldn't be more different. They are loyal to the highest ideals of what Lear can be and exhibit the persistence to continue loving him with all of his failings and poor choices. In this way, critical love is fundamentally hopeful because it has the possibility to be transformative – and even redemptive.

Shannon: Amen, sister!

The relationship between the Fool and critical love is perhaps the most problematic as we navigate the delicate balance between the "critical" and the "love." There is certainly no one more critical of Lear than the Fool, and his damning assessment of Lear's love test exposes the radical decenteredness of Lear's identity through various images that signify evacuation, like an empty pea pod (1.4.189), an egg shell (150–5), an "O" (182), and, perhaps most damagingly, the image of a "shadow" (220). The Fool's truth telling prompts Lear to ask more frantically for external verification by way of a series of questions: "Who am I?" (75) and "Does any here know me?" (215) and "Who is it that can tell me who I am?" (219). Instead of the coherence he desires, Lear is systematically dismantled.

Although the Fool participates in the destruction of Lear's identity, he disappears in Act 3, never to be heard from again. The "critical" overwhelms the "love," rendering this relationship fundamentally less hopeful than Lear's relationships with Cordelia and Kent. However, Shakespeare throws us a provocative monkey wrench: there is speculation that the same actor played both Cordelia and the Fool in the original productions. The demands of a small theater company playing in repertory meant that dramatic doubling was logistically essential. When Lear calls for his Fool in 1.4 – "Where's my fool, ho? I think the world's asleep" (45) – the actor is presumably wriggling out of the elaborate Renaissance dress and into his motley attire. But this doubling is much more significant than just accounting for a shortage of bodies. The actor embodies both the critical and the love, the Fool and Cordelia, and integrates them such that acting itself becomes an act of critical empathy. The player holds both identities in dynamic simultaneity, engaged in the action of critical love, and by doing so offers us a way forward.

Even the play itself maintains a dynamic simultaneity: there is more than one textual version, an editorial reality that creates a doubling of textual meaning that resists reintegration and assimilation. It is as if Shakespeare could not figure out how to end this play because he changes his mind between quarto and folio versions. In *The History of King Lear* (Quarto version, 1608), Lear dies knowing Cordelia is dead, crying "never, never, never" and then "O, O, O, O!" (134). In *The Tragedy of King Lear* (Folio version, 1623), however, Lear bellows "never, never, never, never, never" (5.3.307) in one of the most haunting lines of iambic pentameter in Shakespeare's canon. But in his dying breaths, he is hopeful. He exclaims, "Do you see this? Look on her. Look, her lips. / Look there, look there," before collapsing (309–10). The Folio version is more hopeful, more potent, and more heart-wrenching in its summation of a play where many

Jessica: One of my Shakespeare students, Sally Cunningham, wrote an essay that took my breath away. She argued: "an analysis of critical love in King Lear will demonstrate how hope in someone's dishonoured character can lead to redemption in the form of empathy." She suggests that critical love is what redeems Lear's identity because of his truth tellers' hope. Cordelia's forgiveness redeems him while Kent's continuity provides Lear with the ontological support to be open to redemption.

Lisa: Oh wow, I love this image! ☺

Lisa: Ah yes. I love the way that the conditions of the theatrical moment open up this possibility for analysis and nuance. This is precisely why I ask my students to be actors, dramaturgs and theatrical critics so that they can watch these moments unfold in their own spaces.

Shannon: Is this moment an example of un-critical hope? He thinks he sees her breath, but he's wrong. It is false hope. The audience has to be with him at that moment, too, especially if they know the folk tale or the Holinshed version of the tale, both of which allow the Cordelia figure to live happily. Shakespeare is especially cruel at the moment, setting his audience up to disappoint them.

Lisa: He really does plunge us into Lear's frame of mind that way, doesn't he?

of the characters failed to heave their hearts into their mouths. Both versions, however, fail to offer us renewal. Those left alive at the very end are witnesses and bystanders, not participants and understanders. In the Folio version, Albany is given the final four lines to sum up the play, while in the Quarto version the last quatrain is uttered by Edgar:

> The weight of this sad time we must obey;
> Speak what we feel, not what we ought to say.
> The oldest hath borne most: we that are young
> Shall never see so much, nor live so long. (5.3.322–5)

The words are the same in both versions, but they are expressed by two different characters. While the line "Speak what we feel, not what we ought to say" seems to return us to feeling, to empathy, and to love, the rhyming couplets and the moralizing, fairytale ending strike a note of discordance in what is otherwise an ending that shakes us to our core. Despite my distaste for Lear and my lack of attachment to Cordelia, I weep alongside this heartbroken father as he stoops over his child's lifeless body and howls. Every. Single. Time. What's more, I am nearly inconsolable when Kent, offered the kingdom to co-rule, chooses to say his farewells instead: "I have a journey, sir, shortly to go; / My master calls me, I must not say no" (5.3.320–1). His unflagging loyalty – despite being banished and then denied a highly anticipated reunion with his beloved master – has a quality of critical love that breaks my heart open in the classroom and in the theater.

For Schulz – and, I have argued, for curiosity-centered classrooms – rabbit holes are essential to generating new knowledge. In a defense of so-called short attention spans in the digital age, Schulz asserts:

> The common charge against our online habits is that they are shallow; but, in keeping with the metaphor, rabbit holes deepen our world. They remind us of the sheer abundance of stuff available to think about, the range of things in which it is possible to grow interested. Better still, they present knowledge as pleasure. The modern rabbit hole, unlike the original, isn't a means to an end. It's an end in itself – an end without end, inviting us ever onward, urging us to keep becoming, as Alice would say, "curiouser and curiouser." (para. 14)

In our discussion of *King Lear*, our encounters with rabbit holes and monkey wrenches invite us to revel in complexity and offer us access points into the experience of critical love. We are always in the process of becoming, and that can be terrifying or hopeful depending on how we encounter the monkey wrenches

Lisa: Alice gets bigger and smaller, a growth that shows her different aspects of the world, opens certain doors and pathways that would otherwise be closed if she weren't so capable of transformation. Anything is interesting if you look at it closely enough, I tell my students, and sometimes you have to change your shape in order to get close enough to see it. ☺ In interacting with *Lear*, maybe I need to learn to get bigger or smaller so that I can look at it from diverse perspectives and at different scales. To interact empathetically means to transform the self.

and rabbit holes in our lives. If we can be brave enough to welcome disruption and divergence, if we can make space for both destruction and generativity, then we can free-fall down rabbit holes without having to know where the bottom lies: hope allows us to take the leap with the faith that, when we emerge in a different place and in an altered state, we are immeasurably enriched for the experience.

Keep Falling, Alice.

Lisa: Our new mantra, perhaps? ☺ Certainly T-shirt material. :D

Impossible Choices and Unbreakable Bonds in *King Lear*: Close Reading, Negative Capability, and Critical Empathy

Shannon Murray

In Act 1, Scene 1 of *King Lear*, the initial love test and Cordelia's response to it invoke the most passionate and contradictory responses in my undergraduate classes, and for good reason. In that scene, Shakespeare is doing something extraordinary. He creates a moment in which it is impossible for Cordelia to do the right thing, and he makes it difficult for us as witnesses to that test to come away with simple, easy, and comfortable judgments. When Cordelia is asked, "what can you say to draw / A third more opulent than your sisters?" (1.1.84–5), she answers with her plain-speaking "nothing" (86). And she is dead right. And she's dead wrong.

How wonderful that Shakespeare can take such a simple framework for his play – more folk tale than history – and develop it into one of the most complex in his canon. The thing I want students to leave with is a way to hold on to the complexity of the play, resisting the temptation to simplify, resolve, or shape its rough edges. The ability to recognize and live with complexity – without being paralyzed by it – is one of the most important skills in higher education and in life. *Lear*'s genius is that it gives us so many opportunities to talk about what happens when life and our judgments about it are messy.

What can we do when faced with an impossible situation? A hard choice is one thing, but what about a choice in which neither option is appealing? What if no matter what you do, no matter what choice you make, the outcome won't change, and you can't make things work out for the best? What if you are facing an impossible choice because you happen to be serving a boss, a leader, a country that is autocratic, irrational, or just plain evil? And those are just the questions that Cordelia's position raises. If we think about Lear, we can ask: What do we do if we make a terrible mistake? Are we redeemable or are there time limits on redemption? What if that mistake happens late in

Lisa: "Go with the weird," I tell my classes, pushing them to accept the discomfort Shakespeare creates in such moments and to explore it instead of trying to smooth it all away. As you say, it's important to resist the temptation to simplify and instead to get used to living with complexity. I trust Shakespeare to create such moments for a reason, so that we can, as Aristotle suggested, try out discomfort without actually losing our lives.

Jessica: This is such a crucial question. When I teach *Paradise Lost*, I ask my students what happens if Satan actually repents? If God is truly good and all forgiving and Satan fulfills all the criteria for repentance, is it possible he will be forgiven? Can anyone qualify for redemption?

> **Lisa:** "Use every man after his desert," quoth Hamlet, "and who shall 'scape whipping?" (2.2.516–17).

an otherwise successful life? And what if it happens when a group of baddies are just waiting for us to slip? How much are we responsible for the misery that follows if circumstances rob us of the chance to make things better?

I want to argue that *King Lear's* power lies in the endlessly complex judgments that it requires of us, judgments that can change over time, as we change and age, and that exploring this complexity brings us close to two ideas – negative capability and close reading – both of which nudge us toward critical empathy. *King Lear* is, I believe, a marathon test of critical empathy. I'm not aware of another text that demands such painful and baffling understanding of flawed others. I will look at the opening exchange between Lear and Cordelia, examining it in painfully minute detail – so skip ahead if you like – to show how it can be used as a model of the connections between close reading and critical empathy as well as negative capability and critical empathy.

So, first to the idea of that complexity. When I find myself stuck between the contrary beliefs that Cordelia is right or wrong, or to feel deeply, on the one hand, that Lear deserves what he gets and, on the other, that he deserves pity for his distress, I wonder whether this is something like what poet John Keats was grasping at in his maddeningly cryptic letter to his brother. There he suggests that artists like Shakespeare share "negative capability": "when man is capable of being in uncertainties, Mysteries, doubts, without any irritable reaching after fact & reason" (41). His letter is maddening because the term doesn't appear again in his other work, nor is it more clearly fleshed out in the letter, but it feels like it is nudging up against truth. Here he is talking about the poet's character rather than the audience's experience, but I think the two mirror each other. If the great poet is capable of "being in uncertainties," should he not be able to encourage – even to create – that state of being in his audience? What if we thought of the experience of the ideal viewer of a play like *Lear* as one who dwells in "negative capability"? That would mean that the moment or scene or play demands of us the ability to hold two conflicting, even contradictory ideas or responses in our heads at the same time, without an insistence on settling on one side or the other.

Jessica: I love this formulation: the dynamic simultaneity of two or more things that exist even as they are ostensibly in conflict. Like one giant oxymoron. Fun fact: the word "oxymoron" is itself an oxymoron! Oxy (sharp) + moros (dull) set up the apparent contradiction-in-conjunction. Romeo, overwhelmed with the love of fair Rosaline in 1.1., exclaims: "O brawling love! O loving hate! / O anything of nothing first create! / O heavy lightness, serious vanity!" (166ff). Oxymorons are a figure of speech that can help us explore the concept of togetherness, of difference, which demands that apparent contradictions coexist.

American writer F. Scott Fitzgerald has a similar notion in his startling essay "Crack-up," written for *Esquire* in 1938, about his own mental breakdown. He argues that "the test of a first-rate intelligence is the ability to hold two opposed ideas in the mind at the same time, and still retain the ability to function" (para. 2). That second part is essential: if I am going to maintain two opposing ideas about Lear as a father and ruler, for example, I need neither to crack up nor to throw up my hands and declare judgment pointless. Fitzgerald goes on:

One should, for example, be able to see that things are hopeless and yet be determined to make them otherwise.[1] This philosophy fitted on to my early adult life, when I saw the improbable, the implausible, often the "impossible," come true. Life was something you dominated if you were any good. Life yielded easily to intelligence and effort, or to what proportion could be mustered of both. It seemed a romantic business to be a successful literary man – you were not ever going to be as famous as a movie star but what note you had was probably longer-lived; you were never going to have the power of a man of strong political or religious convictions but you were certainly more independent. Of course within the practice of your trade you were forever unsatisfied – but I, for one, would not have chosen any other. (Fitzgerald)

Fitzgerald is talking particularly about the function of the writer, the artist, as was Keats, but I would argue that the ability both writers praise is equally essential in the reader, the audience. Lear is both monstrous and pitiable; Cordelia is both correct and cold.

In a moment, I'm going to try to show that painstaking and detailed close reading, that old mainstay of literature classrooms, can get us to some practice of critical empathy, but I think it's important to tackle a common jump that I see in my own students, one accompanied by my least favorite word: "relatable." Quite aside from its ugliness, the moment "relatable" gets deployed in conversation or argument, it shuts down discussion, as if once one has discovered "relatability" in a work, we can relax: we have pronounced it worthwhile. And why? Because we have found something in the piece that is like us, mirroring us, connected to our own limited experience of life.

But for me, "relatable" is the antithesis of good critical empathy.

Professor Rebecca Onion identifies the dilemma many of us find when we hear a student declare a play "relatable." On the one hand, it looks like we have succeeded: "Yay! I picked the right, resonant thing to assign! – but I soon noticed that the comment, when made in discussion, cut conversation short. Students would nod at each other across the classroom, clearly feeling like they'd cracked that nut. Yeah! Relatable. That's when the word began to irk me" (para. 2). But I think Charmaine Craig puts it best in a PBS *Newshour* piece. She says: "Partly because I'm culturally and ethnically kind of anomalous, I've rarely related to people in my life. But that doesn't mean I haven't learned from and respected and felt for them. And that's really what I want to say: that there's a difference between relating or liking, in our current sense, and being curious and empathic" (para. 5). She goes on to connect the cult of "relatable" to the rise of "likes" on Facebook: "There's nothing wrong with liking or disliking, but when we only like things we find

Lisa: I agree with the soothing complacency of the "relatable," although I do think that texts can solicit our identification, often by presenting our "selves" back to us, or by using forms that are familiar, for strategic and sometimes even shocking purposes, as we see in *Richard III*, where our identification is solicited by the charming Richard Gloucester, only to be sprung on us like a trap when we can no longer deny that he is monstrous and that our prior admiration of him or identification with him is equally so.

relatable, or we are only interested in people we find likeable, we're implicitly holding up narcissism and conformity, and we're critiquing difference" (para. 3).

Imagine, then, that someone watching King Lear's descent into dementia, isolation, and loss, where all that mattered to him is stripped away, could then reject the play because that experience is not theirs, because it is not relatable. Shakespeare suggests through *Hamlet* that the purpose of playing is to hold up the mirror to *nature*, not to the self. The band R.E.M. gets it right in the song "Losing My Religion": "Life is bigger than you and you are not me" (R.E.M.). Nature is bigger than each of us, and literature's great gift is that we get to see what we are not. Shakespeare gives us a mosaic of complex Otherness; "relatable" looks for the selfie. Here endeth the lesson.

But if "relatable" is the antithesis of critical empathy, how can close reading unlock that empathy, especially in a play like *Lear* that is such a perfect demonstration of the negative capability, the ability to hold multiple contradictory ideas in the mind at the same time? I spend a lot of time on a few passages, and the moment in the opening scene when Cordelia responds to her father's unreasonable request is especially rich. An aging king is about to divide his kingdom in three, and at that moment, perhaps before the event, perhaps on the spur of the moment, he adds a game: each daughter will have to express publicly how much she loves him, "That we our largest bounty may extend / Where nature doth with merit challenge" (1.1.51–2).

Now, if you just tally them up, the reasons Lear's game is wrong, even dangerous, make it clear that Cordelia's decision not to play is on balance the right one. Here's a quick list:

- The game conflates love and material reward: Lear asks his daughters to show him love in exchange for land.
- It makes what should be a private expression public: Lear called a public, state gathering, but he uses it to extort expressions of private feelings.
- It prefers rhetoric over logic or truth; while there is nothing explicitly wrong with rhetoric, the art of finding all the available means of persuasion, in this case Lear is confronted with two daughters who employ rhetoric and one who employs logic.
- It ignores important family law – in fact, the whole idea of dividing the kingdom rather than allowing the eldest to inherit must itself have seemed inappropriate to Shakespeare's audience.
- It separates instead of accumulates property – especially at a time when King James I worked to unite the British Isles, the idea of dividing the country into three would immediately appear politically disastrous.
- It subverts gender expectations: in preferring the voluble elder daughters to a quiet Cordelia, Lear works against a contemporary gender notion that a silent woman is best.[2]

- It is mathematically false: this one has bothered me since I was a smart-alecky high school student. By the time Lear gets to Cordelia, he has already given Goneril and Regan two specific thirds of his kingdom, identified and pointed out on a map. There is only one third left, and anyone can see it. So when he says "what can you do to draw a third more opulent than your sisters," Cordelia is simply speaking the truth when she says "nothing." Even were the math not at issue, she cannot draw a more opulent third: the thirds are already drawn.
- It ignores a religious injunction.

It's this last one that I want to spend some time with, though any on this list could easily occupy a full class, since each one pulls a thread of Renaissance culture, history, or thought. I'll use this one as an example of how rich this moment in the play is.

To begin with, when Lear answers Cordelia's "nothing" with "nothing will come of nothing; speak again" (1.1.89), he unwittingly (or perhaps wittily?) raises a thorny theological question. Did God create the world out of himself or out of nothing, creation *ex Deo* or *ex nihilo*? Cordelia's explanation echoes two, maybe even three moments in the Old Testament and the Church of England's Book of Common Prayer: "You have begot me, bred me, loved me: / I return those duties back as are right fit, / Obey you, love you, and most honour you" (1.1.95–7). In her first line, Cordelia lists Lear's duties in what must be ascending order of importance. Begetting is important but incidental; breeding – upbringing or education – involves more personal choice; but loving is best. He has loved her, bless his heart.

But look at the order in which she says she returns "those duties back as our right fit" – that is, as are most appropriate or fitting: "Obey you, love you, and most honour you." Hers is not the same list, nor should it be. The duties of a king and father will be different from the duties of the subject and daughter. If love, honor, and obey sound familiar, there's a good reason. They were for many centuries the trio English women spoke in marriage vows, as in the 1559 Book of Common Prayer: "Wilt thou obey him and serve him, love, honor, and keep him, in sickness, and in health?" (Booty 292) Cordelia essentially repeats three of those elements of the marriage vow to her father, making that her bond, her vow of connection to him. She has essentially asserted to him her participation in a marriage-like union of father and daughter.

Note that she ends with "honour," and if again that last is in the position of greatest importance, Shakespeare's audience might have heard an echo of one of the Ten Commandments: "honour thy father and thy mother: that thy days may be long upon the land which the Lord thy God giveth thee" (Exodus 20:12). She has said a lot of good, true, and powerful things in that concise and paralleled passage. Lear appreciates

> **Lisa:** This is an interesting iteration of the oxymoron phenomenon Jessica speaks to above. To be a good daughter, she has to be a daughter, a subject, and a wife, all of which demand something different. They don't yoke together comfortably and yet this is what is demanded of her. That is a lot of rhetorical finesse to expect from a child.

none of it. How could that fond, foolish old man miss them? If only he had been better at close reading!

I sometimes wonder, though, if Cordelia might have stopped there. She goes on to say, "why have my sisters husbands that they say they love you all?" Even if Lear had heard her say "I honour, obey, and love you," this next reminder that daughters leave, that fathers lose daughters to husbands, might have drowned her earlier sentiment out. Here again, Cordelia may be echoing the Old Testament, where Genesis tells us that in marriage, "therefore shall a man leave his father and his mother, and shall cleave unto his wife: and they shall be one flesh" (Genesis 2:24). Lear is trapped in that parental anxiety between wishing a daughter married and wishing to keep her as she is: all his. She goes further: "Happily, when I am wed, / That lord whose hand must take my plight shall carry / Half my love with him, half my care and duty" (1.1.99–101). That math never works for me, by the way. Do we halve our love when we love someone new? Surely not. My parents have all my love; so does my husband; and my two children do not split the leftovers. I love them "all" too. Cordelia's words suggest that we have a finite store of love to divide up, as Lear does land. So I feel absolutely that Cordelia is right in what she says; but these lines feel wrong, as if she has both said too much and used the wrong language. (I suppose there's a familial fault at work here; if his math was faulty at the beginning, she responds with a faulty equation.)

To put it simply, everything after "nothing" hurts Lear's feelings. His next two lines are pleading questions: "But goes thy heart with this?" "So young, and so untender?" (103, 105) He has interpreted her simple truth – a married daughter necessarily leaves her father – as unnatural, when it is not only appropriate but an essential part of the scene that Lear himself has constructed. He is the one who has determined that either France or Burgundy will, in this public meeting, become engaged to Cordelia. What she says is not only true; it is in keeping with what he himself wishes for her. And still.

Is Cordelia to blame either in what she says to her father or in how she says it? Kent, the play's good conscience, certainly believes she is correct and has "most rightly said" (182). He is banished for standing up for her. The King of France underscores Kent's judgment by choosing to marry Cordelia not despite Lear's disapproval but because of it. She is, he famously says, herself a dowry, and it is the story of her candor and clear thinking that moves him from love to inflamed respect. This close reading brings me back time and again to my own negative capability: I believe Lear is wrong and I pity him; I believe Cordelia is coldly correct but wish she had mended her speech a little.

Perhaps because of their age, a good portion of my students each time blame Cordelia. Are they harder on her because she

Jessica: Do you think Cordelia ever doubts her decision to say "nothing"? Do you think she has moments of uncertainty? I was reading an article recently on the importance of building uncertainty into the new generation of artificial intelligence "to know when they should doubt themselves" (Knight, para. 1). An essential component of programming "deep learning" is the ability to grapple with complexity and struggle with uncertainty.

Shannon: She seems pretty sure of herself, at least AFTER the "nothing." Before that, there are two moments in the aside when she appears to be working out what to do in this impossible game of her father's: "What shall Cordelia speak? Love, and be silent" (1.1.62).

is young, I wonder? To them, she's cold, rude, inappropriate in her response. They do wonder whether she should've said something else, quit while she was ahead, or chosen another time. Yes, her logic should be seen as better than her sisters' rhetoric, but would a little rhetoric have killed her? I wonder about her intention. It can't simply be to humiliate or embarrass her father, although that is the result. If it is to make him change his mind, to teach him, she goes about it the wrong way. Her sisters recognize two things about their father, both that he has "ever but slenderly known himself" and that the best of his times had "been but rash" (290–2). If Cordelia had seen the same faults in her father – and of course she may not have, since she was the closest of the three to him – she might, as Lear suggests, have "mended" her words a little. My students often suggest that her response smacks as much of pride as of candor. She will tell the truth no matter what, and they point out that the result is civil war and many deaths, including her own. Might the results of the play themselves suggest that Cordelia has acted foolishly if not falsely? Or has she merely miscalculated? What response did she expect from him?

She could surely have understood anger. Right though she may be, she is also a daughter and a subject, and she has spoken impertinently. But perhaps she could be forgiven for not expecting her father to react with such wild finality. Perhaps, like so many of Shakespeare's characters – I think of the character Paulina in *The Winter's Tale* or Macduff in *Macbeth* – Cordelia's greatest failure in this first scene may be a failure of imagination. She could not imagine the kind of reaction she received. A child, and especially a favorite child whose father knows her well, should reasonably expect not to be disowned after so many years of love and over so small a transgression.

I want to interject here with two things that I believe most strongly and that I know affect my judgment of this play. First, the worst thing that can happen to a parent is not the loss of a child; it is losing a child and knowing you are responsible for her death. That is what will happen to Lear. And second, the worst thing that a parent can do is to reject a child. That is what happens to Cordelia. Disowning, disavowing a child is done as an attempt to control behavior. It is almost always the result of an ultimatum: if you do not do as I say, you are no longer mine. It is deeply harmful to a child, of course. But what parents who disown children – and they are still shockingly common – ignore at their peril is that pronouncing the disavowal is a speech act, one that erases their own identities as parents. Lear means to

Lisa: I often travel with students down the "what if" paths of tragedy as we seem compelled to write the parallel universe story of what might have happened if Cordelia had said "lots" or Romeo's letter hadn't gotten lost. Such tragedies seem haunted by their own alternatives. I think often that students feel the anxiety of those moments in their own lives, where they have to make choices and can't know the outcomes. In some ways the tragedies that focus on young people, like Cordelia here, seem to really grasp that way of being in the world, where choices carry the weight of the future and seem so irrevocable. One of the things that Lear can't seem to be able to do is to empathetically put himself in a young person's shoes.

Jessica: Ann-Marie MacDonald's play *Goodnight Desdemona (Good Morning Juliet)* explores alternative comedic endings for two of the most famous tragedies. The premise is that if at the crucial time when all hell breaks loose, everyone gets into a room together and compares notes, tragedy can then be avoided and we are given a festive ending. The tipping points between comedy and tragedy happen in Act 3 for both *Romeo and Juliet* and *Othello*, but in *Lear* the tipping point is eighty-seven lines into the play with Cordelia's "nothing."

Jessica: J.L. Austin, in *How to Do Things with Words* (1955), talks about performative utterances as enacting something by saying it (as opposed to perlocutionary acts, which are persuasive). Disowning a child here is a performative utterance that changes identity – stripping child of parent, BUT in that speech act, the parent strips himself of the identity of parenthood.

destroy Cordelia, but he destroys himself as a father. Both of these notions, I know, affect how I respond to the play and to Lear himself, and both make Lear for me the most devastatingly heartbreaking character Shakespeare ever created. I understand why Lisa is reluctant to teach it. It hurts.

I do believe that Lear committed, of course, the colossal error in judgment, although even he could not have known how monstrous and murderous his other two daughters would turn out to be. But no matter how many ways Cordelia's response seems right, I think it is also *supposed* to feel wrong. Lear's sins and errors are many and varied – from the legal, royal, gendered, parental, mathematical, and scriptural perspectives – but he is also eighty, a very old man tired out by decades of rule. More than that, and despite his older daughters' judgment of him, he is also loved, deeply and steadfastly loved, by the moral centers of the play: Cordelia, Kent, and the Fool. That's really something. Cordelia's refusal to play his game has to be shocking to him. It knocks the stuffing out of Lear: it should shock us too. He is old, exposed, embarrassed. Even if her aim is to educate him, she has flipped the responsibility of a parent to educate the child: she has taken on the parental role. I believe that if it were easier to approve Cordelia's decision in her words, we would have an easy time condemning Lear. And if Lear were less to blame, we would have an easier time condemning Cordelia's behavior. The complexity of that opening means that we can understand his public hurt and feel the *pathos* toward an aging father, and even if we can't excuse his actions, we are invited to share in that hurt, that *pathos* as we witness the suffering that follows from his actions.

Lisa: As so many of us with aging parents do, must be prepared to do ("the calamity of so long life"?). Goneril and Regan do not take on this responsibility for their aging parent in his infirmity. Cordelia does, but in an unhelpful way. Again, as you say, the right thing is not always the right thing in a tragic universe.

Jessica: The Fool accuses Lear of reversing roles with his children: "e'er since thou mad'st thy / daughters thy mothers; for when thou gav'st them the / rod and put'st down thine own breeches" (1.4.162–4).

Shannon: I am indebted to Lisa and Jessica for making me think through my judgments about Goneril and Regan, to extend critical empathy even to murderous, nasty sisters.

The point I'm making is that the richness and difficulty and complexity of that opening scene, even just considering Lear's request and Cordelia's response, make judging the rest of the play a complicated matter. I don't mean to suggest that we don't judge. On the contrary, I think the play cries out for us to try to make distinctions. I'm just suggesting that it makes final decisions about those judgments very difficult, as we empathize by turns with each of the characters – even with Goneril, Regan, and Edmund.

When we read closely, looking at the language, sound, patterns, context, character of one small section of a piece, we are doing the work of deep listening. Almost always, the work invites us to complexity, to seeing how language can sometimes reveal and sometimes attempt to hide. The initial exercise of description – *What do I find in the passage?* – gives way to analysis – *What is the effect of what I've found?* This is an important skill that literary studies offer, one that we can use not just in literary texts but in approaching political speech, advertising, work memos, any moment of human communication. Old-fashioned though it might seem at first, attached as it is to the

New Criticism of the early twentieth century, it nevertheless survives in classrooms today, which haven't abandoned the old questions while asking new ones.

That deep listening to all aspects of the language of another requires the suspension of judgment until as full an understanding as possible is gathered. Done with attention and openness, it is an exercise of critical empathy. Of course, looking at a literary text adds another level of complexity to the act of close reading: reading the speech of a politician and reading the speech of one of Shakespeare's characters are different, specifically because in the literary case we have a "bending author" inventing a situation, a character, and language.

I love that it is about *King Lear*, and about pity for Lear himself particularly, that Lisa, Jessica, and I continue to have the most perpetual disagreements. I find myself agreeing with them even as I disagree, feeling both contradictory judgments at the same time. I love that my sister – not a lover of Shakespeare but someone who took on so much of the care of our grandmother as she slid into dementia – wept when I took her to an outdoor performance of *Lear*. She turned to me and said, "He's like Grandmum." I love that my own judgments and compassion for the play's characters shift as I age, have children, renegotiate family dynamics, and lose that sister. And I love that near the end of the play, Cordelia herself accepts the father who had so foolishly and dangerously rejected her with the lines that I struggle to get out in class without crying. When he asks her forgiveness, telling her that she has cause to wish him dead, her reply is the plain, simple: "No cause, no cause" (4.7.75). In the end, she is our model for empathy, and especially the critical empathy that offers more than a sad emoji before moving on to the next story of woe. Her empathy moves her to action, to risk, and ultimately to forgiveness.

Lisa: I am convinced that Lear is kind of an asshat who never gets all the way to the goalpost in his attempts to understand his own role in the fates of his daughters and friends, even though he can sympathize with their pain and misery (which is some progress, at least). I sometimes think that Cordelia's forgiveness at the end is not one of reciprocal growth or acknowledgment of his growth toward empathy and self-knowledge, but rather an act of grace, a gift given without reciprocity or obligation or dessert.

Shannon: I really agree with that last point: as Shakespeare tells us over and over, the greatest acts of forgiveness are never deserved. Think of Leontes, Posthumus, anyone in *The Tempest*. Cordelia's is beautiful because so many of us would abandon a rotten parent in such circumstances, and she doesn't. So I do think her forgiveness is not a reward for or a result of his growth. I do think that his "You have some cause" is a pretty big admission for this egomaniac, though.

Jessica: You have convinced me that Cordelia requires more credit than I have given her to date. She has resilience, tenacity, and a certain kind of spunkiness to invade England with her husband, France, who supports her and wages war for her/with her. She could have gone off to France and created a new life and a new family but she risks it all because of her (critical) love for her father. If only Lear has been open to a "new reality" rather than a "victory," we might have had a very different kind of play.

NOTES

1 And isn't this a perfect illustration of critical hope?
2 Later he will with devastating irony praise the dead Cordelia for her silence: "Her voice was ever soft, / Gentle and low, an excellent thing in woman" (5.3.271–2).

"Bless Thy Sweet Eyes, They Bleed": The Ethics of Pedagogy and My Fear of *Lear*

Lisa Dickson

I don't teach *King Lear*. In conceiving this project with my colleagues, I realized that I was going to have to confront *Lear* and Lear. Dear Future Self: I'm sorry to tell you, but you will need to think quite hard about why you don't teach *Lear*.

Short version: I am afraid of this play.

Why? I'm not afraid of tragedies. I teach a whole course called Blood, Lust and Tragic Form (colloquially known as Fifty Ways to Kill Your Lover). I did a doctoral thesis on severed heads. I'm not afraid of tragedy or the tragic worldview, in its various permutations. Nor do I shrink from depictions of violence. I've considered the theatrical complications of gore and dismemberment. (Severed heads are notoriously hard to wrangle and often go bouncing into the stalls, much to the audiences' disgust and my unending amusement.) But I am afraid of *Lear*. I once told my students that I don't teach the play to undergrads because, while Shakespeare may be a man for all seasons, not all seasons are for Shakespeare. Callow youth cannot understand the play until said youth has had to contend with an aging parent. This, of course, is a very stupid thing to say. I might as well tell them not to read anything at all that isn't about their exact lives and circumstances. The whole point of literature is to experience lives and circumstances and ideas that are not our own. Dear Past Me: unsay that dumb thing you said, 'kay, thanks, 'bye.

I own the dumb thing I said, acknowledge its wrongheadedness, but, while it is aimed erroneously at my students, it is not *entirely* wrong. It's not that Shakespeare's play isn't for the season of my young students, but that it is too much of mine. I'm afraid to teach *Lear* because the play is a very sharp blade turned on its edge, and I stumble into its unseen keenness and cut myself on it in all kinds of unexpected places. I realize that this is true of most literature that I love. Literature that is good tends to make one bleed; it comes into contact with

Jessica: Sometimes I fervently wish there was a "edit comments" feature in the live classroom. I say things that I think about well after the class is over and wonder, "why did I say that?" or "do I really think that?" As much as those moments are cringe-inducing and keep me awake at night, I think some of the most productive rethinking happens in the spaces where we grapple with the cringe.

Jessica: Despite the fact these affective responses are so present in our discussions of Shakespeare, I am often caught by surprise when it happens. We will be discussing a scene or engaging in a close reading and then all of a sudden a sob catches in my throat and my eyes swim. I used to cover these moments in class, embarrassed at any whiff of loss of control over the cognitive – but now I let those moments happen without shame.

Lisa: And isn't that what Shakespeare is supposed to do? It seems so weird, looking at it this way, that when we get into the classroom we edit out what is so important to the whole project of making drama. It's like looking at the plays "through a glass darkly" or refusing to taste food that is in our mouths. It seems perverse in a way.

Not that I'm advocating having feelings, of course. Feelings are terrible.

Jessica: And yet you have chosen Shakespeare – or Shakespeare has chosen you – and in these plays you have ALL THE FEELS all the TIME.

Lisa: I am a fool.

Jessica: Facilitating those spaces where relevance creates resonances and kinship and the reverberations of our heart strings is a really careful balance. Too much "relevance" and we risk instrumentalizing Shakespeare or erasing what is also strange and unfamiliar. Not enough "relevance" keeps us at a distance and maintains a kind of "I know I should like this because it is cultural capital" kind of attitude that we must struggle against with all our might.

Shannon: Oh, I like this. As always, the middle path?

the skin, breaches it, tells us where the quick is, where we live. Goneril's exasperation with her querulous father grazes across me and suddenly I'm in the car with my dad who is clutching a pillow over his recently cracked-open chest to protect his newly reconstructed heart from the jouncing of my bad driving. Lear plucks at Cordelia's buttons and although I'm sitting in my office chair, I'm out wandering the muddy asphalt of my parents' half-built subdivision because I can't be in the house anymore with a father who has committed the terrible crime of being mortal and, worse, being unhappy about it. It's not that I don't find anything in *Lear* to identify with; it's that I find that a part of me, the part that measures my worth as a child of human beings, identifies too much with the wrong people. This is not to say that I side with Goneril and Regan, or that I don't find their behavior repugnant. I am fully prepared to face the tragic message of the play, to occupy the less-than-radical position that it is wrong to gouge eyes, lock the elderly out in storms, and poison one's sisters. What comes at my unguarded flanks is something else, something sneakier, more wickedly acute and subtle, something that teases out with a sharp point the threads of a more mundane failure of humans to be at all times and in all places the people we hope we are.

This is, I suspect, one of the reasons that Shakespeare's works are important. They are populated by complexities, and at each turn of the clock, they reveal something unexpected.

I'm afraid of *Lear* because I don't want my students to see me bleed.

That says a lot about me, and my particular intellectual and personal phobia, if not outright failure. (If I had a coat of arms, its motto would be *Non ut motus*: I don't like feelings.) In our discussions about teaching, Jessica, Shannon, and I spoke about the power of the question *What do I ask my students to do that I wouldn't do myself?* My *Lear* fear and the context that gives rise to this question also speak to the prevailing culture of teaching and research, the structures of power and authority that scaffold our interaction with art. Every day I seek to help my students feel the relevance of art to their own lives, but I am quite unwilling to feel that myself, at least not in that space where I address them from the front of a lecture hall, whose podium and ranks of raked seating insist that this is where I am meant to stand. In that space behind the podium, this classroom says, I am supported by authority vested in me as the instructor. It is my function to embody that authority. It is a tool that I use to keep people facing the "right way," their minds wedged open and ready to accept input. I depend on that authority to maintain the classroom as a smoothly functioning culture of docile subjects, of which I am one. (I challenge you to find a single teacher who has not had a recurring nightmare of a class that, in response to a directive from the podium, says "no.")

In the space of research, which is to varying degrees demarcated from the space of the classroom, notably as the space of "real" intellectual work, I stand behind a podium of entrenched practices and values, where the architecture of authority is manifested in the tone of the academic voice: distant, aloof, disinterested. Don't get me wrong: I support the idea of intellectual "disinterest" as Matthew Arnold describes it in "The Function of Criticism at the Present Time," insofar as it enables "that more free speculative treatment of things" that often gets oversimplified in the rush to application (707). But the entrenched value system that designates research as "real" academic work also delimits the classroom as, at best, the space where that real work is "applied" and, at worst, the space where we pay our dues in order to enable the real work we would be doing if we weren't stuck in a classroom. To see this system of value in action, one need only to refer to the go-to "reward" for any achievement or service commitment at a university, the course release, a phrase that encodes the idea of escape from an onerous labor.

I have not yet fully come to understand how to occupy that space and the space of my own quick experience with art at the same time. It is exceedingly messy to show up bleeding from wounds. It's risky for a teacher to be a person. What a crime to commit, to turn out to be mortal, after all.

While I was beginning to wrestle with my fear of *Lear* and needing a little bit of courage, I fittingly picked up Parker Palmer's *The Courage to Teach*, one of the touchstone texts of the modern pedagogical movement. I needed a kind voice to help me to grapple with this tricky question of being human in the classroom and Palmer, a Quaker scholar, educator, and philosopher, is the most human and humane of thought partners and guides, one whose voice resonates with the strength and frailty, determination and flexibility required to take up the task of teaching and living what he calls "the undivided life." Good teachers, Palmer tells me, "must stand where personal and public meet, dealing with the thundering flow of traffic at an intersection where 'weaving a web of connectedness' feels more like crossing a freeway on foot" (18). The juxtaposition of the two texts, Shakespeare's and Palmer's, proved to be serendipitous, for *Lear* is very much about the consequences – mental, social, political – of living a divided life.

In his first speech of the play, just over twenty lines long, Lear uses the language of division at least six times, offering to break "In three our kingdom" in order to sever the "cares and business from our age." He will publish his daughters' "several dowers" to prevent "future strife" and to settle the suits of the "Great rivals" of Cordelia's love, France and Burgundy. He will "divest" himself of rule and pit his daughters against each other in a love test "That we our largest bounty may extend" (1.1.37–51). In breaking the nation into pieces, Lear not only offers up his family to a form of verbal civil warfare but effects a self-dismemberment, severing the material, private Natural Body from the ideal, public Politic Body, whose transcendence provides the king with authority. He tries, in other words, to give up kingship while keeping all its honors and trappings, to be a king without the pesky responsibilities of running a kingdom. It is no wonder, then, that infighting and outright war will follow, for Lear has shown his people that it is possible to divide a king from kingship, the man from his rule, from his people, and indeed his own family.

> **Shannon:** Such a strong point, and this hadn't occurred to me before. The foolish thing is that he hopes to avoid division by creating it, surely a doomed enterprise.
>
> **Shannon:** And the division of his retinue works here too – 100, 25, 5, 1.
> **Lisa:** Aha! So true!

In 306 lines of Scene 1, there are twenty-seven references to division, dichotomy, mutual exclusion, and terrible choices. The discourse of division proliferates as the action accelerates and Lear's power is winnowed away. The play becomes lugubrious with references to monstrosity, as proper duty and moral commitment give way to materialist lust and operations of naked force: "Humanity must perforce prey on itself," Albany says, disgusted with Goneril's abuse of Gloucester, "Like monsters of the deep" (4.2.49–50). Cornwall sums up the new state of the union in his commentary on his attainder of Gloucester: "Though well we may not pass upon his life / Without form of justice, yet our power / Shall do a court'sy to our wrath, which men / May blame but not control" (3.7.23–6). In a world where characters "Be-monster" (4.2.63) themselves in their pursuit of power severed from legitimacy and justice, the only means of resistance is to take refuge in the language of oxymoron and paradox, figures whose tortured logic seeks to find truth in the yoking of opposites: "Freedom lives hence, and banishment is here" (1.1.180), Kent asserts as he takes his leave of court. France takes Cordelia as his bride for she is "most rich, being poor" (1.1.249). But such refuge is temporary and exceptionally fragile, like Gloucester's heart, which, "too weak the conflict to support! / 'Twixt two extremes of passions, joy and grief, / Burst[s] smilingly" (5.3.196–8).

When the king attempts to be a king without kingship, the nation collapses. Reduced to the existence of a "bare, forked animal" (3.4.103), left to face the indifferent elements clothed only in the fragility of flesh, Lear and Gloucester come closer to the humanity from which their positions have shielded them. Their *anagnorisis*, a realization that overturns their ways of seeing themselves and the world, is not a result of reason but of feeling: "Take physic, Pomp; / Expose thyself to feel what wretches feel" (3.4.33–4), Lear says on the heath, while Gloucester laments the moral blindness of the "lust-dieted man / […] that will not see / Because he does not feel" (4.1.66–8). As a rumination on epistemology – that is, questions about what we know, what we believe and how we come to believe it – the play asserts that knowledge may *lodge* in the head but is *learned* in the flesh. In the concluding chapter of *The Courage to Teach*, where

Palmer articulates a call for a "New Professional," he makes the case for taking "emotional intelligence as seriously as we take […] cognitive intelligence" (206) and urges us to develop a discipline "to name, claim and aim" that emotional information in order to move toward transformative action and insight (207). I am encouraged by this call to action to look more closely at my emotional responses to *Lear* and to see if I can "mine" those responses for some analytical insight. It is a difficult task. In my classroom, I encourage students to engage with a Shakespearean play in myriad ways, to take it for a walk, to get up and shout it, carry it to the cafeteria and on the bus, to turn it inside out and to remake it in clay or cookie dough or dance moves. I tell them that they must not come at the plays in only one way; to fully know the plays, they must make them live. But in terms of my own engagement, I am less willing to risk and am deeply unwilling to see my own emotional responses to the plays as a source of knowledge. If not exactly bad faith, it is a limitation of the scope of analysis and experience that reflects a divided life.

For Palmer, this division of heart from head is in many ways a product of and is reinforced by the institutional bias toward objective knowledge that "distrusts and devalues inner reality" (*Courage to Teach* 19): "In this culture, the pathology of speech disconnected from the self is regarded, and rewarded, as a virtue" (18). The result for academics is "the pain of dismemberment" that "comes from being disconnected from our own truth, from the passions that took us into teaching, from the heart that is the source of all good work" (21). When I switched late in my doctoral studies to Shakespeare, I did so because I wanted to spend the rest of my life engaged in something that made me soar, that filled me with joy. When I became a scholar of Shakespeare, I learned to scour my work of that very joy. No one can kill a hilarious Shakespearean joke like a Shakespeare scholar. Moving through the world of research, I often find that the voice I use to speak of Shakespeare is what Palmer calls a "caricature": "Our words, spoken at a remove from our hearts, become 'the balloon speech in cartoons'" (18). If I am to take up Palmer's call to "to name, claim and aim" my emotional knowledge, I have to acknowledge that the discomfort I feel about *Lear* is due, again, to my tendency to identify myself in unflattering places. It is my own inauthentic voice that I hear in the

Shannon: You make me wonder whether it's sometimes a good thing, not just cowardly, to divide oneself. Being wholly who we are – or wholly open or wholly honest – at all times would be exhausting; it might even be dangerous. I wonder whether our Shakespeare doesn't give us a clue here. He might tell us that it is always a good thing to live an undivided life – except when it isn't. And that's tougher because we have to think … a lot. (Thinkings are just a little bit less terrible than feelings.)

> **Jessica:** If we think about the use of disguise for self-preservation as a divided self, the difference between comedy and tragedy is that in comedy, someone is always holding your clothes. Viola, in *Twelfth Night*, has the Ship Captain, Portia and Nervosa have one another, Rosalind and Celia can vouch for one another's "original" identities. However, Kent and Edgar have no witness: Kent "razes his likeness" (1.4.4) and Edgar self-mutilates. I always tell my students that they should ensure they always have someone holding their clothes. So in the framework of Palmer's divided life, as long as someone knows your wholeness exists, dividing it for self-preservation is not too risky?

Jessica: Ha! This is so true. It is as if we must suck the delight out of things in order to have any street cred as academics. BUT Sir Philip Sidney, a sixteenth-century writer, courtier and soldier, participates in a long historical tradition that places delight at the heart of teaching; in *The Defense of Poesy* (1579), he exclaims, "Who will be taught if he be not moved with the desire to be taught?" (562). Sidney believed that to move someone was to transform them, and an ideal teacher must generate delight to stir the heart and shape the mind.

> **Lisa:** If I had told my brash younger self that Sidney would become my intellectual boyfriend, I would have been so skeptical. It's so good to know that he will wait for us all to catch up to him. ☺

> **Jessica:** I love Sidney. Elizabeth I found him to be such a pain in the ass (for various reasons, but mainly because he kept pestering her to go to war so he could show off his bravery) that she banished him from court. He got back into her favors by giving her a New Year's gift in 1581 of a whip garnished with diamonds "in token of his submission to the will of Her Majesty." Now that is a way to get back into the good graces of a powerful lady!

opening act of *Lear*, where the pathology of disconnected speech is rewarded with half a kingdom for each sycophantic daughter as Regan and Goneril compete to out-do each other in eloquently empty declarations of love for a self-obsessed father, while the honest rebukes of Kent and the measured response of Cordelia are rewarded with banishment. The consequence of Lear's inability to recognize the true speech of a true heart, and the willingness of his family to collude in the severing of speech from truth, is the collapse of the state into civil war, the family into filial ingratitude, adultery, and sororicide, the king's mind into madness, and the cosmos into the elemental chaos of the storm. Shakespeare is not fooling around. What are the consequences for the classroom and for me?

Like the ramifying fractures within Lear's kingdom, the divisions I live as a teacher ramify outward. In a 2008 study of the personal epistemologies of college students, Jane Elizabeth Pizzolato found that students who have highly developed, "availing" epistemological stances (Muis qtd. in Brownlee et al., 602) in the personal domains of their lives – meaning that they favor learning that transforms them – will nevertheless actively "short-circuit their own abilities" in the academic domain: "To get good grades meant that they sacrificed what was more rewarding in order to do well in their coursework" (Pizzolato 242). Students adopted "extremely narrow" goals, citing "getting the grade" and "passing the test" as the sole perceived value of their labor (240). This is what Ira Shor calls "faux learning," an "unauthentic discourse […] a kind of theater of manipulative discourse where students play at postures they think will help them get by" (51). In other words, the students, like Regan and Goneril, sever their actions from their hearts and are well-rewarded for that act of self-harm. For these students, the definition of success is grounded in an institutionally supported system of self-division in which they live one, instrumentalized life at school and another "real" life elsewhere, in some place "not contaminated or controlled by this dominating process" (17). How crushing to realize that the world of pedagogy where I locate the passion of my heart is simultaneously the place where students learn to put their passions elsewhere.

Shannon: And I never blame students for this self-harming behaviour. We construct or support institutional structures that encourage them to treat grades as an end and learning as a hurdle to get over (or around) and then expect them to love learning for its own sake.

Jessica: Mind BLOWN. We create cultures that short-circuit learning and teach students to self-sabotage in order to get ahead academically. This hurts my heart.

Lisa: Yeah, this one really, honestly left a mark. It literally made me stop, put down my papers, and take a lap because it hurt me like a kick. I've been trying to deal with this observation ever since I first read it and it has radically changed my attitude toward my students and my practice.

Like Lear dividing his kingdom, a teacher who models a divided life can hardly be surprised to see division ramify across the land. Unless I model an undivided life, how can I convince my students to seek it? If I opt for a compartmentalization of feeling from "real" thinking, my authority from the students' agency, how can I expect my students to do anything but reproduce that division? In taking seriously Palmer's call for a "New Professional" who can advocate for and build into the disciplinary practice the value of an undivided life, I am not indulging some new-age fetishization of the "touchy-feely," but rather seeking a way to acknowledge a broader responsibility for cultural change. Fear is not necessarily a bad thing, Palmer observes of his own confrontations with fear: "My fear of teaching at the dangerous intersection of the personal and the public may not be cowardice but confirmation that I am taking the risks that good teaching requires" (*Courage to Teach* 39). What, then, is the nature of this risk? What do we need to do to heal the fractured life?

In *Pedagogy of the Oppressed*, activist and educational philosopher Paulo Freire talks about the "converts" of the revolution, the well-meaning members of the oppressive class who come to join the struggles of the oppressed. For the convert, he argues, there will always be a question of trust, for the oppressors[1] are used to having control of language and its transformative power, and they are afflicted with a nostalgia for power even as they seek to relinquish it: "They talk about the people, but they do not trust them; and trusting the people is the indispensable precondition of revolutionary change" (*Oppressed* 60). As I begin to trace the consequences of my fear of feeling, I turn to Freire and the question of trust because of the way that his description of the "convert" hails me. As the meme goes: "I'm in this tweet and I don't like it." Freire's discussion of the self-divided convert traces the contours of the fear that arises in part from the institutional context that values and rewards objectivity, authority, and control in specific ways, cementing both students and teachers into nonreciprocal relationships of voice and voicelessness. Teachers talk and students listen. When a teacher asks a student to speak and the student answers "correctly," the teacher is verifying her own capacity to transfer information. Very much like Lear's court, where he reserves the right to ask a question for which there is only one answer – that is, unqualified love and ratification of his power and privilege – traditional models of the classroom are echo chambers where authoritative pronouncements are affirmed as the price of entrance into the discipline. This is a bit of a caricature in itself, but the lineaments of the model are persistent. It is one in which the teacher cannot fully trust the students, and vice versa, for trust requires dialogue. Speaking essentially to himself, Lear cannot hear the voice of Cordelia, nor can he understand the truth of her insistence that she loves him "according to her bond" (1.1.91), which, in her mind, is love grounded in the networks of relations – father to child, husband to wife, king to subjects – that bind the nation together.

Unable to repeat the prescribed answer to the question, Cordelia can say only "nothing" (86), for, as Freire asserts, "no one can say a true word alone – nor can she say it *for* another in a prescriptive act which robs others of their words" (88). Demanding that Cordelia speak, Lear admits only the illusion of conversation. In the traditional classroom, the "indispensable precondition for revolutionary change" is missing, and the status quo is reinforced by what Palmer calls "structures of separation": grading, fractured systems of knowledge that silo disciplines and keep them from talking to each other, a culture of competition, obstructionist and byzantine bureaucracy, and so on. As these "limit situations" (Freire 99, 102) are conditions that favor those in power, they present themselves as de facto conditions of the world, and it is difficult for either those with the power or those subject to it to conceive of them as susceptible to change. At points of confrontation, however, a group can begin to make visible – to "name, claim and aim," in Palmer's words – the thematics, the force exerted by networks of values, historical understanding, and commitments that shape the conditions of their lives. When Cordelia says "nothing," she makes visible the inauthenticity of speech in Lear's court, and while she is unable to name it clearly in the language of that space – which is why her critique is annexed in asides aimed outward at the audience – her resistance causes "these situations [to] stand out in relief from the background, revealing their true nature as concrete historical dimensions of a given reality" (99). Even silence is a powerful statement of consciousness of oppressive limits, for "silence suggests a structure of mutism in the face of the overwhelming force of the limit situations" (106). Or, because no matter what clever thing is said in our modern age, we can find that Shakespeare said it first: "Nor are those empty-hearted whose low sounds / Reverb no hollowness" (1.1.152–3). The unbending, unhearing rhetorical momentum of Lear's court runs aground on the beachhead of Cordelia's telling silence and begins immediately to fracture. Lear can only deal with this challenge by essentially closing his eyes to it, banishing his dearest friends in a childish response that he believes will erase opposition from the world.

> **Shannon:** The grading is such a problem. I was struck by a talk Cathy N. Davidson gave on the origins of the number system for student grading: it comes from the beef industry's rankings for cuts of meat.

> **Shannon:** Do you think Cordelia is giving Lear a failing grade – a zero?
>
> **Lisa:** I think, perhaps, that Cordelia is telling Lear that grading is toxic if it's not connected to real values. He wants "Grade A" beef and she is pointing out that his assessment model is flawed.

Lear's reliance on force over listening in this confrontation with an alternative worldview demonstrates not just the persistence of external "limit situations" but illustrates how the external forces of division are only half the story. As Palmer explains, this reliance is symptomatic of a deeper collaboration with structures of separation that is grounded in "one of the deepest fears at the heart of being human," fear of the Other, both those outside of us and the "self-dissenting voice within":

> We fear encounters in which the other is free to be itself, to speak its own truth, to tell us what we may not wish to hear. We want those encounters on our own terms, so that we can control their outcomes, so that they will not threaten our view of the world and self. (*Courage to Teach* 37–8)

One of Lear's problems is that he wants both to be the king and not to be the king, to "still […] manage those authorities / That he hath given away" (1.3.18–19). In this sense, he is the convert "who approaches the people but feels alarm at each step they take, each doubt they express, and each suggestion they offer, and attempts to impose his 'status,'" thereby remaining "nostalgic towards his origins" (Freire, *Oppressed* 61). *King Lear* calls on its title character to become a *true* convert, to heed the call of the Other and to risk transformation. To do so, Lear must confront an Otherness that challenges his very sense of identity in a way so fundamental that he repeatedly expresses his fear that his "wits begin to turn" (3.2.67). Cordelia's resistance, he laments, "like an engine, wrench'd my frame of nature / From the fix'd place" (1.4.258–9). What he sees as ingratitude is his unacknowledged dependency on the Other for his identity, and what he sees as a betrayal is an opportunity for transformation, for "Otherness, taken seriously, always invites transformation, calling us not only to new facts and theories and values but also to new ways of living our lives" (Palmer, *Courage to Teach* 39). Such transformation, *King Lear* demonstrates, is neither easy nor without grave risk, and it entails a radical vulnerability.

Shannon: I love your language of conversion here for Lear's experience. In those terms, though he might have moments of revelation – "I did her wrong" – that conversion moment never quite sticks, so he has glimmers followed by backsliding. William James talks about backsliding in *Varieties of Religious Experience*: "So with the conversion experience: that it should for even a short time show a human being what the highwater mark of his spiritual capacity is, this is what constitutes its importance – an importance which backsliding cannot diminish, although persistence might increase it" (201).

It is this vulnerability that brings me back to the fear of *Lear* and what is at stake in learning to "name, claim, and aim" the knowledge of feeling. When Lear prays not to lose his wits, he is asking for control, which, for him, is identified inextricably with the power of his position. That position lost, he wanders, rails, weeps, and freezes. In traditional educational models, teachers, too, fear a loss of control, where control is identified with structures of authority grounded in the general epistemological suspicion of and resistance to "feelings" as the enemy of objectivity: "As a result, educated people tend to compartmentalize their feelings, acknowledging them in private life, perhaps, but regarding them as dangerous to professional life. Professionals are supposed to be in charge at all times (or so says the myth), and we fear that feeling too deeply will cause us to lose control" (Palmer, *Courage to Teach* 209). And so we ask only questions to which we know the answers and deny ourselves contact with the dissenting Other, even the one who speaks from within. Like Lear, whose absolute power to determine who can speak and whose speech "counts," the teacher becomes dependent on "guiding, ordering, and commanding. They can no longer live without having someone to give orders to" (Freire, *Oppressed* 134). In opting for control, we turn away from the vulnerability that, for Freire, is essential to building trust in the pedagogical space: "The oppressed must see examples of the vulnerability of the oppressor so that a contrary conviction [to the one that assumes the "boss" is the only source of knowledge] can begin to grow within them" (64). Without trust in the Other, there can be no dialogue, and without dialogue, no community, as *King Lear* dramatizes when Lear first banishes his dissenting friends and then is banished himself, until he finds hospitality in a hovel on the heath.

For philosopher John D. Caputo, this vulnerable openness to the Other is the essence of friendship: "taking that risk, putting one's own meaning and self at risk, indeed one's own home, is the only way to let the other come" (*More Radical Hermeneutics* 42). This definition of friendship does not demand the assimilation of the Other into some inflexible, otherwise impervious system governed by only one side, as in Lear's love contest, but rather depends on the mutual respect for difference, difference that, for Palmer, is articulated through concepts of place and function that Cordelia would understand:

> When authentic community emerges, false differences in power and status disappear, such as those based on gender or race. But real differences remain, and so they should, for they are created by functions that need to be performed if community is to thrive – such as the leadership task of maintaining the boundaries and upholding the standards that define community at its best. (*Courage to Teach* 141)

It is true that, as Freire argues, the identities of both the oppressor and the oppressed are defined by their roles in a restrictive system. Palmer, however, reframes the mutually limiting circumstances of that kind of system in terms of "interdependence": "The real threat to community in the classroom is not power and status differences between teachers and students, but the lack of interdependence that these differences encourage" (142). The goal is not to create uniformity (because the uniform is usually designed by the person in power, after all) but to enable differences to create, contribute to, and strengthen the whole. To pretend that differences don't exist is as disingenuous and dangerous as insisting that those differences make me omnipotent in that space, or that the space can't be transformed.

And here, perhaps, is a tentative resolution of my question about how to be both a teacher and a person. It is not required that, to live authentically as a teacher, I must abandon my post for the realm of the subjective, any more than it is required that I excise the subjective in favor of an illusory objectivity. The essential aspect of the role of the king in *King Lear* that Lear himself forgets is that the Body Natural cannot be severed from the Body Politic, for one is the manifestation of the other. To function, the state needs an idea and a body to perform it. I am required to stay there, at that busy intersection of the public and the private, the institutional and the personal, in order to perform my important function in a community of knowledge. It is not necessary to be the sole authority or the most in control. What is required is the willingness to engage the other, to take on the messiness of the situation, "not […] to try to answer or resolve this dilemma by some interesting theoretical move but to experience […] all the paralysis of that impossible situation, and then to begin where you are and to go where you cannot go" (Caputo, *More Radical Hermeneutics* 59). What is required is a model of intellectual friendship.

Shannon: Oh, great teaching metaphor. I use the idea of conversation partners, but I like yours better – much more friendly.

Lisa: This idea comes by way of John D. Caputo and Parker Palmer. I love it, along with the idea of hospitality, the open door.

A teacher must play a role, use her skills to guide inquiry and to create spaces of safety where students can express their truths, not as objects of study or docile subjects of power, but as agents, collaborators, and active participants. To approach the classroom as a space of hospitality, of friendship, I must have faith as "an *a priori* requirement for dialogue" (Freire, *Oppressed* 90) and hope: "Hope is rooted in men's incompletion, from which they move out in constant search – a search which can be carried out only in communion with others" (91). And such communion means to accept the risks inherent to what Caputo calls the purpose of ethics: "to maximize and optimize the possibilities of human flourishing and minimize violence, by allowing for the invention of new forms and the coming of things we have not foreseen" (*More Radical Hermeneutics* 10). I must be willing to occupy a space where students can and will throw up to me unexpected resistances and ways of seeing that challenge the "way things are." I must find ways to recognize these moments, not as failures of my authority or as instances of filial ingratitude, but as moments of "naming, claiming and aiming," of agency and opportunities for transformation. I must respect that resistance in students and learn to recognize it in myself in order to use my own struggles as a means of opening myself to greater respect for those of others, parents, students, colleagues, all those whose interdependence forms the network of a functioning community. As Palmer observes, "If I can remember the inner pluralism of my own soul and the slow pace of my own self-emergence, I will be better able to serve the pluralism among my students at the pace of their young lives" (*Courage to Teach* 25). To live undivided in the classroom, I have to give up the security of an identity defined by my control of docile subjects; I have to put my own meanings at risk; I have to let the Other come.

I have pointed to a few uncomfortable identifications that arise when I choose to take my feelings about Lear and *Lear* seriously, to delve a little bit into the fear that keeps the play out of my teaching repertoire. I come to the text as a daughter who not only feels she falls short of filial duty, but who simultaneously feels aggrieved that parents have the audacity to be people when I need them to be parents, forever. I arrive in the text to hear an echo of my own inauthentic voice, colluding with and competing sophistically for the rewards of a system that ultimately demands the silencing of my joy as the price of both entrance to authority and the acquisition of the approving stamp of "real" work. I become the king of my small domain where a collusion with the structures of authority compounds my inauthenticity by casting me as a "convert" whose commitment to revolution is compromised by a nostalgia for safety and invulnerability. Many of these uncomfortable positions of self-division arise from a lack of the faith that Freire identifies as the irreducible precondition of change. Fear of the Other is the enemy of faith and dialogue.

Let me name, claim and aim some fear: fear that I will speak and the class will respond with a resounding "nothing" and, worse, that I will be unable to hear what they are truly telling me. Fear that my joy will be unheard in the "publish or perish" world of academia. Fear that my joy can be expressed only in asides or can be legitimized only by the statistical analysis of students as objects. Fear that the joy I feel in moments of true learning and intellectual friendship in the classroom, those moments that I believe are the core of the ethics of pedagogy, will be unvalued because the rewards we reap when we step off together into the unfenced whirl of the stormy heath cannot be graded on a rubric. Sometimes I come to the classroom wounded by these fears and can only make it through by stepping back into the safety of objectivity and monologia, that is, the "one word," the comfort of my single, unchallenged, authoritative voice. Sometimes, on bad days, I become Gloucester, convinced that "[a]s flies to wanton boys, are we to th'gods; / They kill us for their sport" (4.1.36–7).

But then something happens. I think I'm alone, speaking to myself, but I'm not. There is a roomful of learners there who are waiting, too, for the Other to come. A voice I should have had faith in all along says in my ear: "Bless thy sweet eyes, they bleed" (4.1.53).

Jessica: [Insert sob caught in throat and eyes swimming.] This is beautiful in its vulnerability and courage, honesty, and critical love. Thank you for visiting *Lear* for this project and for excavating the layers of the personal and the epistemological in the search for an authentic and just classroom.

Lisa: Feelings, wyrdos. They got me! I might be dying.

NOTE

1 Talk about an uncomfortable point of identification! YIKES!

PART TWO

As You Like It

Learning as an Act of Becoming in *As You Like It*

Jessica Riddell

In *As You Like It*, characters are continually in the process of transforming, self-fashioning, and performing – for imagined *and* real audiences. We witness an array of gender-bending, class-transgressing, status-violating acts that expose identity not as a natural or innate quality unique to an individual but rather (to adopt Judith Butler's theoretical lens), a series of performances that draw attention to identity as stylized, socially constructed, and therefore subject to change. While some performances are more self-reflexive than others, even those characters less inclined to critical self-reflection are caught in the whirligig of identity creation: no one leaves the world of this play without being altered in some way.

Transformation, we learn in the first lines of *As You Like It*, is inextricably linked to education; identity is forged through books and refined in experience with a dash of good pedagogy and the unassailable belief that *we can be better than we are*. There is a critically hopeful trajectory to this play that is animated by learners and teachers with varying degrees of expertise, all of whom are on messy learning journeys and navigating contested conceptual terrains. While some characters tiptoe, other characters veritably swagger across these terrains despite the very real possibility that things could at any moment go horribly wrong. In this play we get the very real sense that Rosalind, Orlando, Duke Senior – even Oliver and Duke Frederick – are figuring it out as they go, responding to various situations as they arise, all the while trying to figure out how they are supposed to behave in a world that has turned topsy-turvy.

It is no wonder that this play resonates with undergraduate students (and professors)! Learning is a messy journey, and one of the great lessons of this play is that learning must happen in communion with others over a sustained amount of time,

Lisa: This notion makes this play especially relevant during the COVID-19 pandemic, which challenged us to examine how we behave as social beings, how we present ourselves and how we demonstrate our commitment to one another, all while responding to conditions that change practically minute-by-minute.

Jessica: The performance of identity on social media and virtual spaces has been so stylized – and I do think that the pandemic amplified but also exposed the performative nature of social identity, which gives us a framework for challenging it.

interspersed by moments of failure and despair balanced by revelations and reunion. Indeed, the play dramatizes the limitations of learning when it is pursued as a self-taught endeavor. Book learning only takes you so far, this play seems to suggest, and it is only in engaging with others that one is able to embrace complexity and transform into a better version of one's self.

The play begins with Orlando anxiously fretting about his education – or, in his case, the lack thereof. He is angry that his brother Oliver refuses to send him to university, a direct violation of their father's final wishes. Without a university education, Orlando despairs, he will not be able to develop the capacities he inherited with his noble birth: he laments, "[Oliver] mines my gentility with my education" (1.1.18–19). The subtext here, which "mines" the relationship between identity and class, is nothing short of radical: for Orlando, blood line and a coat of arms do not automatically make a person noble. He believes instead that he can only be a gentleman if he has an education like Jaques de Boys (not to be confused with Jaques, Duke Senior's melancholic courtier), their brother whom Oliver "keeps at school, and report speaks goldenly of his profit" (5–6). Education operates as cultural capital in this play, which finds expression first as "goldenly" and is further reinforced through Orlando's mining metaphor. First, he believes that by denying him an education, Oliver "[under]mines [his] gentility," but he also suggests that education is an act of excavation: to "mine" is to extract something precious, like a vein of gold from a wall of stone. For both mining and education, laborious effort is necessary; digging deep yields value that would otherwise be obscured.

Orlando's conflict with his brother exposes a central preoccupation in the early modern period, which is the belief that the self is something to be made, fashioned, shaped, practiced, performed, and constantly refined through persistent effort. To frame this in contemporary terms, individuals in the early modern period moved away from medieval conceptions of fixed identity (based on class, gender, geography, profession, parentage) in favor of the dawn of a sociocultural understanding of identity as *a state of becoming*. This is a generalization, of course, but it is useful as it reveals a transition that Stephen Greenblatt notes in his *Renaissance Self-Fashioning* (a groundbreaking book that introduced New Historicism and, in doing so, launched an entirely new literary approach):

There is in the early modern period a change in the intellectual, social, psychological, and aesthetic structures that govern the generation of identities. [...] Perhaps the simplest observation we can make is that in the sixteenth century there appears to be

Lisa: Here, too, is an implication that Oliver's actions are a kind of siege warfare, since "mining" doesn't only mean to extract valuable ore but also to plant explosives under enemy territory. So, in a way, Oliver is conducting a kind of civil war against his brother. The education of the individual is in this way a microcosm of the state.

> **Jessica:** I like that interpretation so much because it connects to Shannon's discussions of force against gentleness.

Jessica: This is what psychologist Carol Dweck would call a "growth mindset," which understands intelligence, artistic ability, or athletic aptitude as qualities developed over time through persistence, resilience, effort, and deliberate practice (see also Ericsson). In a wildly different social and historical context than the one in which Dweck writes, the concept aligns well with early modern conceptions of selfhood and mutability.

> **Lisa:** I like how, in both cases, the emphasis is on doing the work. I feel like the consolation for a fallen world in which we are all subject to time and decay – a major early modern preoccupation – is the idea of work, which gives a positive spin to change.

an increased self-consciousness about the fashioning of the human identity as a manipulable, artful process. (Greenblatt 1–2)

Or, in the words of Pistol in *Merry Wives of Windsor*: "Why then the world's mine oyster, / Which I with sword will open" (2.2.2–3). From Orlando's point of view, substitute a book for a sword and the possibilities are almost limitless. But how does one go about fashioning one's identity in this brave new world? One might imagine the disorientation Ben Jonson or William Shakespeare or Christopher Marlowe must have experienced, born as sons of tradesmen (bricklayers and glovers and shoemakers, respectively) but part of a generation of young men who had access to public school for the first time and could therefore shape careers beyond their fathers' trades. In all three cases, these men enjoyed highly successful careers as poets and playwrights with commercial and artistic success that would have been almost unimaginable even a generation earlier.

Accessible education was certainly one of the biggest factors in the uptick of social and class mobility in early modern England. Perhaps not surprisingly, the early modern period also saw the proliferation of self-help books aimed at individuals learning to navigate a whole new ontological terrain. Baldassare Castiglione's *The Book of the Courtier*, Thomas Elyot's *The Book of the Governor*, Pico della Mirandola's *Oration on the Dignity of Man*, and even William Caxton's preface to Thomas Malory's *Morte D'Arthur* all provide guidance and practical advice about how to make it in the world. From Castiglione's "fake it till you make it" angle to Mirandola's defense of the liberal arts as a worthy pursuit, these books share in common the central premise that we can improve and that reading these handbooks can help readers to develop strategies they need to become better versions of themselves.

Things haven't changed much in over 400 years. The self-help book trade is still a lucrative industry and market experts forecast that, by 2022, the annual self-improvement industry in the US alone will be worth $13.2 billion per year.[1] Think about *New York Times* bestsellers like *The 7 Habits of Highly Effective People, The Wealthy Barber, How to Win Friends and Influence People,* and *Women Are from Venus, Men Are from Mars*. All of these books trade on hope. They all share the same formula: projecting into the future, with an anticipated reward at the end, broken down by baby steps. These books are guaranteed to

Lisa: Could we say that, in denying education, Oliver denies Orlando the very means of constructing an identity *at all*, let alone as a nobleman? He doesn't just hollow him out – he explodes him.

> **Jessica:** And yet Oliver confesses to himself and to the audience that despite all his efforts to bar Orlando from formal education, his younger brother has natural (uncultivated) goodness and knowledge (which doesn't make a great case for the power for formal education! Ha!). To hell with the lecture halls, says Duke Senior: the books are in the brooks!

> **Lisa:** True. But with no way to articulate that identity in a language the world can *hear*, is there any there? Hmm. I just hurt my brain.

Shannon: Great list! And I'd add Machiavelli's *The Prince* and Milton's *Of Education* for some alternative views.

> **Lisa:** Yes! And Machiavelli in particular had such a complicated role in English culture. The cynical reading of him, particularly of "the ends justify the means" reverberates even today.

> **Shannon:** We'll come back to Machiavelli in the *Henry V* chapters.

Lisa: This idea of "self-help books" also draws on two different kinds of labor that Orlando notes himself in his opening speech: physical and intellectual. He laments that he's stabled with the animals, like a beast of burden. Education, particularly literacy, is offered in these books as a means of dividing oneself from such burdensome labor. But then, in Arden, is that division challenged by, for example, Duke Senior and even the lion that "teaches" Oliver to be good?

> **Shannon:** I like that. As Jessica says above, the books are in the brooks. Duke Senior insists that the cruel cold can "feelingly persuade me what I am." More self-knowledge than self-fashioning?

> **Lisa:** Hmm. I wonder if we see there two different ways of conceiving identity coming into contact here: the essential and the constructed.

improve your [insert thing you wish to improve here] in [insert # of steps] to make you [insert thing you wish to achieve].

Orlando is the ideal target audience for self-help books. In his case, he wants a job that matches his birth and a salary that matches his abilities. He can't be an academic because his brother won't pay for college. The clergy was a viable option for second sons of noble families in the medieval period but by the late sixteenth century those jobs had dried up. The best job he can hope for is as a courtier, employed in the court or noble household of a powerful man (or woman; compare with Portia in the *Merchant of Venice* or Olivia in *Twelfth Night*).

Orlando needs to figure out how to become a courtier without friends, connections, or mentors.

He needs to look no further than Castiglione.

Castiglione tells his readers to do three things:

1. Exercise the body.
2. Read books written by wise men.
3. Surround yourself with excellent and worthy companions.

This final piece is key: the first two steps don't work without the communal experience.

Castiglione provides very clear instructions on how to become a courtier:

> He therefore that will be a good scholar, beside the practicing of good things, must evermore set all his diligence to be like his mater, and, if it were possible, change himself to him. And when hath had some [introduction], it profiteth him much to behold sundry men of that profession; and, governing himself with that good judgement that must always be his guide, go about to pick out, sometime of one and sometime of another, sundry matters. And even as the bee in the green meadows flieth always about the grass choosing out flowers, so shall our Courtier steal his grace from them that to his [opinion] have it, and from each one that [aspect] shall be most worthy praise. (177)

Orlando's got the first two steps down: he is strong enough to vanquish Charles the Wrestler without much exertion, and he's read a few books (one suspects he skimmed Petrarch's *Il Canzionere* given his truly awful attempts at writing poetry for

---

Shannon: Such valuable advice for twenty-first-century university students, especially the much neglected step 1!

Jessica: I feel like this is good advice for us all! Shannon's maxim – that one should cultivate three hobbies – coupled with Castiglione's advice has inspired me to think about how to live a life that is delightful, messy, and sustainable (as an early modern alternative to the "self-care" narratives and "work/life balance" discussions so prevalent in our cultural zeitgeist).

Lisa: I woke up this morning and ran to my desk to see what had happened to our book while I slept. There's something sustaining in doing work that you love with people that you love. I never felt like leaping out of bed to see essays that I wrote all alone in my tower.

Lisa: This is why picking good companions is so important: Jaques, for instance, decides to change himself into a fool, and succeeds … ish.

Jessica: This is also such a beautiful metaphor for surrounding yourself with inspiring friends who help you make honey. I love thinking about my friends as flowers that yield different kinds of colors, experiences, smells – and by revelling in their company I can gather pollen to create something new, sweet, and sustaining.

Lisa: I'm not crying. You're crying.

Rosalind). But that third piece is elusive until he escapes to the forest: that is where his real education begins. If we pick up on Castiglione's apiary metaphor of bees visiting many flowers to acquire diverse commendable qualities, the forest, as a sanctuary for the exiled court of Duke Senior, provides Orlando with the diversity of courtiers he can imitate in order to emulate.

Orlando's first tutor is Duke Senior, who teaches by modeling gentility and fellowship. His generosity of spirit, expansiveness, and highly developed sense of critical empathy provide Orlando with a master class on how real nobles are supposed to behave. Desperate for food and believing Adam near death, Orlando draws his sword on the duke and his men as they are sitting down to dinner, planning to rob the band of "merry men" (1.1.106). Instead of responding in kind with violence, the duke graciously invites Orlando to eat with them: "What would you have? Your gentleness shall force / More than your force move us to gentleness" (2.7.102–3). When he encounters a model of generosity and benevolence, Orlando finds hope where he has hitherto been hopeless:

> If ever you have look'd on better days,
> If ever been where bells have knoll'd to church,
> If ever sat at any goodman's feast,
> If ever from your eyelids wip'd a tear
> And know what 'tis to pity and be pitied,
> Let gentleness my strong enforcement be,
> In the which hope I blush, and hide my sword. (113–19)

This is a remarkable proposition: Orlando asks the duke to imagine himself in happier times, specifically in communal spaces (at church or at a feast) where empathy and love were given freely. The reciprocal act of being pitied and to pity others in equal measure is presented as a marker of civility; Orlando asks the duke to import his recollection into the present context as proof of Orlando's nobility. Orlando asks the duke to trust that Orlando has seen better days, too. The duke's empathetic response mirrors, line by line, and almost word for word, the language Orlando deploys:

> True is it that we have seen better days,
> And have with holy bell been knoll'd to church,
> And sat at goodmen's feasts and wip'd our eyes
> Of drops that sacred pity hath engender'd:

Lisa: But, significantly, they are courtiers without a court, which kind of raises the question of what makes a courtier at all. What if the education Orlando gets in Arden teaches him not to be a better courtier, but rather to redefine what courtiership actually is?

Shannon: Lovely – and since we know that young men daily flock to this alternative court, there is certainly a thirst for it in this kingdom. Young men (and a few young women) are just looking for the alternative.

Lisa: Yes, again, looking at the margins, as you argue in your essay, is instructive. It's so easy to equate the whole state with its leaders or nobility. But Shakespeare so often fills up the stage with the "general gender" to remind us that there are lots of other energies at work. I love to remind students to think about how the crowds with no lines still speak volumes on the stage.

And therefore sit you down in gentleness
And take upon command what help we have
That to your wanting may be minister'd. (120–6)

This exchange is framed as question and answer ("if" followed by "and") and creates two parallel speeches that have an almost ritualistic or contractual dimension; by the end of the interaction, the duke has hired Orlando as one of his courtiers. This entire interlude – from Orlando's violent sword-brandishing entrance to his new position at Duke's forest court – takes a mere thirty-nine lines and yet constitutes one of Orlando's formative learning experiences.

Duke Senior is Orlando's first instructor. His pedagogical approach hinges on a central premise that nature is the source of knowledge. Indeed, in his first utterance he reveals his belief that nature embeds learning within the physical environment:

And this our life exempt from public haunt
Finds tongues in trees, books in the running brooks,
Sermons in stones, and good in everything.
I would not change it. (2.1.15–18)[2]

According to Duke Senior, lessons are located in the landscape, in the form of orations, books, and sermons, and are a source of goodness that stands in contrast to the contamination found in the "public haunt" of the court. For the duke, knowledge is innate, natural, intuitive – and as free and ubiquitous as the trees and running brooks. However, there are limits to his epistemology. After all, he's been overthrown and is now languishing in a forest with his buddies pretending he's Robin Hood. It is almost as if the duke missed the first two chapters of Castiglione (1. Exercise the body; 2. Read books by wise men) and skipped right to the part when you surround yourself with wonderful friends. Learning is communal but effort is also required. One suspects the duke has not learned very much in the forest, perhaps because he has not yet internalized his failures and integrated them into experience in order to build the resilience necessary to get off his duff and do something with himself. In case we're tempted to indulge the lovely old duke, Shakespeare does not allow us to forget that his daughter, whom he left behind, is under constant threat of exile, poverty, violence, and death.

If Orlando has any hope of learning how to navigate the complexities of the world, he needs a better tutor.

Rosalind is much better suited as a professor. After all, teaching and learning are hardwired into her character, introduced in

Lisa: The speed of this moment makes me consider how a student's whole experience of a subject can turn on a moment's interaction or an unexpected connection and how much that process cannot be *planned*, even though its ground can be *prepared* by creating learning spaces where students can be greeted with friendship.

Shannon: Fitting, since Senior is such a Stoic, as I suggest in my chapter. Happiness for the Stoic is a life lived in accordance with nature. There's such a fruitful intersection here between this stoicism and contemporary ecocriticism.

Shannon: Shakespeare mentions Robin Hood but never actually writes a play about him: I would love to have seen what his Robin Hood or King Arthur plays might have looked like had he gone with those well-worn and time-tested tales.

Lisa: Would watch. Netflix, please call Shannon.

the first words she speaks in the play. When her beloved cousin beseeches her to be happy, Rosalind replies, "Dear Celia, I show more mirth than I am mistress of, and would you yet I were merrier: unless you could *teach* me to forget a banished father, you must not *learn* me how to remember any extraordinary pleasure" (1.2.2–5, my emphasis). In this moment, Rosalind believes that some things, such as learning how to forget her banished father, are unteachable. (And yet, when she escapes the court disguised as Ganymede, her father almost entirely slips her mind.[3]) For the time being, however, Rosalind is intractable. Celia tries to counter her cousin's melancholy with a reproach that Rosalind doesn't love her enough to imagine a different perspective: "I could have taught my love to take thy father for mine; so wouldst thou, if the truth of thy love to me were so righteously tempered as mine is to thee" (9–12). In other words, Celia accuses Rosalind of being a bad student. If you loved me enough, she laments, you would've learned the lesson like an eager pupil. Rosalind quickly makes amends and promises Celia she will try to rejoice in her happiness despite her own lowered status. As a distraction, Rosalind suggests that she will devise "sports" for their entertainment and suggests falling in love as a fun pastime (21–2). A mere 100 lines later, Orlando enters right on cue.

If Rosalind is a bad student, she is a highly motivated teacher. Although she purports to fashion Orlando as a courtier (and a lover), her real mission is to groom him as a husband. Poetry is the medium through which Rosalind teaches him. This choice of subject matter might seem odd to a modern audience, but it is perfectly – and pedagogically – early modern. Sixteenth-century writer, courtier, and soldier Sir Philip Sidney believes poetry is the subject best suited for transforming learners. In *The Defense of Poesy* (1579) he argues: "Poetry therefore is an art of imitation, for so Aristotle termeth it in the word *mimesis*, that is to say, a representing, a counterfeiting, or figuring forth – to speak metaphorically, a speaking picture – with this end, to *teach and delight*" (583, my emphasis). Taking a page from Sidney, Rosalind teaches Orlando by harnessing the art of imitation; disguised as Ganymede, she critiques his poetry to test, instruct, and delight.[4] She's not really training him to be a poet, and she's not actually training him to be a lover. Petrarch's formulation of courtly love is out of place in her realistic, eyes-wide-open approach to the world. Instead, she is training Orlando to be a good learner (which will, one imagines, make him a suitable husband). Poetry is the subject matter of instruction but Rosalind's learning objectives are designed to develop a much broader set of competencies.

Rosalind doesn't merely critique Orlando's poetry.[5] She uses the theater, and role playing in particular, to provide Orlando

Lisa: Can one be a good teacher if one is not a good learner?

Shannon: She seems to start as a reluctant learner, but as Jessica says, she changes – and that is good learning!

Lisa: True! I remember being a new teacher and thinking that if I had to learn something I was failing as a teacher. Experience has proved this to be *very untrue*.

Shannon: I love it when Shakespeare writes bad verse on purpose: the laughable lines in the play about Pyramis and Thisbe in *Dream* or Benedick's abortive attempts at rhymes when he really is in love, for example. How fun for Shakespeare to remind us that those who truly feel something might not be able to write it well – and the corollary, that those who write it well might not actually feel it.

Jessica: I wonder if Shakespeare got joy from making bad art? The bad poetry here is a source of entertainment (we laugh at the maker) but there is also something so earnest about the endeavor. As someone who recently took up the hobby of painting, I get joy out of the making of art that I know is not objectively good.

Lisa: I think what Rosalind is trying to dig out is the sincerity of the missive, and the refinement of his technique – or yours – is not in service of the technique but of the connection to joy and to others.

with experiential learning opportunities in order to ensure he transforms as a learner and a lover. Play-acting was a controversial medium in the early modern period. Anti-theatrical pamphleteers, like Stephen Gosson (*The School of Abuse*, 1579; *Plays Confuted in Five Actions*, 1582), Philip Stubbes (*The Anatomy of Abuse*, 1583), and William Prynne (*Histriomastix*, 1633), condemn the theater as a site of moral pestilence. Stubbes claims that plays

> corrupt the eies with alluring gestures: the eyes, the heart: and the heart, the bodie, till al be horrible before the Lord. […] These players behauiour polluteth all thinges. And of their playes he saith, they are the feasts of Sathan, the inuentions of the deuill, &c. Councels haue decrieed verie sharply against them, and polluted bodies by these filthie occasions haue on their death beddes confessed the daunger of them, lamented their owne foule and greeuous faulles, and left their warning for euer with vs to beware of them. (83)

Countering the Puritan condemnation of the theater as a spiritual plague, Thomas Heywood mounts a lofty defense of drama in *Apology for Actors* (1612) and in so doing offers a series of moral anecdotes designed to prove that plays benefit society. In one moral exemplum, Heywood claims that a woman in Norfolk confessed to the murder of her husband while watching a play that featured a woman poisoning her husband and then being haunted by his ghost: "She was so moved with the sight thereof / As she cried out, the play was made by her, / And openly confessed her husband's murder" (qtd. in Collier 345). The anecdote was widely reported in the late sixteenth century and was almost certainly the inspiration for Shakespeare's "Mousetrap" play in *Hamlet*. Heywood points to this incident as evidence of the affective impact of drama as a model of moral engagement and instruction.

On both sides of the debate, Puritans and theater advocates alike believe that drama has a transformative effect on members of the audience. The general consensus is that, for better or worse, members of the audience are not passive spectators but rather actively engaged makers of meaning. Rosalind banks on this when she sets off to transform Orlando, and she inadvertently transforms herself in the process.

When Rosalind first encounters one of Orlando's poems hanging on a tree, she calls it a "tedious homily of love" (3.3.137–8) and mercilessly criticizes the meter: "some of them had in them more feet than the verses would bear" (146–7). She goes so far as to call his poems "lame" (149), at least until the shrewd Celia transforms Rosalind from reader to fangirl. The usually composed Rosalind falls to pieces as soon as the author's identity is revealed:

> Alas the day, what shall I do with my doublet and hose? What did he when thou saw'st him? What said he? How looked he? Wherein went he? What makes him here? Did he

ask for me? Where remains he? How parted he with thee? And when shalt thou see him again? Answer me in one word. (196–9)

Rosalind fires off ten questions in rapid succession with the hilariously impossible final command: answer everything with one word. She is never more human than in her discombobulation, and she wants to know two things: "Does he know I'm in the forest?" and "Is he still cute?" (206–8). Celia, enjoying herself immensely, prolongs the story about her encounter with Orlando. One imagines this playful torture could go on for some time were it not for the unexpected arrival of Orlando that forces Rosalind to quickly pull her proverbial shit together. On the fly, Rosalind decides to perform the part of a cheeky servant in order to teach him a lesson: "I will speak to him like a saucy lackey, and under that habit play the knave with him" (268–9). Her first reaction is not to reveal herself and requite his love, but rather to imitate in order to educate.

She sets up Orlando in a roundabout way, drawing him in as a co-conspirator in her desire to "cure" whomever is writing verses into trees:

There is a man haunts the forest that abuses our young plants with carving "Rosalind" on their barks; hangs odes upon hawthorns and elegies on brambles; all, forsooth, deifying the name of Rosalind. If I could meet that fancy-monger, I would give him some good counsel, for he seems to have the quotidian of love upon him. (324–30)

Orlando immediately claims authorship and demands to know what advice Ganymede has for him. Instead, Rosalind does a close reading of his appearance and declares that Orlando has no markers of a man in love: no "lean cheek," no dark circles under his eyes, no disheveled appearance (337–40). In fact, her devastating dismantling culminates in an accusation of self-love: "you are rather point-device in your accouterments, as loving yourself than seeming the lover of any other" (345–7). Her fear, barely masked by her sauciness, is that Orlando lacks sincerity and is merely in love with love itself. Rosalind certainly has cause for suspicion since this kind of lover animates many of Shakespeare's plays: a non-exhaustive list of easily exhausted lovers includes Romeo with Rosaline, Orsino with Olivia, Demetrius with both Helena and Hermia, and even Claudio with Hero. Rosalind must test Orlando's love to ensure this is no fleeting fancy.

Rosalind suggests Orlando will be cured of his lovesickness if he pretends that Ganymede is Rosalind and woos him

Lisa: A good learner, willing to accept feedback. Has Rosalind created a safe learning space, do you think?

Jessica: She is a bit harsh for my pedagogical preferences. She evaluates Orlando for what he is missing (not externally demonstrating the marks of a lover), not what he has made or has to the potential to express. Her teaching evaluations might be low.

Lisa: Yes, berating is not a good strategy. Challenging Orlando to delve into his motives, expectations and beliefs about love, though, is valuable. But she's a new teacher and maybe can learn about, as Shannon says in her essay, the educative value of kindness.

Shannon: She surely has reason – and not just in stories – to doubt the faithfulness of men. Neither her uncle nor, at a stretch, her father have stuck by her.

Jessica: This is so true. She has been abandoned and rejected by two men who should know better, so her stakes here are high. I recently came across an article that started with "extreme independence is a trauma response" (Weiner) and that these people often adopt co-dependent relationships with people who rely on them for their survival. Rosalind and Celia perhaps?

in her stead. Although Orlando protests that he does not want to be cured, he entertains Ganymede's proposition by asking how this might be accomplished. Rosalind-as-Ganymede's account is a harsh condemnation of fickle women, undercut only by the fact we know Rosalind is parodying, in the most exaggerated manner, men's perception (and fear) of women:

> He was to imagine me his love, his mistress, and I set him every day to woo me. At which time would I, being but a moonish youth, grieve, be effeminate, changeable, longing and liking, proud, fantastical, apish, shallow, inconstant, full of tears, full of smiles; for every passion something, and for no passion truly anything, as boys and women are, for the most part, cattle of this colour; would now like him, now loathe him; then entertain him, then forswear him; now weep for him, then spit at him; that I drave my suitor from his mad humour of love to a living humour of madness, which was to forswear the full stream of the world and to live in a nook, merely monastic. (365–77)

Lisa: Who is also, in this case, a parody of Rosalind. She "teaches" him to woo the parody, but his willingness to learn is what woos her, the real her. The "subject matter" isn't really the point, it seems. The cultivating of the learning mindset is.

Shannon: He does seem a little slow to catch on to the flow of the role play, doesn't he?

Jessica: Is Orlando playing dumb or is he just dumb (in the most delightfully earnest of ways)?

Lisa: Or maybe just inexperienced, which is not the same as dumb. Not a lot of courting going on in his stable. But maybe he could teach Ganymede a thing or two about good husbandry.

This scene – where we see Rosalind disguised as Ganymede disguising himself as *Rosalind* – bends the limitations of dramatic transvestitism in the most subversive ways. In the midst of the almost disorienting shape-shifting lies the heart of the matter: Can you become a better version of yourself? The relationship between performance and pedagogy is nowhere clearer than Rosalind's attempt to educate Orlando.

Rosalind implements her love simulation in 4.1. Orlando is an hour late, which is not a great sign; so when Orlando says he will die of love, Rosalind deflates this stale Petrarchan conceit with an almost ruthless flourish: "The poor world is almost six thousand years old and in all this time there was not any man died in his own person, *videlicet*, in a love cause. […] Men have died from time to time – and worms have eaten them – but not for love" (4.1.81–3, 92–3). Orlando struggles to keep up with Rosalind's wit but as soon as he is out of sight she collapses under the weight of her true feelings, showing that she is not immune to sighing and crying. When she swoons at the sight of the bloody handkerchief covered in her lover's blood, she risks exposing her true identity to Oliver. Once Oliver detects Rosalind's counterfeit in 4.2, the play very quickly untangles itself to a comedic conclusion with a record four weddings in one. Orlando is tried, tested, and emerges as a true lover and worthy spouse for one of Shakespeare's most savvy heroines.

Rosalind proves herself a master of self-fashioning in the vein of Castiglione's *sprezzatura*, which exudes "a certain [nonchalance], to cover all art withal, and seem whatsoever he doth and sayeth to do it without pain, and, as it were, not minding it"

(Castiglione 177–8). The concept of self-fashioning and performances of selfhood feel all too familiar in the context of our twenty-first-century digital world, where a new generation of selves-in-the-making perform public versions of themselves on various social media platforms for diverse audiences. Instagram feeds are populated with perfectly posed, airbrushed pictures taken at optimal angles and manipulated through filters, culminating in a highly stylized visual narrative of a life meant to convey perfection in its various forms. As one of my student collaborators remarked recently, "when I look at other people's Instagram accounts, I think, "I'd be happy if I lived *that* life."

While Instagram audiences know how much work goes into that performance of self in the public domain (because they are constantly engaging with and through that process), they are still prone to be wowed by it, a response that Castiglione observed in his sixteenth-century work: "I believe grace is much derived, for in rare matters and well brought to pass every man knoweth the hardness of them, so that a readiness therein maketh great wonder" (178). In other words, everyone knows how much effort is required to self-fashion, and yet performances that appear effortless and natural are still lauded. Castiglione warns us not to get caught showboating: "contrariwise to use force and, as they say, to hale by the hair, giveth a great disgrace and maketh everything, how great soever it be, to be little esteemed" (178). Even if the performance is exceptional, if the audience gets a whiff of artifice or exertion, no matter how worthy such exertion is on its own, the performance is rendered worthless. One of my lovely students reflected: "it would be so much easier if things were innate and natural. This knowledge [that effort and persistence are fundamental to improvement] is just so *exhausting*."

Shannon: Even #nofilter becomes performative.
  Lisa: Modern *sprezzatura*. So artful it seems artless.

Lisa: It seems to me that this idea somehow underlies the university's love affair with grades and final exams, an "airbrushed" version of a student that elides all the messiness of transformation that learning entails. Imagine going to see *As You Like It,* only watching the final scene, and declaring that you know anything at all about Orlando. And yet, for our students, that transcript is meant to tell the whole story.

I hear you. And, interestingly enough, so does Oliver. Oliver's jealously of his brother lies in the suspicion that Orlando is just naturally better than him:

> I hope I shall see an end of him; for my soul – yet I know not why – hates nothing more than he. Yet he's gentle, never schooled and yet learned, full of noble device, of all sorts enchantingly beloved, and indeed so much in the heart of the world, and especially of my own people who best know him, that I am altogether misprized. (1.1.147–53)

Oliver erases the messiness of Orlando's learning journey, ascribing to his younger brother all the qualities of natural, innate gentility. There is a tension in the play between self-fashioning and innate abilities, between performance of selfhood and fixed

Lisa: Unlike Orlando's "growth mindset," Oliver's is a "fixed mindset" that believes that intelligence is unchangeable, that feedback is dangerous and that labor can't really change your "smarts."
  Shannon: Yes! And how wonderful that Shakespeare gives Oliver a transformational moment of his own – even if it can seem a little convenient to a shrewd twenty-first-century reader: heroic self-sacrifice and love at first sight combine to set him on the growth path.
  Lisa: This is why I have a little hope that Duke Senior's court 2.0 will be less open to usurpation, because there are newer, more flexible young people returning with "newfangled" ideas from abroad.

identity. The play seems to suggest we can hold both at the same time and that transformation is possible for all of us. The audience is implicated in a hopeful trajectory that draws attention to our own messy learning journeys as we navigate contested conceptual terrains. In the epilogue, Rosalind calls upon us to be both taught and delighted by this pedagogical play:

> My way is to conjure you, and I'll begin with the women. I charge you, O women, for the love you bear to men, to like as much of this play as please you. And I charge you, O men, for the love you bear to women – as I perceive by your simpering, none of you hates them – that between you and the women the play may please. (Epilogue 9–15)

This is not merely a cheap appeal for applause, but something more profound. Sidney exclaims: "Who will be taught, if he be not moved with the desire to be taught?" (562). He believed that to *move* someone was to *transform* them and that an ideal teacher must generate delight to stir the heart and shape the mind. For Sidney, teachers "giveth so sweet a prospect into the way" (562). Rosalind educates us all with a careful balance of intellectual rigor and playful revels that leaves us all moved and transformed, hopefully for the better.

NOTES

1 "Americans spent $11 billion in 2008 on self-improvement books, CDs, seminars, coaching, and stress-management programs – 13.6% more than they did back in 2005, according to Marketdata Enterprises, an independent Tampa-based research firm that tracks everything from adoption agencies to funeral homes. Latest forecast: 6.2% annual growth through 2012. We should see better 5.6% average yearly gains from 2016 to 2022, when the overall market value should increase to $13.2 billion" ("What People Are Still Willing to Pay For," para. 2).

2 Although many versions of the play attribute this last line to Duke Senior, the 2008 Oxford University Press edition gives it to his lord, Amiens.

3 In 3.4., Rosalind runs into her father in the forest, but her preoccupation with Orlando makes this encounter almost an afterthought: "I met the duke yesterday and had much question with him; he asked me of what parentage I was. I told him of as good as he: so he laughed and let me go. But what talk we of fathers when there is such a man as Orlando?" (3.5.31–4).

4 The importance of delight cannot be understated in the process of teaching and learning. Sidney exclaims, "Who will be taught, if he be not moved with the desire to be taught?" (562). He believed that to move someone was to transform them, and an ideal teacher must generate delight to stir the heart and shape the mind. At the core of this philosophy is the idea that the heart and mind are inextricably bound in the pursuit of knowledge, in both its acquisition and creation. Rosalind educates Orlando with a careful balance between intellectual rigor and playful revels. For Sidney, teachers, like poets who are his subject matter, "giveth so sweet a prospect into the way" (562).

5 Curiously, drama falls under the category of poetry for Sidney, since theater, like verse, creates a "golden" world.

"Sweet Are the Uses of Adversity": Duke Senior's Arden as a Hopeful Creation

Shannon Murray

If you could choose to live in any one of Shakespeare's created worlds, which would it be? I'll put it another way: Which of Shakespeare's worlds do you wish our world resembled? For me, the place is the Forest of Arden and the reason is Duke Senior. In *As You Like It*, Shakespeare imagines a world in which gentleness overcomes violence, where our leaders can remain their best selves and still lead us.

As You Like It is my favorite of Shakespeare's comedies. It is also the one that I find it hardest to teach to my satisfaction. Perhaps it is because I love it as an almost sacred text – one that gives me hope for the world, a moral framework I can aspire to, and wonderful wonderful wonderful characters – that makes any classroom attempt less than my idealized conception of what it should be. Any conversation about *As You Like It* should be transcendent, light, and profound at the same time, an idealized world that recognizes the real but isn't hobbled by it. But I know that the reason this play matters for me is one particular production: the Royal Shakespeare Company in 1985, with Juliet Stevenson as Rosalind and Fiona Shaw as Celia. It was, in my memory, both simple and beautiful: simply beautiful. How could I hope to recreate that transformative experience for my students in a seventy-five-minute, twice-a-week classroom?

So here is how I deal with it now. I want to get to two things, and I try to remember that everything else is secondary. The first is what kind of an amazing, delightful, resourceful, clever, magnetic heart of the play Rosalind is. I won't

Jessica: I haven't always loved this play. My conversion (I do very much like it now) is not fully complete because I am MAD at Duke Senior for making merry with his little band of brothers while his daughter faces persecution and even death at the hands of his increasingly unstable brother. It is the same brand of anger I nurse against Lear, but at least he has moments of realization (if not redemption) around his role in others' misery. How much has Duke Senior learned by the end of the play remains a bit of a loose thread (but if anyone can convince me, it is the wyrdos!).

Shannon: I am so stuck in thinking of him as a wonderful example of the Stoic, or the humorally balanced human – the ideal of equanimity – that I worry less about him learning and like the fact that he is consistent. The one thing I don't talk about, though, is the limits of that stoicism. I may want to be at peace with the way the world is, but I also know that sometimes anger is the most appropriate response. What if this were a different world and Duke Frederick got through without the hermit and conversion? Would Duke Senior's loving generosity have kept them all alive? In the world of this play, absolutely; but in ours?

Lisa: I feel this, too, as though the more I love something the more disappointed I will be when I try to teach it. But I wonder, also, if, aside from recognizing that we can't ever do everything, we could trust that the students in any given classroom will find their own magic that may be completely different from our own, and maybe my job is less to take them than to follow them.

Jessica: I am more convinced about Duke Senior when we relieve him of his duty as a parent and a person and instead think about his embodied philosophy. That makes sense that as a character he is less "of this world" and more a lens through which to see (possibly new) worlds.

> **Shannon:** I see what you mean. Does he know that Rosalind will eventually be threatened, I wonder? We know Celia begs to have her stay as a companion. I want to give him the benefit of the doubt, as I do poor Macduff or Paulina, though they could be guilty of a failure of imagination: yes, he's bad, but he couldn't possibly be THAT bad! Is that a place where hope becomes dangerous, uncritical?

> **Lisa:** Hmm. Yes. The place where hope becomes uncritical. There is this question of responsibility, or my need for Duke Senior, in his withdrawal to Arden, to still give something to the world. Maybe what he gives is an example. Maybe what he gives is a cautionary tale about what happens when you attempt to build something in the absence of a consideration about the contexts that always complicate any beautiful vision.

Lisa: I wonder if this is why there are so many adaptations of the plays based on extrapolating from small moments and characters. All seem to bring with them a lived-in world that we only get to glimpse.

> **Shannon:** Nice thought. There is the notion that these "piggy-back" adaptations allow us to look at a space the original author missed, as a kind of correction of a fault in humanity, like Bronte missing that Bertha Mason is a human being, for example. But I'd stick up for Shakespeare here as someone who so often says "look over there" at characters we might otherwise miss. That makes the adaptor's job easier.

> **Jessica:** Erin Shields (award-winning Canadian playwright) is working on a play that tells the stories of Goneril and Regan a decade before their father has his epic retirement meltdown. In her podcast interview on *Wyrd Words*, she laments that we don't have enough time with these characters. Is that the case for Duke Senior too? Or is he as fully developed as he needs to be to do the work he needs to do?

talk about her here, because lots of other people have done that already. The second is a remarkable thing that happens in the margins of the play – with Rosalind's father, Duke Senior, who is, I think, the play's soul.

That relatively minor character may seem like an odd focus for an essay on *As You Like it*. True, Rosalind is always the best reason to read or see this play. She is the perfect creation: smart, funny, good, resourceful, brave. Her fun in the forest disguised as a boy makes me wish Shakespeare had written her more scenes of banter with Orlando. It's always with a sense of disappointment that I see her return to her own clothes and to her real life, even though, as her father's only heir, her presence reassures us that Arden and the court will be in good hands. Beyond the banter and the pleasure of disguise and revelation, though, this play offers a radically hopeful idea about the good life and how best to live it, and Duke Senior is the moral and philosophical anchor of that hope.

He is also a reminder of how sharp Shakespeare is at the margins of his play. Duke Senior has only a little more than a hundred lines, and yet his character is fully realized through just a few profound moments. Maybe it should come as no surprise that Shakespeare paid such generous attention to minor characters. What we understand of his own career as an actor suggests that he tended to play such roles, old men like Adam in this play, minor functionaries, the kind of part that might in more traditional drama have served merely to swell a scene or two. Any playwright in such a part might well think of the whole person at the heart of any such role. I am reminded of what actor and director Athena Stevens said when asked why we keep doing Shakespeare instead of turning to new playwrights and new stories: "Because he was a human being who saw the full humanity in other human beings" – no matter how small their roles seem to be.

Duke Senior is Rosalind's father, and his loss is our starting point. His younger brother, Duke Frederick, usurps his dukedom, and the older brother flees the court to take refuge in the forest. Senior is by rights the highest ranking character in the play, although his actual political power has been limited by the now more powerful bad duke. Still, powerless though he is, young men leave comfortable homes to join him in exile. What he loses in power he makes up in for in gentle charisma. In the terms of the play, it is his presence, his response to his losses and to the losses of others, that make him a model not only for the characters in this admittedly unreal play but for all of us in very real life.

A look at one of his early scenes suggests why.

The first time we see him, his speech sets the tone for the men he leads and for the mode we'll find in the Forest of Arden:

> Now, my co-mates and brothers in exile,
> Hath not old custom made this life more sweet
> Than that of painted pomp? Are not these woods
> More free from peril than the envious court?
> Here feel we not the penalty of Adam,
> The seasons' difference, as the icy fang
> And churlish chiding of the winter's wind –
> Which when it bites and blows upon my body,
> Even till I shrink with cold, I smile and say,
> "This is no flattery" – these are counsellors
> That feelingly persuade me what I am.
> Sweet are the uses of adversity
> Which like the toad, ugly and venomous,
> Wears yet a precious jewel in his head,
> And this our life exempt from public haunt
> Finds tongues in trees, books in the running brooks,
> Sermons in stones and good in everything.
> I would not change it. (2.1.1–18)[1]

Lisa: It seems that power and charisma and quality of character are split into two parts in this play, Frederick and Senior. We see in other plays how dangerous someone can be if power and charisma are united, as in the case of Richard of Gloucester or Claudius, both usurpers. Senior seems to be cultivating charisma and quality of character but those alone cannot guarantee the stability of the state or access to state power.

Jessica: Rosalind and Orlando both have charisma, too; their natural energy puts them at risk in political spheres when the people in power are jealous of the charisma they lack. Oliver hates Orlando because he is "enchantingly beloved, and indeed so much in the heart of the world, and especially of my own people, who know him best, that I am altogether misprised" (1.1.144–7). Duke Frederick justifies his decision to banish Rosalind because "her very silences and her patience / Speak to the people, and they pity her" (1.3.75–7). He fears Rosalind's brightness makes his own daughter look dull in comparison.

Lisa: And the deciding factor here is that Orlando and Rosalind are good people. I wonder if the distinction rests on whether charisma is directed at connection to another, as in Duke Senior's or Rosalind's case, or if it is in service of the self, as in the case of Frederick. Is it an underlying principle of community that separates charismatics?

I love this speech. This is a soul in exile not just making the best of a bad situation but truly seeing the virtues in the trials he and his fellows live through. The woods are better than the court because what Duke Senior and his men feel in nature is the truth: there are no flatterers to lie or to tell him he is more than he is. Cold and wind have the honesty to tell him his true nature as a human, and he is deeply grateful for the self-knowledge. So many times in his plays, Shakespeare allows a character – a Lear or a Hamlet – to strip away some accepted element of human life to see what is underneath the "accommodations" for Lear or the "paint" for Hamlet. In those moments, Shakespeare asks us to think about what we truly are, what our default settings are. Here, Duke Senior is doing that, and stripped of comforts, he would not change his condition.

It's important to note that he's not merely being foolish; there's no "it's all good" rubbish cliché here. The speech is itself honest about suffering and hardship as it is; this is not a false pastoral world of eternal spring. The Forest of Arden is cold, deer are killed, and cottagers pay absentee landlords and have little to eat themselves. He is asserting that that hardship itself is a teacher, as are the trees, brooks, and stones. Sweet are the uses of adversity. This is critical hope, and it is contagious.

It is also, I think, a moment at which old-fashioned and new-fangled approaches to Shakespeare can meet happily. While Duke Senior's attitude is an ideal focus for ecocriticism, for some of Shakespeare's audience, it may have been shorthand for the "philosopher," specifically the stoicism of Emperor Marcus Aurelius or Roman writer Cicero, who saw that the best way to live was "according to nature," a frustratingly open phrase. How lovely is this idea from Cicero:

> As the Stoics hold, everything that the earth produces is created for human use; and as human beings too, are born for the sake of human beings, that they may be able mutually to help one another; in this direction we are to follow Nature as our guide, to contribute to the general good by an interchange of acts of kindness, by giving and receiving, and thus by our skill, our industry, and our talents to cement human society more closely together, human being to human being. (qtd. in Boerhaave 350)

The contemporary ecocritic might hesitate at the idea that all of nature is for human use, but the rest is pretty sound – and pretty hopeful in a moment of climate crisis. Be kind to each other by, among other things, looking to nature as our guide. Ecocriticism in Shakespeare studies, as theorist Gabriel Egan suggests, looks at five questions, one of which is how our understanding of the nature of life differs from that of Shakespeare and his contemporaries (12). In early literature, we can find plenty of examples of characters whose behavior toward nature might look like a cautionary tale for our own time. But Senior chooses – by necessity, it's true – a life *in* nature rather than one dominating it. Notice that he does not, as Prospero does, take over other people's dwellings or even build buildings, erecting a little replicate empire in his new world of exile. Instead, he attempts to fit himself, quietly, into nature and to learn from it. He is even reluctant to kill animals for food "in their own confines" (2.1.24). Killing deer in the forest would be like usurping the rightful owners of that forest, and both Senior and Jaques feel the parallel to their own usurpation. This merry band is a step away from vegetarianism, and Duke Senior can embody a Stoic and an ecocritical stance at the same time.

Lisa: In an interview with Krista Tippett, Parker Palmer talks about two kinds of suffering: suffering that saps life, that comes from "forces of distortion" and injustice that force one away from where one wants or needs to be (*Soul of Depression* 19:16); and the suffering that comes from standing for something and facing resistance, which is "a life-giving way to suffer" (30:20). Some suffering must be resisted or ameliorated or escaped. I wonder how this idea fits with the suffering that the characters in this play experience.

Jessica: I can't help but feel that some of the suffering in this play is performative, and that the performance of suffering is entertaining to the Duke. For example, he finds amusement in Jaques's grief at the death of a stag (a spectacle that entertains him when it is reported by two lords who observed Jaques weeping alongside the animal as it died).

Lisa: Where, I wonder, does he think his food comes from, when he ate venison at court?

Luckily for his daughter Rosalind, Duke Senior's way of looking at the world has the effect of gentling his future son-in-law as well as his other companions in the forest. In Act 2, Orlando has escaped his murderous brother with his good servant Adam and, as he desperately searches for food, he finds the exiles at dinner. Mirroring the treatment he has received in the court, he threatens the duke: "He dies that touches any of this fruit / Till I and my affairs are answered" (2.7.99–100). The duke's reply is courtesy itself: "What would you have? Your gentleness shall force / More than your force move us to gentleness" (102–3). Think for a moment what this means. In distress themselves and suffering from lack of food, the leader of this band insists that in the wilderness, gentleness can overcome force. This is, for me, the center of the play, and it is the core of what could be called either its most hopeful message or its least realistic one. The court, which should be civilized, delights in rigged blood sports and establishes itself on foundations of jealousy, suspicion, and fratricide. The forest, in opposition, is a place of gentle order, self-control, and compassion.

Jessica: I love that the Duke uses a chiasmus to do the work of recoding behaviours and social norms. Repeating gentleness and force but inverting them is an effective pedagogical technique to school Orlando on how to be a good courtier ("gentleness shall force / more than your force move us to gentleness").

Lisa: This is an act of recentering, isn't it? Offering a different starting place from which to measure the world.

And Orlando is altered by the encounter. He assures them that he has behaved only as he assumed they would: savagely, as befits a savage forest. Their kindness moves him to imitate that behavior instead, and he urges them toward empathy, toward seeing his plight through theirs:

Speak you so gently? Pardon me, I pray you:
I thought that all things had been savage here
And therefore put I on the countenance
Of stern commandment. But whate'er you are
That in this desert inaccessible,
Under the shade of melancholy boughs,
Lose and neglect the creeping hours of time –
If ever you have look'd on better days,
If ever been where bells have knoll'd to church,
If ever sat at any goodman's feast,
If ever from your eyelids wip'd a tear,
And know what 'tis to pity and be pitied,
Let gentleness my strong enforcement be,
In the which hope I blush, and hide my sword. (106–19)

A wonderful line: "Let gentleness my strong enforcement be." As they met his force with gentleness, he now tries to enforce their gentleness through hope and empathy.

Lisa: I wonder whether this meaning of the word creates a bit of a loophole for Senior, who, in figuring his circumstances as bad luck or misfortune, does not need to contemplate whether or not his way of being in the world might have set him up for usurpation.

Lisa: And after we have chatted about this idea, now I wonder if I've missed the mark in the above comment. Why should I blame Duke Senior or demand that he change in order to "be effective" in the "real world" instead of asking how the so-called "real world" should change to accommodate him? What if we began to demand a different world instead of wondering how to fit into the existing one?

When Orlando exits to get his companion, the duke is left to muse on this meeting, in a way that focuses on the suffering of others:

> Thou see'st we are not all alone unhappy:
> This wide and universal theatre
> Presents more woeful pageants than the scene
> Wherein we play in. (136–9)

"Unhappy" here probably carries the now largely lost sense of "unfortunate" or "unlucky" more than the contemporary sense of general misery. They are not the only ones to have fallen on bad times, then. He does feel the empathy Orlando had hoped for. Because it is followed by the justly famous "All the world's a stage" speech by Jaques, these four lines of the duke's are easily missed. They introduce the stage-play-world metaphor that Jaques picks up, expands, and marries with the idea of the seven ages of man:

> All the world's a stage,
> And all the men and women merely players:
> They have their exits and their entrances
> And one man in his time plays many parts,
> His acts being seven ages. At first the infant,
> Mewling and puking in the nurse's arms;
> And then the whining schoolboy with his satchel
> And shining morning face, creeping like snail
> Unwillingly to school; and then the lover,
> Sighing like furnace, with a woeful ballad
> Made to his mistress' eyebrow; then a soldier,
> Full of strange oaths and bearded like the pard,
> Jealous in honour, sudden, and quick in quarrel,
> Seeking the bubble "reputation"
> Even in the cannon's mouth; and then the justice,
> In fair round belly with good capon lin'd,
> With eyes severe and beard of formal cut,
> Full of wise saws and modern instances –
> And so he plays his part; the sixth age shifts
> Into the lean and slipper'd pantaloon,
> With spectacles on nose and pouch on side,
> His youthful hose well sav'd – a world too wide

For his shrunk shank – and his big manly voice,

Turning again toward childish treble, pipes

And whistles in his sound; last scene of all

That ends this strange eventful history

Is second childishness and mere oblivion,

Sans teeth, sans eyes, sans taste, sans everything. (139–66)

I love that Jaques encapsulates the whole of a human life in the line "this strange eventful history." It is a tour de force performance, an example of Jaques's one-upmanship, as he takes the metaphor that Senior casually lobs and slams back an extraordinary and detailed answer. But notice how unhappy all the examples Jaques offers are. The infant is "mewling and puking," the schoolboy is reluctant to learn, the soldier and lover focus their attention on false things, and in age, we are "sans teeth, sans taste, sans eyes, sans everything." It is a triumph as a speech, but it is also thoroughly pessimistic, selecting not the worst but certainly the most foolish elements of human experience. The speech worries me as an example of an often-quoted bit of Shakespeare gone wrong, taken from its dramatic context and allowed to stand on its own as a statement of the play itself or even of the author. However, the context shows us again that while Shakespeare is a great poet, he is an even greater dramatist.

Look again at Duke Senior's lines, and you'll see how Shakespeare actually undercuts Jaques's speech. For the duke, a contemplation of Orlando's behavior and situation makes him sympathetic, able to put the unhappinesses of his own experience into perspective, reminding his followers that there are others in the world who suffer. This is one of the shifts that I find most valuable and most moving in Shakespeare: the reminder that there are others in the world, that their experience is both like and unlike our own, and that they therefore deserve attention. The reductive "strange eventful history" in Jaques's version is for the duke a "wide and universal theatre." While Jaques reduces the whole of the experience of childhood or age to one small and unhappy example, the duke reminds us of the many different kinds of experiences that humans have in the world – the "more woeful pageants than the scene / Wherein we play in" – and urges us to be aware of them. Jaques offers a diminution of human experience. The duke offers one that is enveloping, expansive, and attentive to difference. I like the latter much better, and it is certainly the duke's universal pageant that I want to play in, not Jaques's strange eventful history.

But which is correct? I have two answers to that question. In this little debate of competing worldviews, Jaques appears the winner, and certainly the number of pop culture

Lisa: Yes! I love the way that the juxtaposition of speeches, as you show here, is as much an engine of meaning as the speeches themselves. Drama is cool.

Jessica: Context matters! One of my students shared that her grandmother used to recite this speech, whisky in hand, rolling the words around on her tongue in a thick Irish brogue. This student did not know where and how it lived before our course. When we did a close reading, it was the first time she had heard it out loud since her grandmother died. She shared afterward that the way in which it was bookended – by Duke Frederick and then the arrival of Adam – made her feel closer to her grandmother and her belief in the magic of literature.

references Jaques gets would seem to support that conclusion. He gets the last word, he gets the most lines, and, if we were just adding up the strength of his rhetoric – his ability to pick up and extend the argument, to develop two commonplaces into a fresh new conceit – that ability would also make him the winner. But remember what I said about Shakespeare the dramatist?

I think we do Shakespeare a disservice any time we separate the language of his characters from the context they find themselves in. By itself, Jaques's speech appears to be a persuasively negative view of the whole of human existence, but look what happens just after he stops. I like to imagine the slightest of pauses after his last word, a moment in which Senior and his followers might find themselves seduced by the linguistic strength of Jaques's argument: Yes, they think, isn't life miserable? If we are lucky enough to live to old age, we'll be even more miserable than we are now. But who then appears? Orlando has used the time taken up by these two competing views of the world to collect Adam and carry him onto the stage. This is a visual and powerful response to Jaques's last lines. Countering the argument that old age is mere absence, "sans everything," is a profound alternative. Remember that Adam has already saved Orlando's life, sacrificed his own meager savings to follow and support Orlando in his dangerous flight, and traded the safety of his home for the insecurity and physical hardships of travel in the wild. Along with Celia, he is one of the models of sacrifice for one's beloved in the play. And in return, Orlando risks his own safety to get him food and then physically carries the old man onto the stage, where the duke instructs him to set down his "venerable burden" (167). Thus Shakespeare refutes Jaques: this is *also* old age, one that is courageous, loving, self-sacrificing, and worthy of veneration.

Jaques's speech is undeniably great, but the context Shakespeare sets for that speech should complicate our response to it. If we just take that speech as the play's final word on life, we have to ignore both the compassion of the speech before and the vision of meaningful old age that follows it. Surely this juxtaposition suggests that Shakespeare wants the reductive, unpleasant vision to be countered. I'm not convinced that either side is truly defeated, though. Jaques's view of the world is memorable and persuasive precisely because at many times we can look at human life and think what a sad thing it is. That is true. But the simple and moving beauty of Adam's presence is also true. This also is what human life is: great in its compassion for others. We may find that we have equal evidence on any day for an optimistic or a pessimistic view of human life. I will always hope to choose the optimistic. But I also really value in Shakespeare his ability to introduce to our minds two opposing but possibly true things at the same time. Maybe, then, asking simple questions in class that demand a simple

Lisa: Here is the "life-giving" suffering that Palmer talks about. Suffering that comes from standing for something. I think Senior, as a teacher, has a lot to learn from Celia and Adam. They take on a different kind of suffering, one with agency, one that tries to make the world safe for their values.

Jessica: I really like this reading of Adam's agency as self-sacrifice; handing over his life savings and setting out to the forest is an act of self-determination, founded on the hope that he will be 1) contributing to the greater good and 2) also be taken care of by a benevolent master (before there were registered retirement savings plans).

answer is not the best way to highlight this virtue in these plays. Instead of "Which worldview is correct?" or even "Which worldview do you prefer?" the better question would be: "How does this play make us feel the truth of both positions?"

My argument here makes clear the challenge involved in reading or teaching Shakespeare. I do believe it is possible to read with the drama in mind, to imagine how the stage looks at any moment. But I also know that it is possible to ignore the dramatic when the poetry is so darned good. The trick is to read like a director. But I also want to highlight the fact that as a dramatist, one of Shakespeare's great virtues is his insistence on context for understanding. I believe that one of the most important ideas for a liberal education is the ability to live with complex answers to complex questions without requiring a simple answer. Shakespeare gives us so many examples of this to work with; the trick is to make sure that we attend to those rather than latch onto the simple conclusions.

I've looked at the heart of this little scene and the complexity of reading that famous speech in its dramatic context. Now I want to look at force and gentleness. When the duke meets Orlando's threats with "Your gentleness shall force / More than your force move us to gentleness," he brings up a principle that works throughout this play: it is possible that love can overcome hatred, kindness can overcome unkindness, and gentleness can overcome force. On the surface of it, all of this might seem impossible, but the play gives us example after example to the contrary. When Rosalind is to be sent away from court at the beginning of the play, Celia tries to comfort her: "You know my father hath no child but I, nor none is like to have; and, truly, when he dies thou shalt be his heir: for what he hath taken away from thy father perforce I will render thee again in affection. By mine honour, I will, and when I break that oath, let me turn monster" (1.2.15–19). This must be one of the few times in a Shakespeare play that a character swears an oath at the beginning of a play and isn't foresworn by the end. What Celia offers is the simplest way to right the wrong that begins the play: when she inherits the dukedom, she will simply give it to Rosalind. Her father's force will be overturned by her own gentleness.

Strangely, the idea of a strong gentleness appears again at the end of the wrestling scene. There, of course, the apparently weaker contender beats the stronger, in a mini version of David and Goliath. At the end, Rosalind and Orlando see each other for the first time and fall in love in another example of strange overthrow. Orlando says to himself, "O poor Orlando! thou art overthrown: / Or Charles or something weaker masters thee" (1.2.234–5). Love is presented as a wrestling match in which the weaker can overthrow the stronger, but Rosalind has already said, "Sir, you have wrestled well

Jessica: And this is the exercise of critical empathy, which is to make room for differing perspectives without erasing or reducing or projecting. The spaces between worldviews create discomfort, and the challenge becomes: how do we sit in the discomfort, not merely to acknowledge difference but find beauty and insight in those spaces.

Lisa: And there's the additional idea that these positions will be true in different ways in different contexts. As Shannon shows in her discussion of the ways that Jaques's famous speech means differently when read in the context of Duke Senior's speech and Adam's arrival, context makes things waaaay messier, productively.

Lisa: Does Duke Senior's use of gentleness as a means of open generosity modify this martial paradigm of love as a sort of conquest, whether mutual or not?

Jessica: Martial masculinity is defined and measured by performance and action (fight, wrestle, shoot, ride); the courtly lover is, by contrast, founded on the principles of submission and passivity (longing, pining, sighing). Here we see a lovely reframing – another option – of masculinity as gentle conquest.

Lisa: This openness or directedness toward the Other is really the concept that winnows all different kinds of wheat from the chaff, whether that be charisma, power, conventions, social rules, etc.

and overthrown / More than your enemies" (228–9). So, love is a thing in which the weaker may overthrow the stronger, but in mutual love, both parties are overthrown. The scene in the forest, then, is probably the third occasion on which we see the love, the gentleness, or the apparently weaker side win over the stronger, the more violent or forceful.

A fourth and fifth occasion are yet to come. When Orlando's brother, Oliver, follows him into the forest in order to kill him at Frederick's command, he sleeps, and during that sleep, his life is threatened by both a snake and the lioness that the serpent has startled. Orlando considers leaving him – "Twice he did turn his back and purpos'd so" (4.3.124) – but turns back again to kill the lioness threatening his brother and in the process is injured by her. Almost instantly upon waking, Oliver sees what Orlando has done and repents. Of course, in the dialogue between force and gentleness, the lioness loses; it was not grace or kindness that she meets. Instead we are to see Oliver's rescue as Orlando's self-sacrifice, his willingness to risk himself even for the brother who intends to kill him. The forgiveness implicit in that act is moving, especially in Oliver's telling. No wonder Celia falls for him.

Once this process of "overcoming" has been established as the dominant principle of the play in general and of the Forest of Arden under Duke Senior in particular, the play's odd and sometimes mocked happy ending makes more sense. You'll recall that Duke Frederick decides to march on the forest, to put Duke Senior to the sword. But as the report of Orlando's other brother, Jaques de Boys, puts it, Frederick gets to the outskirts of the wood,

Where, meeting with an old religious man,
After some question with him, was converted
Both from his enterprise and from the world,
His crown bequeathing to his banish'd brother,
And all their lands restor'd to them again
That were with him exil'd [...] (5.4.151–6)

Well, that was easy. Think about other Shakespeare plays that involve usurpation and political overthrow: *Hamlet, Macbeth, King Lear, Coriolanus, Julius Caesar*. Even in *The Tempest*, there is more threatened – even if little but time is lost – in the attempt of one brother to overthrow another. Here, though, the problem threatening the forest is solved at the outskirts of the forest by a sudden conversion. In other plays, I might be tempted to call this out as a kind of *deus ex machina*, an unprepared-for appearance by a character who resolves conflict out of the blue. Here, though, this kind of event is perfectly prepared for by the various episodes we have already seen in which gentleness overcomes violence. What else could work in the circumstances? It makes no sense to have Duke Senior mount an army in response; nor would it be in keeping with the play to have him defeated by the oncoming army. Here, the first and also final threat of force is overwhelmed by a godly old man (please note the usefulness of the old again). And so, in his last act in the play before becoming a hermit himself, Frederick gives over the dukedom again, willingly and without violence.

The world of *As You Like It,* of the Forest of Arden, is one in which patience and gentleness defeat violence and force. It is, to paraphrase Canadian literary critic Northrup Frye, not the world as it is but as it ought to be, a world that our gods would wish for us if they were worth worshipping. It is the world as I would like it. And I persist in believing that it is not foolish to imagine worlds better than the one we have, and then to imagine how we might get there.

Jessica: Are we encouraged to think that when the play ends and everyone returns to court, the gentleness will rule over force? That when Duke Senior resumes his position at the apex of political power, this time will be different? (And are we allowed to feel a little sorry for Duke Senior, who has to back to "adulting" when he seemed perfectly content in the forest?)

Lisa: We know that his style of rule was not "effective" before. It seems to me that the hope is not necessarily with Duke Senior's return, but that the next generation – Orlando, Rosalind, Celia – all have seen a different way to live and may bring those aspirations and recentering energy with them. As Rebecca Solnit says in *Hope in the Dark*, "the change that counts in revolution takes place first in the imagination" (26).

In my *Henry V* chapter, I mention the interview with Krista Tippett, in which John Lewis talks about the civil rights movement and its focus on the "beloved community." In that movement, he says, they imagined what the world they wanted would be like and then they behaved as if it were already here (Lewis). That seems to me a triumph both of imagination and of hope. It also requires a third ingredient: a leader able to conjure that vision of the future in words, to capture it with language, to make it focused, concrete, sharp. That is a rhetorical act, an act of persuasion as well as an act of imagination: to see the world as it ought to be and then to convince others to follow into the future. I see that kind of vision and persuasive charisma in Shakespeare's Henry V; in Duke Senior, written at about the same time, we have a much less morally suspect one. His principles of gentleness and equanimity, love, and stoicism persuade young men to leave

Lisa: As usual, my suspicious nature is softened by Shannon's gentle persuasiveness.

comfort and join him in exile, and they might persuade us to imagine, for a moment, what this kind of world would be like if we all met swords with offers of hospitality. That's the kind of world I would want to live in. Delightful though it would be to imagine myself a Rosalind, I could be much more useful as a Duke Senior.

NOTE

1 Although many versions of the play attribute this last line to Duke Senior, the 2008 Oxford University Press edition gives it to his lord, Amiens.

Something Wicked: Verse and Bodies in *As You Like It* 5.2

Lisa Dickson

"Again!"

The students have arranged themselves in a line, shoulder to shoulder, at the front of the class. They begin again:

> SILVIUS: [...] And so am I for Phoebe.
> PHOEBE: And I for Ganymede.
> ORLANDO: And I for Rosalind.
> ROSALIND: And I for no woman. (5.2.80–3)

Okay. It's go time. Act 5. As the Player in Tom Stoppard's *Rosencrantz and Guildenstern Are Dead* reminds us, "Generally speaking, things have gone about as far as they can possibly go when things have got about as bad as they can reasonably get" (Stoppard 2.314). And things at this moment are reasonably bad. Four lovers are finally all together on stage and the misalignment of their affections that has been comic fodder for most of the play has brought them all to a crisis point. Silvius has it bad for Phoebe, who only has eyes for Ganymede. Ganymede, who is really Rosalind in disguise, is not into anybody, but Rosalind is head over heels for Orlando, who loves her back, except that he gets tongue-tied at the thought of actually talking to her. Ganymede has been educating him, man to man, about how to woo Rosalind by pretending to be "Rosalind," a typical "cold maid" who resists his charms. So, in this exchange, Rosalind is Ganymede who is pretending to be "Rosalind." The only thing standing between Rosalind and the object of her affections, Orlando, is herself, that is, Ganymede-"Rosalind," who is the only version of herself who can talk to Orlando without fainting. It's a bit of a mess, in other words. Everyone loves someone who does not love them back. Except when they do. Oy.

The lovers declare themselves for their beloveds in three fast-paced rounds (5.2.80–98).

"Faster!" I shout at the actors. "Who are you looking at?"

"And so am I for Phoebe and I for Ganymede and I for Rosalind and I for no woman!"

"Faster!

"AndsoamIforPhoebeandIforGanymedeandIforRosalindandIfornowoman!"

The student playing Rosalind stumbles a bit on "And I for no woman." There are too many syllables. The iambs are broken.

"Faster!

"*AndsoamIforPhoebeandIforGanymedeandIforRosalindandIfornowoman!*"

"Where is Rosalind?"

They stop. What?

"Who are you looking at when you speak?"

They point down the line, Silvius to Phoebe, Phoebe to Ganymede, Orlando back to "Rosalind," Rosalind to … empty space? To Orlando? He is indeed "no woman." But Rosalind *is* Ganymede and Ganymede is not for Orlando. Where is she standing? The dialogue is the passing of a hot potato. Down the line, it demands, and demands it three times in rapid succession, enough to really get on a roll: once to set the terms, a second time to set the pattern, a third to create an expectation that will be broken in the comic payoff. The rule of three. The students sensed this when they arranged themselves in a row at the front of the room. But Rosalind is a problem, a knot or an eddy in the flow. Worse, she's in two places at once. Or is it three? Ganymede and "Rosalind," beloved, and Rosalind, invisible in her disguises, loving "no woman," in limbo.

The students rearrange themselves to put Rosalind between Orlando and Phoebe. Better, but the hot verse-potato rhythm resists. It's still awkward to change direction like that, to bend the flow back on itself. Then we decided to map out the "Rosalind problem" by passing a physical "hot potato" back and forth – a pencil, a book – as each speaker indicates the object of their affection. The result: Rosalind's "I for no woman" litters the front row of the lecture theater with debris – there is no one there to catch her line. Someone suggests that, since Rosalind is the problem, Rosalind should be fixing it. They make Rosalind jump from place to place in the line so that she can be Ganymede beside Phoebe and then Rosalind (or Ganymede-"Rosalind"?) beside Orlando. That slows everything down unless Rosalind really goes for it. There's something hilariously wonderful in the spectacle of Rosalind literally jumping from one place to another, sometimes jumping the wrong way, knocking people over, making a royal mess of the tidy repetition that Shakespeare has written for them. Really, Rosalind, have you no respect for verse?

Shannon: I love this so much – it is not only feeling the play in your body but working out the stage puzzles together.

Lisa: It happens every year when I get feedback from students: it's the classes where we pushed the tables aside and just hashed out a bunch of options in physical ways that they always remember. We do such a disservice to ourselves when we lock everyone into desks.

Out of breath and standing in the wrong place, Rosalind gasps, "This is impossible!"

Yes. Yes it is.

The room goes quiet.

Then:

"Oh!"

The beautiful regularity of the verse structure gets all snarled up in the impossible physicality of the thing. Rosalind can be Ganymede or Ganymede-"Rosalind" *or* Rosalind, and could do it just fine when all of these personae were not occupying the same space. But it was inevitable that at some point everyone would arrive on stage together. Things have gone as far as they could reasonably go, and Orlando has, after all, declared that he "can live no longer by thinking" (5.2.48). It's Act 5. That's the convention, after all, or, as Stoppard's Player points out, "It is *written*" (2.316). The structure of the verse, its three rounds of repeated potato-passing, is revealing to us that being three people at once is way easier *said* than *done*. Aye, there's the rub.

Throughout the play, this has been the nail in the floorboard that unravels your sock, this incompatibility of rules and life, saying and doing, playing and being. Orlando laments constantly that he has the name of a gentleman but lives like swine. He writes poems like a conventional lover, but his sonnet is missing a quatrain and it's on a tree instead of in a book. He has the heart of a nobleman but is not a nobleman, and his nobility is violent and uncontained by the conventions of social behavior. He threatens Duke Senior with his sword because he "thought that all things had been savage" in the woods (2.7.107) and must be schooled in the art of mercy and courtesy. Orlando *needs* the rules of verse to give him the means to express his nobility.

Having the opposite problem, Rosalind struggles against the restrictiveness of rules that are the condition of her world. She is oppressed by the conventions that govern her sex and keep her dependent upon the mercurial power of the usurper, Duke Frederick. She loves Orlando as a woman but he will only speak to her if she's a man. While Orlando's submission to convention makes him more himself and more capable of acting in the world, Rosalind can only act in the world – own property, be a landlord – if she is "acting," and her former "real" self, who has chosen exile in the face of execution, is doubly displaced. So, who is the real Rosalind? Where does she stand? The strictures and regularity of convention both enable and disable the

Jessica: This play (and this scene in particular) seems to push at early modern notions of gender, where females were considered less developed versions of males. Could Rosalind-as-Ganymede-playing-Rosalind imagine having an easier time gliding back and forth across the continuum in various states of becoming? Or does she get stuck along the way, no longer able to move between gendered expressions so seamlessly?

Shannon: This works so neatly with Jessica's chapter on education. Orlando is not going to come to self-knowledge or education, it seems, without rules and teachers.

> **Lisa:** Yes, and I wonder if it's because the world those rules delimit are his birthright – they're made for him – while those rules always already exclude Rosalind, so entering into them always means being largely "unsaid."

Jessica: We have contemporary accounts (in chapbooks, plays, and records of lawsuits) of women dressing as men, getting into brawls, running businesses, and even marrying women. Mary Firth (aka Moll Cutpurse) was a historical figure who inspired Dekker and Middleton's *The Roaring Girl*, a play about a marriage plot that involves Moll, a notorious cross-dressing but benevolent woman well acquainted with London's low life.

> **Lisa:** Yes, in the case of the various Molls, they were less in disguise than they were flat out flipping the bird at compartmentalization. Rosalind's disguise subverts gender norms by upholding them with a wink.

expression of the self; playing is at once as superficial as the melancholy Jaques donning a fool's motley and as deep as Rosalind's "manly" wit that can only be expressed in costume. Conventions restrict *and* they give shape to the matter of being, depending on where you're standing. These functions continually jostle each other uncomfortably and comically (because the best comedy is one that jostles our comfort), and one of the ways that Shakespeare discomfits us is by playing tricks with the conventions of language and the stage.

In 1983 – bear with me here – Disney made a film based on the Ray Bradbury novel called *Something Wicked This Way Comes*. I don't remember anything about the film except for the score which, in my memory at least, featured an almost subliminal sound of footsteps – something wicked this way coming – that increased in intensity throughout the movie as the wicked thing came closer. This is an *extradiegetic* sound effect, which means that it's a part of the film but outside the world that the film portrays, like the musical score that influences how we experience the film but the people *in* the film don't hear it. The effect of the extradiegetic sound of approaching footsteps was to freak me out more than the creepy action did, not least because I couldn't really tell why I was so freaked out. It twanged my nerve endings until, when the wicked thing finally arrived, I shrieked and threw the popcorn I was popping all over the kitchen. Shakespeare's use of verse and the conventions of poetry and theater is like the almost-subliminal footsteps of a wicked thing that is *in* the world of the play, insofar as it is the linguistic matter of which the play is constructed but isn't *of* the world of the play. There's something very Rosalindish about this wicked thing called verse: like her, it's both there and not there, inside and outside of the scene. The tensions Shakespeare creates pluck expertly at our nerve endings almost subliminally, nearly invisibly, until we grab them by the lapels and drag them into the light by, for instance, making students jump around until they are exhausted.

Jessica: Anti-theatrical pamphleteer Stephen Gosson (1582) rails against cross-dressing, in which "proportion is so broken, unity dissolved, harmony confounded, that the whole body must be dismembered and the prince or the head cannot choose but sicken" ("Plays Confuted" 110). Gosson's concerns are around the precarity of social order. The signs that mark different positions seem all too easy to appropriate.

Lisa: Gosson can scare himself even more when it becomes clear that the precariousness he ascribes to cross-dressing applies to *anyone* playing *any* role and indeed to representation itself. A student once did a remix for my class that was a series of overlaid masks that, when successively removed revealed … nothing.

The repetition and hot-potato-passing of this moment in 5.2 is a fun bit, but its real significance becomes apparent when we put actual bodies in it, when we see and feel how difficult and exhausting it is for Rosalind to occupy three places at once. It doesn't seem to be such a big deal when you read it because our readerly mind glosses over the gaps and tricky bits, and we don't have too much trouble with the triple exposure that Rosalind represents because we can flip between her identities quite easily in our mind's eye. But once you have to contend with the laws of physics and the capacities of bodies in an extant space, the tidiness of continuity and the smooth unfolding of patterns represented by the verse reveal themselves to be far more problematic than they first appeared. Also revealed is the analytical potential of what Ann Cooper Albright calls the "kin-aesthetic imagination" in the service of which we can mobilize our physicality "as a research tool or guide" (103, 107).

Sometimes, the students' reaction to this moment is to assert, occasionally with a tone of grievance, that Shakespeare's made a mistake. Why would he write the verse in this way if it means that the staging is going to be such a problem? Shouldn't he know better? Our first instinct when confronted with one of these wicked moments in Shakespeare's work is to find a way to normalize it, to smooth it out and make it tidy, to find an explanation that makes the weirdness square with our expectations of verisimilitude, our sense of realism. Fog is very useful in this regard. I can't count how many times students turn to fog to resolve problems. It's foggy on the battlements at the beginning of *Hamlet*, which is why Francisco and Barnardo can't see each other even though the stage is ten feet across; it's foggy in the fens in *Titus Andronicus*, which is why Marcus stands there spouting poetry while Lavinia bleeds out from multiple wounds. My response to student grievance in these moments is to fall back on my faith in Shakespeare. I trust him. Trust that he knows what he's doing and go with it, I tell them. Embrace the weird.

> **Shannon:** It's also so fun and joyful – no small thing in learning. Teaching plays gives us so much scope for play in the other sense, and play is so important for learning at any age. I want to be in your class.
>
> > **Lisa:** I want to be in your class.
> >
> > **Lisa:** I love the way that Rebecca Solnit thinks about joy in *Hope in the Dark*: "joy is a fine initial act of insurrection" (24).

> **Shannon:** I'm with you. I always think of Ben Jonson's comment in *Timber, or Discoveries*: "I remember, the players have often mentioned it as an honour to Shakespeare that in his writing (whatsoever he penned) he never blotted out line. My answer hath been, would he had blotted a thousand. Which they thought a malevolent speech" (52). Well, yes, it is a little malevolent, or envious, perhaps, of a gift tied as much to nature as to art. Jonson embraced the fit and decorous, not the weird.
>
> > **Lisa:** So maybe the weird is where it's at. There's something to be said for a thing with cracks in it, places where you can put your fingernails in and give it a pull, oddities that show where the art has pushed against convention and the rules. The "fit and decorous" have their place, but they can be so static. No one wants to play rough with the perfect. As the Talking Heads sang, "Heaven, heaven is a place, a place where nothing, nothing ever happens."

The tension between the demands of the verse in this scene and those of the physical players tasked with embodying them is not a bug; it's a feature. A great deal can be discovered if we let Shakespeare's wicked thing come this way. This willingness sometimes means leaving the door open to the unexpected. In creating this weird collision of words and actions, Shakespeare is asking us to hope. He's asking us to think about the difficulties of being human in a world that makes contradictory demands of us, where ideals are often at odds with pragmatics, where having a "local habitation and a name" means living astride these contradictions and somehow still getting to work on time. These are the challenges that students, on the threshold of their adulthood, grapple with daily. "There are lots of competing truths battling with one another for their place in the sun, and the truth is that we have to learn to cope with the conflict," John D. Caputo reminds us, concluding: "The skies do not open up and drop The Truth into our laps" (*On Religion* 21). Finding truth, living it, is a lot of *work*.

Which brings us back to Rosalind, whom we could never accuse of not having a work ethic. We left her with a stitch in her side on lap three of the race:

"AndsoamIforPhoebeandIforGanymedeandIforRosalindandIfornowoman!"

The next lap is where the rule of three gets its payoff:

PHOEBE (*TO ROSALIND*): If this be so, why blame you me to love you?
SILVIUS (*TO PHOEBE*): If this be so, why blame you me to love you?
ORLANDO: If this be so, why blame you me to love you?

ROSALIND: Why do you speak too "Why blame you me to love you?"

[Who do you speak to, "Why blame you me to love you?"]

ORLANDO: To her that is not here nor doth not hear. (5.2.99–104)

The pattern we've been rolling along with collides with a brick wall, here indicated by the absence of an addressee in Orlando's speech tag. Rosalind notices it and points it out, like that one person in *Something Wicked This Way Comes* who sees the wicked thing coming while everyone is looking somewhere else.

There are two ways that editors have presented Rosalind's startled question. Alan Brissenden of the Oxford World Classics edition gives us "Why do you speak too" but notes that an earlier editor, Rowe, "emended *why* to "who," which is reasonable in light of Orlando's reply" (n. 5.2.100). It just sounds weird to answer "*Why* are you speaking" with "To her." That does not answer the question as posed at all. Brissenden justifies keeping the *why* on the grounds that Orlando "is off in a reverie" and therefore the unspoken "[Because I am speaking] to her that is not here" is implied. This is one of those places where we have to balance the weirdness of Shakespeare's words as they come down to us through the vagaries of centuries of editorial practice against the Ockham's razor of simple sense-making. It makes more sense to amend "why" to "who" and to save us the trouble of imagining dialogue that is not there.

But then again, imagining stuff that is not there is entirely the problem that all of these characters are having at the moment. So maybe it's more interesting to keep the conversational misfire intact as another wicked moment that adds to the increasingly confused situation engendered by Rosalind's multiple identities. Rosalind herself is a living non-sequitur.

Consider an interesting word in this round of declarations: "you." Each speaker directs the line at the object of their unrequited love – Silvius to Phoebe, Phoebe to Ganymede – except

---

Cécilia: The Oxford edition we have is the second one but without the comma ("Who do you speak to 'Why blame you me to love you?'").

Lisa: Dear reader, please meet in this marginal exchange our wonderful Wyrd Apprentice and research assistant, Cécilia. She is a wicked thing hidden in the lines of this book.

My version says: "Why do you speak too, 'Why blame you me to love you?'" (5.2.101–2).

Here, we see how we have to grapple with editorial accretions and variations, as complexity, context, and history are "baked in" to our experience of the text. This little editorial exchange between me and Cécilia, our Wyrd Apprentice, is yet another layer of "living and breathing" in the process of interpretation.

Jessica: "Imagining stuff that is not there" is the work of theater; we as audience members must harness our imaginative forces and fill in the "blanks" in a way that is done for us in film and television. The "wooden O" we are asked to animate in *Henry V* seems to extend here to producers of meaning inside the world of the play, too.

Jessica: I never noticed how many times "you" shows up in this scene (58 times), especially in contrast to the more intimate "thou" (once). French preserves the distinction between the formal singular "vous" and informal "tu." The English language has phased out this difference but the distinction was very much in place in the early modern period. This begs the question: why is everyone so formal with their intended beloveds in this scene?

Shannon: Imagine how tangled the meter would be if he used the second person singular: Why blamest thou me to love thee? Challenging though Lisa's tongue-twister is, it would be worse with the "est" to contend with. Is this another place Shakespeare thinks practically of the work his actors have to do?

Lisa: I wonder if the formal "you" also indicates the degree of idealization going on in the scene. Also, I agree with Shannon that the body and its capabilities are really present in that choice. I hadn't thought of that aspect of the "you" before.

Orlando, whose "you" sort of hangs in the air. If I ask the students, "Where does Orlando look?" they debate hotly whether he looks off into the middle distance or at Ganymede-"Rosalind." Alan Brissenden reminds us that Orlando, in a bit of a swoon at the thought of his love, addresses a Rosalind who is not present at all and exists only in his "reverie." We play that out. Orlando speaks dreamily to the air. In asking, "Who do you speak to, 'Why blame you me to love you?'" Rosalind is simply pointing out that he looks weird doing that. In this scenario, Rosalind is safe. Orlando hasn't made the connection between Ganymede-"Rosalind" and herself. In this case, the somewhat manic urgency of her subsequent breathless planning to resolve her situation seems a little disproportionate to the moment.

The second option is more wicked, weird, and fruitful. If Orlando looks not dreamily into nothing but rather at the actor playing Rosalind-"Rosalind"-Ganymede, things get way riskier for Rosalind. If Orlando looks right at Rosalind-"Rosalind"-Ganymede, the question of who, exactly, Orlando is addressing when he looks at her is a messy one. We play it as though Orlando is addressing "Rosalind" as enacted by Ganymede. Again, the tension wilts and all the momentum of the earlier jumping about bleeds away. Rosalind herself is never really at risk here as she's already playing "Rosalind" and her cover is intact. Nobody real can get hurt. The stakes are low. As in the normalizing turn to "reverie" (the mental equivalent of "fog"), the address to "Rosalind" relaxes us just fine and also anesthetizes the scene. There's no real discomfort here and no comic payoff.

If, however, Orlando addresses Rosalind, the tension built up by the energetic friction of Rosalind's leaping from one self to the next discharges powerfully, and this moment is marked, wickedly, by a trick with the verse that provides a moment of slow-motion emphasis. In response to Rosalind's question, Orlando says: "To her that is not here nor doth not hear." Because, as we've seen, bodies are a great site for research, I make the students put down their books and clap the stresses in this line as they say them. The first three iambs are a remnant of the preceding verse pattern and show us that Orlando is still on those rails, but then the line slows down in the three spondees that follow: "doth not hear." I once asked Alexandra Bennett, an actor friend of mine, how she can remember Shakespeare's poetry *and* emote at the same time. She said that it's because the emotion isn't *on top* of the words; it's *in the words*. Orlando's response is a perfect example of this truth, as the rhythm of the line makes each word drop, *thump, thump, thump*, as Orlando comes wickedly closer, closer, closer to a revelation. Footsteps. Something wicked. Something wondrous. The student playing Orlando, now hearing this stretching out of time as he speaks it, *switches mid-line* from talking to "Rosalind" to *almost* talking to

Shannon: Nice. In that valuable BBC series *Playing Shakespeare*, John Barton talks about the verse as more aid than poetry: "it's there to help the actor. It's full of little hints from Shakespeare about how to act a given speech or scene. It's stage direction in shorthand. [...] Shakespeare was an actor, and I believe that his verse is above all a device to help the actor" ("Using the Verse" 1:57).

Lisa: One year when my students were doing their end-of-semester scene performances, a student arrived in class in an unruly black wig and slouchy cardigan. We all knew exactly who she was supposed to be.

Rosalind. He almost sees her through her multiple disguises. The ponderous footfalls of the spondees are the sound of his epiphany.

Something wicked has come.

No wonder, then, that Rosalind snaps into action to bring the play of personae to some kind of resolution. She's almost been found out, not on her own terms, as she has laid them out to Orlando earlier in the scene, but by the power of the verse. She's slipped up, marvelously, terrifyingly, hopefully. The tissue between her various personae has been worn threadbare by the demands of *acting* and her self shows through. As the patterns of the play demonstrate, this revelation is inevitable; the physical, undeniable body betrays her constantly, as when she hears of Orlando's wounding by a lioness, and she faints. She tries to play it off as "counterfeit," but here again her costume is worn thin. Oliver calls her out: "This was not counterfeit: there is too great testimony in your complexion that it was a passion of earnest (4.3.166–7). Only as a figment of reverie is Rosalind safe; as a physical being in extant space, she must *act*; that is, she must take action, *do* something as only a real person can. She can live no longer by thinking. The play's comic trajectory pushes all of its players through the counterfeit of "acting" toward the act-ual.

And here begins the "comic" denouement. In spite of Rosalind's revolutionary iconoclasm, the pattern, the verse, will out her. Her multiplicity is exhausting and unsustainable ("This is impossible!" the actor gasps, worn out from all that jumping). The verse wins. There's a kernel of tragedy in there for feminists and their allies who lament that Rosalind's exuberant agency will be stripped away with her boy's clothes: she will cease to be a landowner with tenants and will become a wife, the property of Orlando, a conventional woman bound by the conventions of womanhood. In the final act, verse returns *literally in the form of a god*, Hymen, who, in coming to join the lovers, does so in rhyming couplets. "Then is there mirth in heaven / When earthly things made even / Atone together" (5.4.100–3). "Atone together" reads here as "at one together," in a little visual pun that gestures toward the collapsing of Rosalind's multiplicitous selves into a singular identity as Orlando's wife, "if," Phoebe says, "sight and shape be true" (5.4.112). Form and content, surface and substance, playing and being are collapsed in this pageant of marriage where the oaths of the wedding vows are actions that change the world and the being of those who speak them: saying "I am your wife" in the context of the ceremony makes one a wife. The earlier tensions between speaking

Shannon: This moment always reminds me of *Way of the World* by William Congreve, when the irrepressible Millamant accepts Mirabel's proposal, saying, "if I continue to endure you a little longer, I may by degrees dwindle into a wife" (4.5). I don't want Rosalind to dwindle, even as I suspect she is capable of fashioning a new kind of marriage for them both.

Lisa: That is a perfect phrase, "dwindle into a wife." Again, I like the crack in the play that lets the light in, Rosalind's epilogue, and all the ways that the play pushes against convention so that it cannot close again perfectly, like a suitcase at the end of a vacation that you can't zip up because of all your souvenirs.

Jessica: Shakespeare stages many masques with similar stylistic conventions but slightly different hosts: Hymen presides over AYLI, while Juno, Iris, and Ceres host the wedding masque in *The Tempest*. Why does Shakespeare need a mythical *deus ex machina*? Is it to save Rosalind from herself, restore social order that has been exposed as arbitrary, or something else more "wicked"?

Lisa: What if it's a sly way of noting that the only way to stuff everything back in the box is literally to invoke a god from outside the world? The world, left to itself, will be excessive and resistant to wrangling, and, since gods are unlikely to show up in the regular world, maybe we can hope for a little more messiness. As Rebecca Solnit says in *Hope in the Dark*, "Joy sneaks in anyway, abundance cascades forth uninvited" (24).

and acting, the verse and the people playing it, are resolved in favor of the verse that is ordered, regular, tidy, and that rhymes in couplets as all the messy, excessive, disguised, and displaced characters are rhymed in couples with their appropriate mates.

Except.

Except that Rosalind returns in an epilogue in her wedding finery to speak as the boy she is and to kiss the men as "If I were a woman" (Epilogue 15–16). What the verse has set right, the theater sets awry. The "if" in "If sight and shape be true" is where something wicked achieves escape velocity. The sight of Rosalind is not commensurate with the shape of the boy beneath the clothes. In the speech, Rosalind, no longer reduced to a singular identity, regains her multiplicity as a costumed actor in a theater, *of* the play but, here in the epilogue, not quite *in* it. The unruly physicality of the embodied actor wickedly disturbs the "reverie" of conventional identity and opens up the space again by being in it. As W.B. Worthen argues, this is the irreducible quality that defines theater: "Theater goes well beyond the force of mere speech, subjecting writing to the body, to labor, to the work of production" (9).

This is the power of the body in theater and in the classroom. Of course, it must be said that sometimes this "hot potato" exercise does not come off so smoothly. In fact, very often it does not come off at all, at least not without a fair bit of prodding and coaching. Students' glorious unruliness – which sometimes manifests itself as impenetrable reticence or an immovable deferral to my authority – makes the learning space risky: we never know at the outset where – or who – we will be at the end of the day. In many ways, it would be so much easier to gaze into the middle distance and teach as in a "reverie," where people exist only as figments, to speak monologically, in a single, authoritative, immovable voice, into the darkened lecture hall and to avoid the messy physicality of students. Teaching would be risk-free if not for students, if one never had to figure out whom to look at when saying "you." Figments are obedient to the will, but they are not alive. To be present, to speak with students, to explore the play *in time and place*, is risky.

And in such risk is the potential for empathy, for hope, both of which ask us to put our selves on the line in a way that opens us – broken open, Parker Palmer hopes – to something different, something wicked, and sometimes to something dangerous. I can relate to the frisson, the terror and the relief, encoded in those spondees when Orlando almost sees through "Rosalind" and Ganymede to the Rosalind that animates them. I can begin to imagine those moments for so many of my students struggling to figure out who they are and who they want the world to see when the world says "you." Having left my own queerness at the door for most of my career, I can imagine those students for whom this moment represents a joyous assertion of self and love and visibility. For others, it may mean something altogether more terrifying. I consider how a trans student might balk at "playing a girl" because, as Shannon has pointed out, "gender neutral" casting is never really neutral. I see how a gender-fluid student might revel in Rosalind's protean mastery of her multiplicitous selves or lament the collapse of all of that into the singularity of conformity. The *physicality of the verse,* and through it the play's revelation of the difficulty of being a person, of figuring out who to be and where to stand, places us all at that moment of epiphany, on the threshold of an encounter with an Other we are just beginning to see. The pell-mell comic energy in this scene dramatizes an opportunity for empathy. Furthermore, its relentless forward momentum toward an insistent but unstable presence is a kind of hopeful opening to an as-yet-unmade future, for, as Ros King observes, feeling the body in Shakespeare's verse attunes us to the "difference [...] between observing a state and experiencing a process" (394). Opting to step out of "reverie" into the complexity of embodiment means opting for risk, if we are willing to trust that space of discovery as Shakespeare trusts the stage.

In the comic denouement of the play, convention snaps all of the pieces back into place. But that's not all that happens in this play. In the classroom, the strictures of regulation, authority, and power don't go away but they are not the only thing in that space. From the tensions between the disembodied "reverie" and the lived embodiment of learning arises an ebullient celebration of the power of creativity to bend the rules – not always to breaking – to declare the power of poetry both to create order and to prove that there is always something else, in the gaps and tensions, that escapes. "We never are what we are," John D. Caputo asserts; "something different is always possible" (*Radical Hermeneutics* 35).

Jessica: Rosalind's cross-dressing is supposedly for her safety and survival, but she also revels in her doublet and hose. Her dramatic transvestitism allows social worlds to renew, to shed light upon life, the meanings it harbors, to elucidate potentials. The subversion and inversions of festive play projects an alternate conceptualization of reality.

Shannon: Even Ophelia sometimes gets it right: "Lord, we know what we are, but know not what we may be" (*Hamlet* 4.5.43–4).

Lisa: So, maybe it's fitting to end an experience of the play with lots of questions: Will Duke Senior be any better at ruling when he goes back? Will Rosalind "dwindle" as a wife or flex against conventions until they give? The play opens up into the future, provocatively and tantalizingly.

PART THREE

Henry V

Henry V: Prophecy, Hope-Speak, and Future-Speak

Shannon Murray

Introduction

> I am not saying that hope can change the world all by itself. What I am suggesting is that hope is a necessary condition of our work as educators attempting to bring about change. Hope problematizes time by opening it up to our intervention, allowing us a starting point from which we can articulate and move toward a shared vision for the future. (Jacobs 794)

I began my chapter on *As You Like It* by asking what kind of a world you would like to live in. I'll start this one with a connected question: what kind of a future do you imagine, and how do our leaders help conjure, make concrete, that future? What I love in Dale Jacobs's idea about hope here is the connection to time. Hope "problematizes time" so that we move toward "a shared vision of the future." His wonderful essay makes a distinction between "hope-for" and "hope-in." "Hope-for" is individual, self-focused. We might hope for recognition or money or love, but those hopes are wishes for the self. The kind he celebrates is "hope-in," a hope that includes others, and it may not even require the self to benefit. It is the hope for a better life, a better world, even after one's own death. My own hope in higher education or in the importance of grappling with Shakespeare both fall into the "hope in" something beyond myself – I hope.

So, what does this have to do with *Henry V*? To start with, we have critical questions about critical hope in this book. Is it

Jessica: As Shakespeare moves into the later stages of his career, TIME becomes a character, a theme, and a vehicle for other kinds of processes. In *The Winter's Tale,* jealous Leontes needs to stew in the consequences of his toxic masculinity for sixteen years before his daughter and wife and kingdom are restored. Transformation takes time. Rehabilitation takes time. Does hope need to be located within time (past, present, future)?

Lisa: Are "hope-for" and "hope-in" incompatible? Complementary? Mutually modifying? Can your hope in higher education sustain what you hope for yourself?

Jessica: I like that idea of hope in something (e.g., the power of higher education to make the world more equitable, diverse, just) can fuel hope for your role in enacting that future-facing vision.

possible to teach hope in any useful way in a university course, even a university literature course? (I think so.) Where are the limits on hope? Is hope always a good, always a virtue spurring us on to good action, or can it also be twisted for bad purposes? (I fear it is merely neutral.) And where are the connections between empathy and hope? Is one stronger with the other, or are they discrete ways of approaching the world? *Henry V* seems to me to be a wonderful play to use to question hope because Shakespeare makes his national hero much more complex than he has to be: a brilliant orator who repeatedly shakes off responsibility for events he is actually responsible for; an apparently beleaguered commander who is actually an invader himself but who is able to employ the status of victim when it is convenient; someone devoted to appropriate behavior even when it appears to hurt him personally who nevertheless gives an order to kill prisoners. He is also someone who uses the language of hope, of a shared vision of the future, that embraces both egalitarian celebration and a deeply twisted violence. But I'd argue that his brand of hope is uncoupled from empathy, and the result is short-term victory and long-term failure.

For me, Henry V is both an example and a cautionary tale, a model and a monster. Before I go on, I ought to offer my potential conflict of interest here. My first encounter with him was in 1977, in the Regent's Park Open Air Theatre in London, and I fell instantly in love with the character. My younger sister, Suellen, and I returned again and again, even in the English drizzle, to watch Henry dazzle us with his honor, his wit, and his charisma. Of course he was right, we thought, and of course he was to be followed. In the years since, I have returned to *Henry V* so many times, reading, watching, and teaching the play, and my response is, I hope, more layered than in that early infatuation. I can see past some of Henry's rhetoric and can talk wisely about wariness and rhetoric and moral ambiguity. But a shocking amount of that early attraction persists, especially when I see a good performance. Give me a great Agincourt speech and I am my sixteen-year-old self again, fully believing in Henry, in honor, and in his cause. That's what I love to wrestle with now and to have my students wrestle with, and I fully believe that it is Shakespeare who invites, even requires that wrestling, by taking what could be a simple hagiography of a national hero and a famous victory and insisting that we look at it with a critical eye. That Henry can continue to seduce me is the power of great oratory (and sometimes of great performance!), and it is also the warning: that rhetoric can turn us against what we know to be true and right and that not all hope is good. That's what I want to look at here, the moments when critical hope, unyoked from critical empathy, can be dangerous.

Jessica: The dark side of hope is a shadow that looms over this book. The authors of this book imagine a host of hope warriors determined to make the world more inclusive and equitable for all. Assuming that all those who wield hope do so through the lens of human rights and sovereignty for all people and planet is presumptuous at best, downright dangerous at its worst. Just as rhetoric can go rogue, hope can be dangerous when it is used for the powers of seduction or coercion.

Lisa: Which is why Aristotle was so careful to yoke rhetoric to ethics, and why Plato was so suspicious of Sophists like Gorgias. Gorgias reminds us in his *Encomium of Helen* that oratory is an enchantment that can transform us and carry us away, as Helen was abducted by Paris.

Jessica: YES! Rhetoric (persuading and listening) can lead us to reason that transcends power of coercion or seduction. But tie rhetoric to power and all sorts of humans can run amok.

Henry Rouses

In an interview with Krista Tippett, John Lewis talked about the civil rights movement and its focus on the "beloved community." In that movement, he says, they imagined the way they wanted their world to look, and then they behaved as if it were already there (Lewis). That seems to me a triumph both of imagination and of hope. It also required a third ingredient: a leader able to conjure that vision of the future in words, to capture it with language, to make it focused, concrete, sharp. That is a rhetorical act, an act of persuasion as well as an act of imagination: to see the world as it ought to be and then to convince others to follow into the future. It is to say not "we should go to a mountaintop" but "I have been to the mountaintop." The beloved community may still be a dream, but it's a dream and a vision worth hanging on to, especially in troubling and troubled times. Hope-talk, I think, gets stronger the more we need it.

Henry V's famous speech to the troops before the battle of Agincourt is perhaps an odd parallel here for John Lewis's vision or Martin Luther King Jr.'s Mountaintop speech, but it is the mode rather than the message of Henry's speech here that interests me, the varied deployments of future-speak. Henry is a Machiavellian hoper, less absolute in his goals than he is situational or contextual. He will conjure a paradise or a hell, hope or despair, depending on what his goal is. And although I can forgive a lot of Henry, I'm grateful to Shakespeare that he never lets me wallow in my historical crush. (Henry's troops may be beleaguered underdogs, but they got that way because Henry was invading another country after taking bad advice and succumbing to pique.) He is, as the Victorian William Hazlitt calls him, an "amiable monster," a man "ready to sacrifice his own life for the pleasure of destroying thousands of other lives" (130, 133). For me, Henry's greatest strength is as a kind of prophet, conjuring a future that his audience might want to live in or shun. Reading his "future-speak" is a helpful warning that hope can be dangerous when it is deployed for a bad end – like saying you want to make your country great again even if it means others will suffer.

So, what actually happens in that rousing address to his troops? In her chapter, Jessica talks about how extraordinary Henry's rhetoric is here, but I want to look more at tenses, both

Lisa: Oh man, the phrase "Machiavellian hoper" has sent me into a tailspin!

Jessica: When Milton created Satan more than sixty years later, he was doing just that kind of work. How much of that work is gaslighting yourself and others? What is the line between self-determination and self-delusion?

Lisa: Yeah, for Henry, I will somehow suspend my rule never to be entertained by likeable villains. And that, as you say, requires a lot of unpacking and comes with all kinds of uncomfortable questions about commitments and complicities.

Jessica: It took me a long time to see Henry through this lens. Maybe it is because I am awfully suggestible or defer to authority but I was buying everything he was selling for years. I didn't have a "wait a sec" moment until much later as it dawned on me that old white men at the head of institutions don't always have the best interests of *all* in mind …

Shannon: … nor do young white men, in this case.

Lisa: And that statement, of course, depends on defining "your country" in a very particular way, in a way that somehow makes some people your fellows and some not. So much of what Henry (and others we shall not mention) does is definitional, drawing boundaries and setting conceptual terms and premises from which to extrapolate in order to get what he wants. This is what the long-winded "Salic Law" rigmarole in 1.2 is all about.

Shannon: I agree. The placement of that rigamarole – and the whispering conspirators that start the play – help us take away some of Henry's guilt in invading a country. It also reminds us that they are about to start a war, sacrificing arms and legs and heads chopped off in battle, as soldier Michael Williams points out, and that war is declared on pretty iffy grounds.

here and in a few other key spots where Henry is imagining the future. Taking his cue from his "cousin" Westmoreland, he moves from imagining a battle in which he fights with as few men as possible – the fewer men, the greater share of honor – to not wanting to share: "for the best hope I have" (4.3.33). What does that mean, I wonder? I have hope for the outcome of the battle? For dying in battle and getting fame and honor from it? The best hope. But while that early section is "I" speak – all about Henry's place – he quickly remembers his audience and switches to others – and to the future. Now he imagines the "he" who "outlives this day and comes safe home" (41). That imagined soldier will live to be proud, to "stand a-tiptoe when this day is named / And rouse him at the name of Crispian" (42–3). He will become more than he is; he will expand.

Notice that it is not the battle of Agincourt that rouses that soldier: it is the name of the saints whose day it is. That's one of those strong attachments to yearly ritual that most of us have lost now – marking the year by the saints in the saints' calendar. The battle happens to take place on the feast day of Crispin Crispianus. All kinds of things will be associated with any saint for whom a day is celebrated, but Henry imagines a secular celebration, an attachment of this battle, this famous battle, to the saint's day. Are we to imagine potential martyrdom? (Both Crispin and his twin Crispinian were beheaded.) Probably not. But here's the thing: saints' days happen yearly. Although we have since had a purge of saints from that packed annual calendar, at Henry's historical moment, the year is saturated with saints, and from now on, Henry imagines, these two rather obscure martyrs will be associated with the battle about to happen – from the now to the near future and repeated yearly on the vigil.

Henry's next move is to a slightly more distant future. Imagine you have come home; you are proud of the name of Crispian. But now imagine that you live a long life – you "see old age" – and every year, you invite your neighbors to join you on the eve of the battle's anniversary. And that's when life gets joyous. There is feasting. There are neighbors, happily partaking, and then there is the necessary storytelling: "Then will he strip his sleeve and show his scars / And say 'These wounds I had on Crispin's Day'" (47–8). I am reminded of the presentation of wounds in *Coriolanus*, as a demonstration of the soldier's experience but also his seriousness and suffering. My favorite line in the whole speech is "he'll remember, with advantages, / What feats he did that day" (50–1). I imagine Henry channeling Falstaff at that moment, remembering with grudging affection Falstaff's ability to tell a convincing but exaggerated story of his own feats, as when he "kills" Hotspur. Henry, that intellectual magpie, learns from everyone, indiscriminately. So, the memories of the day just ahead will live on, but not just with the survivors, since "this

Lisa: And he does some tricky sleight of hand here, too, doesn't he? By noting how *future* storytellers will puff up the tale and make it heroic, he conveniently deflects from the fact that he is doing so *in the present*, in this very speech! You will aggrandize yourselves for reasons later, he seems to say, but I am not doing that now for reasons. No, not me.

Jessica: The relationship between time and storytelling is so bendy in this speech! Henry is telling the story of the day (at the beginning of the day) through the lens of an imagined future where these stories (told by others) are filled with nostalgia. It is like the narrative version of Rosalind's identity-bending tour de force that Lisa talks about in her *AYLI* chapter. And yet here Henry locates himself in the eternal present; he is an all-seeing and all-knowing (reliable) narrator freed from the shackles of linear chronology. In this way, he becomes God (at least, in Boethius's estimation of the eternal present).

story shall the good man teach his son" (56). Note that those who come safe home now have not just neighbors, feasts, and old age to look forward to. They now have imagined progeny. And note too that feats and scars make a full narrative. They have become a story. Passing that story on from one generation to the next guarantees its survival, long past that day or old age, or even their own sons, who presumably will tell the story again and again: "And Crispin Crispian shall ne'er go by / From this day to the ending of the world / But we in it shall be remembered" (57–9) – from today to coming home to old age to the next generation to the world's end. Now that's hopeful.

The speech takes the soldiers and the larger audience through at least four time periods in a kind of rhetorical time travel: now, home, old age, world's end. They are asked to imagine themselves – oh so subtly – dying, living, aging, and being remembered in that narrative until the end of time itself. Part of the power of the speech lies in its secondary audience: Shakespeare's. That audience knows the battle; they know who will win, against overwhelming odds, and they are living proof of his prophetic words. People will – and still do – remember Agincourt and Crispin's Day.

Note the simplicity of the future he has them imagine. Home, yes, but with scars; no one is getting through this day without wounds. But the scars become talismans, signs of belonging. Once you imagine scars, you can imagine neighbors, imagine feasts, imagine a yearly festival, shifted from marking a saint and martyr to marking a glorious battle that you survived. Imagine community, community centered on you and your achievements. It will be such an important day that more will be remembered than actually happened; it will be the Woodstock of the War of the Roses. Henry has taken men convinced they would be washed off at the next tide – what a great passive metaphor! – and made them agents, survivors, heroes.

> **Lisa:** "We kept more promises than we made" quoth someone whom I will not name.
>
> **Jessica:** Ah yes, "he who will not be named" was also never named in Stephen Greenblatt's wonderful book *Tyrants: Shakespeare on Politics* (2018) and yet looms largely on every page. I wonder if it is an act of rebellion, a small victory, or perhaps even disingenuous to avoid explicitly referencing such a character – and what they will say in future historiographies about this choice?

Now, Shakespeare and Henry both want to have it both ways here. The strength of that speech – the conjured hopeful future, the narrative that will live on in retellings – seems to be the efficient cause of the victory the next day. But Henry also shares the victory with God, requesting that the hymn "*Non nobis*" be sung. That hymn of humility suggests that all is not from us but from God alone, and it echoes what Henry says three times when he hears how many French and few English were killed in the battle: that it was God's victory and not theirs, that God fights for the English. Here Henry's habitual shifting of responsibility from himself to some other body appears at its best, its most humble and pious, but more of that later.

What about the French in all of this? What about their future-speak, their hope, their prophetic narratives? If this play is in one way a battle between two competing notions of the future, why do the French lose – ignoring, of course, the weather, the heavy armor, and the longbow that seem to have been vital together in the actual battle? They too have a notion about the future: "A very little little let us do and all is done," says the Constable (4.2.33–4), with more confidence than hope, before the battle. Two things are missing though, here and in the conversation in the French tent the night before. The first is a *shared* vision of the future, one that involves all the hearers and not just the speaker. And the other is a leader able to make people see through his words that imagined shared future. The Dauphin, the apparent leader here, is mocked by his fellows and seems much more interested in his horse than in his fellow soldiers. Compare that to Henry, who claims he cares nothing for garments or gold: "such outward things dwell not in my desire" (4.3.27). The French are fragmented, lacking community, lacking a leader with imaginative power.

This brings me back to that helpful distinction Dale Jacobs makes in that article about hope and pedagogy I began this chapter with:

> As individuals, we may want (hope-for) tenure, a raise, or a new computer, but this kind of individual wanting does not involve the kind of hope-in (a collective idea) … is, hoping is not tied to having (hope-for), a state of mind that is closer to desire. Hope-in rests in a collective, rather than individual, future. It is this kind of utopian hope that I believe is imperative for us to articulate and to see as aligned with the kind of pedagogy expressed by hooks and others. (786)

Jessica: Oh, brilliant. So the "hope-in" is more sturdy and robust than "hope-for."
Shannon: I think so – because it is more outward-looking than self-interested.

Henry's speech demonstrates "hope in" his soldiers and their futures, even in the face of hopeless odds; the French, though, when they look ahead at all, express "hope for" themselves.

Henry Woos

But this isn't the only time Henry has such an effect on others. The play shows him repeatedly constructing a vision of the future. In Agincourt and in the wooing scene at the end of the play, Henry's future-speak is meant to appeal, and the shared future is an attractive one (5.2). At Harfleur and in the scene of the tennis balls, though, Henry's method is the same: he demonstrates the same ability to conjure a future so real as to effect change in the hearer (3.3; 1.2). But in these last two, his purpose is the opposite of hope. The hearers are to despair, to see the imagined future and work to avoid it rather than to help make it.

Look at the wooing scene first. Left with the French princess, Catherine, during the postwar negotiations, Henry tries to win her love as he has won the war. This is an unnecessary seduction, surely, and it always seems to me oddly out of place, no matter how charming and disarming the actor playing Henry is. After hours of war and politics, we get talk of love; after four acts composed largely of men doing manly things, we get two women. Most odd of all, the representatives of England and France are offstage negotiating a treaty that will without doubt include the marriage of Henry and Catherine. What's more, in the few scenes we've seen with Catherine through the play, she has been learning English. The Dauphin and his father may have thought that they would win the war, but Catherine clearly has her doubts. She is already preparing for a future, practical gal that she is, that would require her to speak English. She is at least resigned to the idea. But the scene plays itself out as if she has some agency, some ability to choose. What's going on here?

The simplest answer might work here: Henry's desire is not just to win her through battle and political agreement but to win her consent and her love. That would be more persuasive if she appeared to have other options should she say no. And Henry uses some of the same strategies here that he does on the battlefield, including conjuring a shared vision of the future. In what looks at first like a terrible case of foot in mouth, he claims he is not the enemy of France: "for I love France so well that I will not part with a village of it, I will have it all mine: and, Kate, when France is mine, and I am yours, then yours is France, and you are mine" (5.2.169–72). Note two shifts here: from the present to the future – I will have all of France – and from his possession to hers – Kate will possess both Henry and all of France. Not a loss, then, but a gain. Marry me and conquer France yourself.

He also, by the way, promises her a better-looking husband, because age, "that ill / layer-up of beauty," can't touch him because he is already unattractive. "Thou / shalt wear me, if thou wear me, better and better" (221–2, 223–4). My appearance can only improve, he promises, in yet another example of Henry's hopeful future-speak. This is a line that works whether a plain or a handsome Henry is cast. It can either read as a truth – "I'm so ugly I can't get any worse" – or as a charming self-deprecation. Either way, Henry wins. (Except that he dies in just five years, which suggests he is a talented rhetor but a flawed prophet.)

When Kate agrees to agree – "then it shall also content me" (241) – he offers to kiss her and then adds one even larger vision of their future together: "O Kate, nice customs curtsy to great kings. Dear Kate, you and I cannot be confined within the weak list of a country's fashion: we are the makers of manners, Kate;

> **Jessica:** She is so practical that the vocabulary she learns is based on body parts, as if she knows the political landscape is written on her body.
>
> > **Lisa:** And that it can be "carved up" in this blazon like chines of beef.

> **Lisa:** There's a great parallel here with Exeter who, when the French king asks "what follows" if the French do not submit, replies: "Bloody constraint," "widows' tears, the orphans' cries," "dead men's blood" (2.4.96–107).

> **Lisa:** And there's that definitional boundary-drawing again.

> **Lisa:** That's a terrific distillation of that bit of charming verbal acrobatics.
>
> > **Jessica:** Gaslighting or an invitation to self-determination?
> >
> > **Shannon:** Both, I'd say.

> **Lisa:** Me, watching Tom Hiddleston say this line: "Um … How?"
>
> > **Shannon:** More than one attractive performer uses this line as a chance to charm with perhaps insincere self-deprecation. Looking at you, Branagh.

and the liberty that follows our places stops the mouth of all find-faults" (260). Icky though this little exchange can look now – he will destroy the first (of many?) customs of the country he has overthrown and stop her mouth with a kiss – in the play, it works. He asks her to imagine herself the empress of a larger kingdom, with a better-looking husband, in which they together will construct the way citizens behave, their very manners. From "you" and "I," he switches to "we," and with that, he catches her mind with a vision of their shared future. This guy is good.

But it's all a bit suspect, isn't it? He gets what he wants by giving her the appearance of agency. He persuades her to kiss him by pretending that she has the power to remake custom, when it is to both English custom and Henry's desire that she acquiesces. It is a version of the future and of personal responsibility that works, even if she and the audience see that it's sketchy.

Henry Threatens

Henry's great talent among many is that he can conjure a vision of the future and make others see it and want to live in it. But he can also create a hellish version of the future when it suits him. Henry's future-speak is not wholly hopeful. It is only so when that shared vision fits his purpose. Think of other times in the play when he is equally adept at creating a vision, almost a prophecy of the future, but as a horrific threat rather than an inspiring promise. When the Dauphin tries to humiliate Henry with a reminder of his profligate past, Henry imagines a blindingly higher rise from that earlier fall:

> For that I have laid by my majesty
> And plodded like a man for working days,
> But I will rise there with so full a glory
> That I will dazzle all the eyes of France,
> Yea strike the Dauphin blind to look on us.
> And tell the pleasant prince this mock of his
> Hath turned his balls to gunstones, and his soul
> Shall stand sore chargèd for the wasteful vengeance
> That shall fly from them – for many a thousand widows
> Shall this his mock mock out of their dear husbands,
> Mock mothers from their sons, mock castles down;
> Ay, some are yet ungotten and unborn
> That shall have cause to curse the Dauphin's scorn. (1.2.276–88)

It is an impressive moment, and the fact that he ends this sec-tion with a rhyme suggests that he knows it: it's a kind of punc-tuation mark, an indication of his absolute control over his material. This imagined future is of a horror, the desolation of families, the razing of castles. And just as he moves from the immediate future to the distant in his Agincourt speech, here he prognosticates past those who will witness this terror to those "yet ungotten and unborn" who will curse the Dauphin. It's also just such classic Henry that, although he has already made his mind up, surely, to invade France, this future-speak also contains his characteristic shifting of blame. "It's not my fault if I go to France and kill lots of people; the Dauphin's mock did it."

And he creates the same kind of desolate future when he speaks to the governor of Harfleur, in a truly shocking series of threats:

> If I begin the batt'ry once again
> I will not leave the half-achievèd Harfleur
> Till in her ashes she lie burièd.
> The gates of mercy shall be all shut up,
> And the fleshed soldier, rough and hard of heart,
> In liberty of bloody hand shall range
> With conscience wide as hell, mowing like grass
> Your fresh fair virgins and your flow'ring infants.
> What is it then to me if impious war
> Arrayed in flames like to the prince of fiends
> Do with his smirched complexion all fell feats
> Enlinked to waste and desolation?
> What is't to me, when you yourselves are cause,
> If your pure maidens fall into the hand
> Of hot and forcing violation?
> What rein can hold licentious wickedness
> When down the hill he holds his fierce career?
> We may as bootless spend our vain command
> Upon th'enragèd soldiers in their spoil
> As send precepts to the leviathan
> To come ashore. Therefore, you men of Harfleur,
> Take pity of your town and of your people
> Whiles yet my soldiers are in my command;

Lisa: I am always struck by this weird, dangerous alchemy of poetic language that can enclose the most chaotic, most disordered and disordering things within calming and ordering structures. In this way, Henry, the amiable monster, is like poetic language itself.

> **Jessica:** Claudius does this in 1.2 of *Hamlet*, where he uses poetic devices (chiasmus, articulus antitheton) to reframe very disorderly things (dirge in marriage and mirth in funeral!). Ugh.

Whiles yet the cool and temperate wind of grace

O'erblows the filthy and contagious clouds

Of heady murder, spoil and villainy.

If not – why, in a moment look to see

The blind and bloody soldier with foul hand

Defile the locks of your shrill-shrieking daughters;

Your fathers taken by the silver beards,

And their most reverend heads dashed to the walls;

Your naked infants spitted upon pikes,

Whiles the mad mothers with their howls confused

Do break the clouds, as did the wives of Jewry

At Herod's bloody-hunting slaughtermen. (3.3.87–121)

It's a challenge for directors to stage a likeable Henry who also threatens wartime rape and infanticide and claims it will all be the victims' fault. What a picture of inhuman cruelty is painted here. Violent tortures and deaths are imagined for pure maidens, fresh-fair virgins, shrill-shrieking daughters, flowering and naked infants, mad mothers, and aged fathers, while responsibility is shifted away from the man who will give the command and onto his soldiers, to a personified war, or to the residents of Harfleur themselves.

So many of the strategies I wanted to praise in his St. Crispin's Day speech are employed again here: the future-speak, the vivid narrative into which the hearer is invited to see himself. But this is despair, not hope, that he means to create. And there is no empathy here at all, no sense of communal purpose when even the soldiers would be bent on individual destruction and chaos. A great orator, Shakespeare warns us, can give us Agincourt or Harfleur, bands of brothers or infants spitted upon pikes.

Lisa: And many productions have done so – Laurence Olivier's WW2 version (1944), for instance, which is so clean and fair, so bloodless and jingoistic. It does its job as a good bit of morale-boosting for the citizens of a devastated England, but mostly by cutting all the most searching parts out.

Shannon: Yes, like Olivier cutting the killing of the prisoners or the exposure of three English traitors, because, of course, there are no traitors among the English. The *Hollow Crown* version is interesting because it keeps the uncomfortable bits.

Shakespeare might have made this a simple hagiographical play, but he's not a simple guy. If he had wished, he could have filled the theater with people happy to see a righteous Henry in a righteous war, but he didn't. Instead, he gives us a Machiavel, but one who seems to want to manipulate in a good cause. He gives us an orator equally capable of a vividly hopeful and a nightmarish future for his auditors. He gives us a man (whom we have followed through three plays) we can admire even as we see him playing us. And in the end, we can see that this glorious and powerful leader has not actually succeeded in creating the future he imagined, as his Chorus says:

Thus far with rough and all-unable pen

Our bending author hath pursued the story,

In little room confining mighty men,
Mangling by starts the full course of their glory.
Small time, but in that small most greatly lived
This star of England. Fortune made his sword,
By which the world's best garden be achieved,
And of it left his son imperial lord.
Henry the Sixth, in infant bands crowned King
Of France and England, did this king succeed,
Whose state so many had the managing
That they lost France and made his England bleed,
Which oft our stage hath shown – and, for their sake,
In your fair minds let this acceptance take. (Epilogue 1–14)

I'm not sure I detect Shakespeare's physical self anywhere in his plays as clearly as here – just in that word "bending"! It immediately conjures the picture of a body curved over the paper these lines are being written on. And at the end, the stage itself is referenced, as are the plays that Shakespeare has already written, from *Henry VI, Part 1* through *Richard III*. The ending has a cyclical effect, harkening back to the history plays that have gone before, and reminding us of how this all turns out – with the hunchback's carnage and the Tudor triumph.

But the other thing about this conclusion is how deeply despairing it is. It points to the pointlessness of all the events with which we have just been fully engaged. Henry V will die soon, and the result of this invasion of France will be England's suffering. This pointlessness is nicely highlighted in the *Hollow Crown* version, filmed for television in 2012, which begins and ends in Henry's funeral. Shakespeare stops short of explicitly denouncing war or territorial appropriation, but I can't help remembering the arguments of Michael Williams to the king the night before Agincourt:

> **Lisa:** Yes, by reversing the order of history in his completion of the Plantagenets plays, he constructs an arc that moves from fractiousness to unity, as all those multiplicitous, backbiting lords from the *Henry VI* plays are distilled to and displaced by this one, great, triumphant English personality.
>
> **Jessica:** The "bending author" is bending time in his history plays. A favorite Tudor maxim was "Truth is the Daughter of Time" (used often in Elizabethan spectacle to draw a providential line between Henry VIII and his resilient daughter, Elizabeth I). Shakespeare is playing with this notion here, too.

But if the cause be not good, the King himself hath a heavy reckoning to make, when all those legs and arms and heads chopped off in battle shall join together at the latter day, and cry all "We died at such a place" – some swearing, some crying for a surgeon, some upon their wives left poor behind them, some upon the debts they owe, some upon their children rawly left. I am afeard there are few die well that die in a battle. (4.1.129–36)

Clearly, Henry is not the only one capable of creating vivid and memorable images of future horror (though I detect some of his magpie wit in picking up and reframing the vision of the "latter day" in his "from this day to the ending of the world"). Looked at this way, we see a charismatic leader leading his country to a war that ultimately leaves his England weaker than when he started. How's that for a cautionary tale?

Conclusion

It feels like a long way from the days when my sister and I would stalk the *Henry V* actors from the Regent's Park Open Air Theatre. Although my own response to the play was pretty simple at the time, I know that the play lasts and can be played again and again, for different purposes and in different historical moments, precisely because it resists the simple judgments that a straight, jingoistic piece would deserve. Henry can be both a charismatic and pious leader and a genial monster. I can both cheer the famous victory of the underdogs and be rightly uncomfortable at the invasion of another country on suspect pretexts. I can be appalled at the barbarism of the French who kill boys and shocked when Henry orders the slaughter of prisoners, making up two different excuses. I can find Henry's wooing both charming and creepy.

Playing up these conflicting responses, responses that Shakespeare seems purposefully to provoke, makes the play so much fun to talk about in a class, where individual students find themselves defending or attacking one element or another. As always, it is because the classroom is a space for so many voices that discussions of Shakespeare are so satisfying there. I hope explorations of complex plays like this help train cautious minds, minds able to recognize when they are getting played, how rhetoric can be both attractive and dangerous, making us feel what we wouldn't think. Here as in his other plays, Shakespeare can make strong and active citizens in a democracy, thinkers able to make good choices but also to hold two conflicting ideas in their heads at the same time.

But more than in so many other plays – even those with manipulative speakers like Iago or Richard III – this play gives us a picture of someone who deploys hope when it is convenient, despair when it is not. We see the uses of hope both when it is connected and when it is unconnected to empathy, and we see the uses of hope-for and hope-in. Not all hope, the play seems to suggest, is equal. True critical hope needs not only to understand the situation fully and help make a better future; it also needs to be linked to critical empathy. One without the other will never create the beloved community.

Lisa: I hear Plato here, condemning the poets for enlisting our feelings against our reason.

Jessica: This differentiation is key. Hope can have a dark side and can be used, like rhetoric, for purposes that are selfish, self-serving, or harmful to others. Knowing all this, and being able to appreciate the differences, underlines the importance of "critical" as a prefix paired with hope.

Orators of Hope or Rhetors Gone Rogue? The Ambiguities of Persuasion in *Henry V*

Jessica Riddell

"What hill are you willing to die on?"

I pose this question when I teach *Henry V* in my Shakespeare and Critical Hope course.

"And how can you persuade others to join you?"

Henry V uses words to persuade his men to literally run into the mouths of cannons. How does he do it? Why would these men be willing to die for words? If the pen is indeed mightier than the sword, the orator is mightier than the general in early modern and postmodern contexts alike.

Rhetoric, until recently considered an antiquated subject and a relic of the medieval curriculum, is now enjoying a comeback with increasing relevance in our "post-truth" world.

In fact, developing rhetorical literacy has never been so urgent.

This generation of young people is facing some of the toughest and most thorny challenges one can imagine: the climate crisis, income inequality, gendered violence, homophobia and transphobia, food and water insecurity, large-scale warfare, and geopolitical instability. Compound this with the rise in disinformation campaigns, information warfare, fake news, and post-truth politics and the sheer multitude and complexity of these pressing issues is overwhelming.

The cognitive and emotional load that our students are asked to carry is enormous. I worry constantly about how I can even begin to help them navigate a world that *feels* radically more unstable than the one in which I grew up. Nobody taught me

Shannon: That's why I love the suggestion Paul Hanstedt makes in *Creating Wicked Students* – that in order to address problems like much too shifting and complexity for simple or single-disciplinary answers, we need to help our students think wickedly.

Lisa: And we of the old school, the establishment, the institution, etc., must then learn to deal courageously and openly with the results of that work of fostering wicked thinkers: the next generation telling us that we did a lot of things wrong and that we are responsible for fixing our mistakes.

Lisa: Is it? Or is it that we are now way more connected to the stories of others, through the global information and economic systems that are less able to support our blissful ignorance of the effects of our choices on people far away?

Jessica: This is such an interesting question that pushes up against the "good old days" narrative. Your insight reminds me of Steven Pinker's *The Better Angels of Our Nature: Why Violence Has Declined* (2011) where he argues that "humans are now living in the most peaceful era in the history of our species" (Stetka, para. 1). I DO think this generation is dealing with the unprecedented urgency of wicked problems, like climate change, in ways that the late 1970s–1980s felt more … insulated?

Shannon: Shakespeare is such a good mentor when we approach complex problems, isn't he? The plays rarely tell me what to think but rather how to think about what I think.

Lisa: And orators of reckoning, too, I would say. Their vision of the future is not one of "moving on" and "getting past" the violations of the day, but of reckoning with the past in the name of justice in order to move forward. Critical hope is never just about tomorrow.

how to do this in graduate school, I despair. And then a little voice in my head says, "or did they?" In these moments, Parker Palmer's advice in *The Courage to Teach* urges me to connect with "the mentors who evoked us and with the subject of study that chose us" (22) to make sense of the forces that converge in our lives.

Looking through my early modern lens, I realize that Shakespeare provides us with a master class in rhetoric that offers a road map for navigating – and tackling – some of our most pressing social issues. Plays like *Henry V* teach us to appreciate the dazzling power and peril of rhetoric. Shakespeare shows us characters who weigh their words and waste them so that we can, through example and instruction, unlock the power of our own voices and evaluate the force of others' "words, words, words" (*Hamlet* 2.2.185).

Cue rhetorical rabbit hole.

In a mere fourteen months, Greta Thunberg went from a fifteen-year-old protesting by herself in front of the Swedish Parliament to addressing world leaders at the United Nations and condemning them for their inaction on climate change (September 23, 2019). Greta is riding a wave of youth advocacy that has become part of our cultural zeitgeist: "the spirit of our times" is now animated by young people who have become our orators of hope.

In 2014, at the age of seventeen, Malala Yousafzai became the youngest person to receive a Nobel Peace Prize.

Along with their classmates, David Hogg and Emma Gonzalez organized the largest protest in US history with over one million people participating in March for Our Lives in March 2018.

Since she was eight years old, Autumn Peltier has been a driving force in the fight to protect water in Indigenous communities in Canada. The teenage activist from Wiikwemkoong First Nation on Manitoulin Island in Ontario has been a tireless advocate for water security and urged the General Assembly to "warrior up" when she addressed the United Nations in March 2018, at the age of thirteen.

While the social issues differ – climate crisis, female access to education, gun control, decolonization, and water security – they all have something in common: these orators of hope are all trained in rhetoric. In entirely circumstantial and yet tantalizing ways, we might even trace faint lineages of linguistic performance back to Shakespeare.

Greta Thunberg's mother, Malena Ernman, is an internationally acclaimed opera singer, and her father, Svante Thunberg, is a classically trained stage actor, producer, and writer, even performing in *Romeo and Juliet* at the Royal Dramatic Theater Dramaten in Sweden ("Svante Thunberg").

Malala Yousafzai's parents founded a chain of schools and provided her with an intensive education in Western literature, including Shakespeare. When she returned home after being shot by the Taliban, Malala granted an interview to Reuters and "pointed out a shelf in her room with books including Shakespeare's *Comedy of Errors* and *Romeo and Juliet*, as well as a copy of the television series 'Ugly Betty' – she was, after all, a teenager!" (Ahmad, para. 5).

David Hogg and Emma Gonzalez attended Marjory Stoneman Douglas High School, where they were trained in performing and liberal arts (Riddell, para. 8). In fact, the school board has an exceptional drama program and a "system-wide debate program that teaches extemporaneous speaking from an early age" (Gurney, para. 4). Every student in middle and high school in the district has access to a public-speaking program. In fact, David Hogg and Emma Gonzalez were so effective at public speaking in the wake of the tragic shooting that they were accused of being "crisis actors" by the Conservative media (Uyehara, para. 5).

Autumn Peltier's training in oratory is situated in Indigenous knowledges and is part of a powerful storytelling tradition that is thousands of years old. Her great-aunt Josephine Mandamin, founder of the Mother Earth Water Walkers, was an Anishinaabe elder, water activist, chief water commissioner of the Anishinabek Nation, and an exceptionally powerful orator. When she passed away in February 2019, she was hailed as "Water Warrior Grandmother Josephine Mandamin" and remembered as a visionary who dedicated her life to cleaner water and greater water protection (*Water Docs*).

All of these orators of hope have been educated on the power of persuasion and coached in public speaking from elders who have mastered the art of rhetoric, drawn from Western or Indigenous traditions and knowledges.

Their experience in rhetoric should not devalue their advocacy efforts; instead, their training should reinforce the enduring belief we can persuade people to think and see differently than they do in the hopes of a better world for all.

And yet rhetoric – when it *is* used in our contemporary context – is loaded with negative connotations. In the political sphere, rhetoric is lobbed about as an insult to undermine the sincerity of an individual by suggesting that their words are empty, artificial, or out of touch: "they are full of rhetoric" or "that is just empty rhetoric" is an easy way to win an argument by challenging the "authenticity" of the words – and by extension, the speaker (authenticity is, itself, a rhetorical tactic, wielded by those trying to differentiate themselves from charges of artifice that accompany oratory and public speaking).

Lisa: It's a battle over what gets to be "real," who gets to say what's "real," who has a "real" voice. It is fascinating how, at this moment of crisis, this power struggle turns on the language of theater: I – the Man, the authority, the establishment, the adult – speak *real* words; you – the child orator, the disruptor – are "just" doing theater. In the political theater (ha!), theater is reduced to "fake" (Plato's view), whereas these young orators are using its spectacular power to "move" the world (Sidney).

Shannon: You make me think of other good or neutral terms – "liberal" or "academic," for example – that get a similar sort of reductive treatment.

Lisa: I would add "semantic," which is a word often used to dismiss arguments as unimportant. *Henry V* demonstrates that semantics are crucial. How we speak things into the world shapes what we see as possible.

Silencing opponents by accusing them of "rhetoric" can be tied to anti-elitism (and its twisted sister, populism) – yet these are not new charges. As far back as there was rhetoric, there was a suspicion that people could use words to alter another person's reality for various purposes, for the good, the bad, and the downright nefarious. The Sophists mentioned in Plato, for example, were condemned for using arguments without substance: rhetoric gone wrong or, at the very least, gone rogue.

So what is rhetoric? In its most basic form, rhetoric is the ability to persuade. According to the ancients, reason gives us purpose (*telos*), and rhetoric is the instrument of reason. For Aristotle and his contemporaries, rhetoric is *reason-in-action* and can help us move beyond the vagaries of the power of coercion and seduction so that we can reach a higher, transcendental plane of existence.[1] In Aristotle's formulation, if you use rhetoric for purposes other than striving for eternal, intelligent, and divine knowledge, you are doing it wrong. If you are deploying rhetoric to seduce or coerce for your own needs or desires, this represents a deformity or arc away from the rational; in classical terms, deploying rhetoric for your own gain dilutes your purpose, detracts from your end goals, and degrades your life's work.

Orators of hope imagine a world better than their own for others.

Rhetors gone rogue manipulate the world for the betterment of themselves at the cost of others.

Shakespeare deploys rhetoric in a range of ways on this spectrum: as a vehicle of hope and as a weapon of coercion, as a platform to expose our darkest inclinations and a stage that promises to lift us to a higher state of being. He offers us a master class in rhetoric that asks us to hold two oppositions – the dual capacity of language to hope and harm – together without splitting apart. In fact, this tension is often beautiful, breathtaking, and always entertaining.

Lisa: If this model were a vertebrate, this would be its spine: the connection of individual action and talents to collective benefit or deficit.

> **Jessica:** I really like this metaphor of a backbone to help illuminate the structure of rhetoric – and how the spine guides what we are saying and how we use rhetoric.

Lisa: Which makes Henry an excellent case study as he, too, has a "dual capacity … to hope and harm."

> **Shannon:** Yes, and he does in the *Henry IV* plays as well. (A lot of his friends end up dead.)

Shannon: He does it in the sonnets too, which we haven't really been talking about much in this book. I give my students rhetorical "cheat sheets" when we tackle them, and we go from "I like what he did there but I don't know why" to "oh, I see what he was doing there," once we know the rhetorical and poetic terms.

> **Lisa:** Yes! The timepiece becomes more beautiful when you can see all the intricate gears and flywheels interacting inside it!

Henry V and the Power of Linguistic Chameleons

While there are a number of masterful orators in Shakespeare's canon who fall into one of the two categories I've proposed – orators of hope and rhetors gone rogue – Henry V is perhaps the most ambiguous. Depending on how we interpret his rhetorically sophisticated performances, he can occupy either position. He is the rabbit-duck of Shakespeare's protagonists and the power of his shape-shifting relies entirely on his mastery of language.[2]

The play *Henry V* marks the fourth and final installation in Shakespeare's wildly popular tetralogy. The three previous plays in the series dramatize Richard II's overthrow and death, the ascension of Henry IV, and the difficulty Henry IV has holding onto the throne, which is complicated by the mischievous adventures of heir apparent, Prince Hal, and his lecherous, drunken friend, Sir John Falstaff. The future Henry V and Falstaff, the latter hailed as one of Shakespeare's greatest comedic characters, party their way through Cheapside with a naughty band of ne'er-do-wells for the better part of *Henry IV Part 1* and *Part 2*. In the opening lines of *Henry V*, we learn that Prince Hal has discarded his old friend when he becomes king, and this act of betrayal was too much for the old knight to bear: according to Mistress Quickly, Falstaff dies of a broken heart (2.1.85).[3]

When we encounter the newly reformed Henry V in the opening lines of the eponymous play, the audience must reconcile his past escapades with the beloved historical king and military conqueror memorialized in Holinshed's *Chronicles*. Shakespeare has to ensure the lovable rascal and prodigal son from *Henry IV Parts 1* and *2* is still recognizable while also bestowing upon the new king the appropriate royal authority. Shakespeare manages this tightrope walk by employing a relatively new Renaissance political ideology inspired by Niccolo Machiavelli, one of the first great modern voices in political and moral theory. Machiavelli's *The Prince* is full of advice on how the ruler should skillfully use whatever resources are available to maximize his own power and reduce the power of his enemies.

Although *The Prince* was banned in England during Shakespeare's lifetime, the Machiavel became a popular stock character on the early modern stage, especially in revenge tragedies. In Shakespeare's canon, the Machiavel puts his or her own personal survival and power above any traditional moral restraint. The Machiavel takes on a variety of forms, including the melodramatic villain (*Richard III*), motiveless maligners like Don John and Iago, shrewd political operatives like Bolingbroke, Goneril, Regan, and Claudius, as well as figures of enormous psychological complexity and ambiguous morality like Prince Hal (*Henry V*) and Macbeth.

However, the primary characteristic of the Machiavels in Shakespeare's plays is that they are linguistic chameleons. First and foremost, they are experts in navigating different discursive worlds. Learning from the most masterful linguistic chameleon, Henry V, provides us with a master class in rhetorical literacy: studying Henry V's rhetoric shows us how to create worlds and shape realities. The play also asks us to acknowledge not only that language can be used for purposes of good, bad, and the downright nefarious, but also that such purposes can operate in dynamic simultaneity.

When we meet Henry early in the play, he is dealing with an image problem. His past exploits are still fresh in the minds of his subjects; he must harness all his linguistic prowess to

Shannon: As a student, I remember thinking that this sort of death was a too convenient way to get rid of a character: until I read the mortality bills for the period. "Grief" was one of the consistently noted causes of death. Shakespeare was just following the medical science of the time.

Shannon: This works so nicely with the discussion of self-fashioning in your *AYLI* chapter. Henry is such a master at shaping his own self, and woe to those who can't see what he is up to. Fortunately, as audience members, we get to glimpse his strategies – or at least we think we do …?

Lisa: What is our responsibility as educators who take as our core object of study this mercurial thing called language?

Jessica: Now more than ever we need to design for information literacy. Our students need a "cheat sheet" for differentiating between the good, the bad, and the nefarious. We are bombarded with information from all kinds of sources (dubious and legitimate commingled). We must engage in these conversations and provide tools for individuals to do the critical work themselves.

signal his identity transformation, both to members of his court and for his enemies in France, and assert his royal legitimacy. The Dauphin of France, determined
to undermine Henry's image rehabilitation campaign, sends Henry a case of tennis
balls to mock him for his past indiscretions; the suggestion here is that the superficial,
fun-loving Hal should stick to parties and leave serious matters like war to the grown-
ups. The Dauphin bites his thumb at the new king in a very public manner and Henry
must respond.[4] Henry uses this opportunity to flex his rhetorical muscles and turns
the tennis court into a conceit (an extended metaphor) to juxtapose sport and war:

> When we have matched our rackets to these balls,
> We will in France, by God's grace, play a set
> Shall strike his father's crown into the hazard.
> Tell him he hath made a match with such a wrangler
> That all the courts of France will be disturbed
> With chases. And we understand him well,
> How he comes o'er us with our wilder days,
> Not measuring what use we made of them. (1.2.261–8)

The complexity of the conceit, which deploys the technical language of early modern
tennis and repurposes the terminology for war, is one of Shakespeare's best set pieces.
The "crown" as a metonymic extension of kingship (and control of France) doubles
as the scoring system in tennis (the normal stake was a *couronne* or crown). The "haz-
ard" operates both as the threat of war and the aperture in the back walls of the tennis
court. If the ball gets stuck in this opening, the opponent scores a point (n. 263, p.
115). The "wrangler" – a quarrelsome player disputing the call or point – is repur-
posed for the Dauphin, who has chosen the wrong opponent with whom to bandy
balls (and yes, there is a double entendre with tennis balls and testicles. Manhood is
on the line in this high-stakes contest). "Chases" are both military pursuits and a way
to score points (referring here to when the tennis ball bounces a second time without
being returned).[5] The court is simultaneously a place of sport and a place of politics.
However, the next section of Henry's speech marks a transition, where he rebukes the
Dauphin for trivializing a matter that has serious (deadly) consequences:

> And tell the pleasant prince this mock of his
> Hath turned his balls to gunstones, and his soul
> Shall stand sore chargèd for the wasteful vengeance
> That shall fly with them – for many a thousand widows
> Shall this his mock mock out of their dear husbands,
> Mock mothers from their sons, mock castles down;

Ay, some are yet ungotten and unborn
That shall have cause to curse the Dauphin's scorn. (281–8)

Henry turns the Dauphin's mock on its head, repeating the word four times in the space of two lines in order to transform its meaning irrevocably. The meaning of "mock" morphs from a "joke" to the cause of the "death of dear husbands" as a result of the joke (mock out = "bring to a specified state or condition by mockery" [OED n. 4]); "mock" is then used as a verb that separates mothers from their sons (mock = "to put a stop to, to hinder" [n. 5]) and has the power to tear down castles (mock here functions either as a "piece of trickery or deception" or "to jinx" [n. 1b]). Henry deploys *antanaclasis*, the rhetorical trope in which a word is repeated with a shift in meaning, in order to transform the meaning of "mock" and, by extension, our perceptions of the English invasion of France. This is a *LOT* to pack in to one speech with very particular goal: Henry wants us to believe that any violence that occurs is the direct consequence of the Dauphin's scorn. This is, of course, a tricky bit of revisionist rhetoric since we all witnessed Henry's decision to "bend [France] to our awe, / Or break it all to pieces" (1.2.224–5) *before* the French Ambassador arrives with the tun of tennis balls. But if we take a page from Machiavelli, one should never let the truth get in the way of effective rhetoric.

In this encounter, Henry demonstrates his ability to use language to shape other people's perceptions. An unflattering interpretation might assert that Henry gaslights his subjects to justify an unjustifiable war, while a more sympathetic reading positions Henry as a moral and restrained monarch in contrast to the Dauphin, styled here as a trivial dandy taking cheap shots from behind the robes of his powerful father. In this second version, Henry's retaliation is justified not only as restitution for his lost honor but for all English men *and* French families (if you notice, Henry pointedly shows concern for mothers and sons and husbands in France since they are, as he claims, his subjects too).

Lisa: This is where a *narrative-structural* reading of this whole first act really pays off. The way Shakespeare doles out the action does so much to establish the ironies and ambiguities that are the substrate of the play. The rhetorical strategies Henry deploys here tie in with the *stylistic* elements and demonstrate how all of these domains work together and are illuminated by each other, so that the house has many doors.

Jessica: Some of my students were unfamiliar with this term at first blush. When I explained that gaslighting was manipulating someone so that they question their reality, perceptions, or memories, they quickly understood the concept and could identify the behavior immediately (aided by contemporary illustrations such as Fox News and "he who shall not be named").

If Henry warms up with his tennis ball speech, he finds his voice at Harfleur. As he leads his men into battle, he must literally persuade them to run into the mouth of a cannon for him. He has to be so persuasive that his speech short-circuits the basic human instinct for survival. His exhortation in the heat of battle can be divided into three strategies. The opening section uses rhetoric to transform his men into soldiers:

Once more unto the breach, dear friends, once more,
Or close the wall up with our English dead.
In peace there's nothing so becomes a man

As modest stillness and humility,

But when the blast of war blows in our ears,

Then imitate the action of the tiger.

Stiffen the sinews, summon up the blood,

Disguise fair nature with hard-favored rage.

Then lend the eye a terrible aspect,

Let it pry through the portage of the head

Like the brass cannon, let the brow o'erwhelm it

As fearfully as doth a gallèd rock

O'erhang and jutty his confounded base,

Swilled with the wild and wasteful ocean.

Now set the teeth and stretch the nostril wide,

Hold hard the breath, and bend up every spirit

To his full height […] (3.1.1–17)

Henry uses simile, which draws parallels between two dissimilar things but maintains a clear distinction. In contrast to metaphor, which says x = y (my beloved is a rose), simile suggests connection while maintaining differentiation using "like" or "as": x // y (my beloved is *like* a rose). In these two examples, one beloved is eminently more kissable than the other. In this speech, Henry mobilizes five similes to encourage his men to assume a new identity for battle:

1. Predatory animal: *imitate* the action of a tiger, accompanied by a list, an *articulus*, of the features of the tiger they should emulate
2. War machine: become *like* a brass cannon
3. Impenetrable natural object: men should adjust their facial features *as* a galled rock intimidates sailors
4. Historical warrior: "*like* so many Alexanders"
5. Racing animal: "*like* greyhounds in the slip"

Henry uses simile rather than metaphor in order to highlight the performative nature of martial masculinity; the identity of a man must be different in times of war and times of peace. In order to maintain a civil society, men must only imitate animals, not *be* animals, since they must return to their original identities once the battle is over. The transformation, while, temporary, encourages them to adopt a persona that makes them capable of risking life and limb in battle.

Shannon: Such a nice point to make about the difference between simile and metaphor here: each of these is a disguise to put on, a part to play, rather than an identity. That's what Coriolanus gets wrong, isn't it: he is always what he is, not bothering to suit his behavior to the moment. Always interested in acting, isn't our playwright?

Lisa: I agree. He sets up the idea of acting and then troubles that premise: when you're spitting babies on pikes, the differentiation in a simile means f**k-all. From the point of view of victims, "acting like" a monster still makes you a monster. And this recognition is precisely what Henry counts on when he turns his rhetoric on Harfleur. So Shakespeare gives us this brilliant deployment of simile and then, in the next brilliant speech, shows its emptiness, especially if we get a sympathetic presentation of the people of Harfleur on stage.

Word patterning (also known as schemes in classical rhetoric) also plays a crucial role in this speech. Henry uses *epanalepsis*, a word repeated at the beginning and end of the same sentence, to build momentum: "*once more* unto the breach dear friends, *once more*." Then he ratchets up the rhythm as the speech progresses, relying more and more on the sounds of words as he gets ready to "let slip the dogs of war" (compare with *Julius Caesar* 3.1.273):

> On, on, you noblest English,
> Whose blood is fet from fathers of war-proof,
> Fathers that like so many Alexanders
> Have in these parts from morn till even fought,
> And sheathed their swords for lack of argument.
> Dishonour not your mothers; now attest
> That those whom you called fathers did beget you.
> Be copy now to men of grosser blood
> And teach them how to war. And you, good yeomen,
> Whose limbs were made in England, show us here
> The mettle of your pasture; let us swear
> That you are worth your breeding – which I doubt not,
> For there is none of you so mean and base
> That hath not noble lustre in your eyes. (3.1.17–30)

Henry shifts his strategy from performativity to parentage, signaling this change with a scheme called *epizeuxis*, a figure of repetition with no intervening words. This scheme gives the appearance of natural emotion and is used to demonstrate great intensity of feeling: "On, on, you noblest English." In the first part of the speech, Henry urges his soldiers to become something they *are not* (tigers, cannons, cliffs), but in this second section, he invokes soldiers to remember who they *are*: that is, English Men born and raised in England from a lineage of battle-tested fathers and honorable mothers.

Their military masculinity is "fet" (fetched, derived) from their fathers, which is important enough that Henry emphasizes paternity through a clever use of *anadiplosis*, in which a word near the end of the clause begins the next clause. *Anadiplosis* is Greek for "doubling back": therefore, using this scheme echoes the lineage of fathers and sons engaging in warfare for their king, effectively repeating throughout English history. In doing so, Henry connects these soldiers to a legacy far greater and further reaching than this one moment in time. This is nationalistic propaganda at its most explicit: Henry asks his men to prove they are "worth their breeding." Here Henry introduces a theme of meritocracy in war, suggesting that war can make a lowly farmer noble. Through language he suspends class hierarchies and (temporarily) bestows the highest honors on the lowest-ranking men. Henry's command of language has the power to (re)create identity and redefine social class, reaching its culmination in his famous "St. Crispian Day" speech a little later in the play.

In the third section of his Harfleur speech, Henry uses rhythm to urge on his soldiers and lends these lines a metrical quality akin to the beating of a drum: Henry builds momentum in the middle section with alliteration (the repetition of the initial consonant in two or more words, usually used for emphasis) with blood pumping phrases like "but when the blast of war blows" and "hold hard the breath, and bend up every spirit" (5, 16) and then finishes with short, choppy sentences, an accelerated tempo, and a final battle cry:

> I see you stand like greyhounds in the slips,
> Straining upon the start. The game's afoot.
> Follow your spirit, and upon this charge
> Cry "God for Harry! England and Saint George!" (31–4)

Who amongst us would falter in the face of such rousing rhetoric? Henry promises that we can become tigers, make our mothers proud, honor our fathers, become noble – all with Harry, England, *and* St. George behind us!

And yet, because Shakespeare is always throwing a monkey wrench into things, the scene immediately following undercuts the rhetoric of war with a deflating parody, and gives us an inkling that Henry has not persuaded *everyone*:

> *Enter Nim, Bardolph, Pistol, and Boy*
> BARDOLPH: On, on, on, on, on! To the breach, to the breach!
> NIM: Pray thee corporal, stay. The knocks are too hot, and
> for mine own part, I have not a case of lives. The humour
> of it is too hot; that is the very plainsong of it.
> PISTOL: "The plainsong" is most just, for humours do abound.
> Knocks go and come, God's vassals drop and die,
> *[Sings]* And sword and shield,
> In bloody field,
> Doth win immortal fame.
> BOY: Would I were in an alehouse in London. I would give
> all my fame for a pot of ale, and safety. (3.2.1–11)

While Bardolph seems to be buying everything Henry is selling, rushing toward battle with his sword raised and his brow furrowed as per instructions, he is comically

---

Shannon: Poor Pistol, Bardolph, Nim, and the Boy don't ever see the fruits of this idea, do they? Shakespeare doesn't shy away from the sad conclusion that, for most of those soldiers who were "not of name," little changes when the battle ends.

Lisa: "Not of name" brings me back to Judith Butler, who notes in *Precarious Life* that nationalism is grounded on a determination of whose loss is "grievable" and whose isn't, and how "grievability is publicly distributed" (34). Here, and in the Agincourt speech, Henry gestures toward the possibility that everyone is "grievable" *as Englishmen*, but when the rolls of the dead are read out, the "general gender" are "none else of name."

Shannon: Not me. I can be suspicious and clever as I want when I read, but I get sucked in every time I see a production.

Lisa: Stephen Gosson is sitting on your shoulder whispering about how spectacle is corrupting your mind! :D (Compare with *School of Abuse*.)

interrupted by his companions. Nim flatly refuses to be swayed and Pistol does a quick calculation of the value of immortal fame in the face of mortal danger and is unswayed. While we know these three are rogues and scoundrels, there is an opportunity to feel real *pathos* when the Boy yearns for the comforts of a pot of ale in Cheapside in the midst of a terrifying war far from home. Shakespeare places these two scenes side by side to catch us in our own suggestibility. A moment ago we were ready to run into battle with Henry as our chief hope warrior and now we long for the creature comforts of peacetime. Shakespeare asks us to hold both of these as truths without suggesting one is more right, more just, more true.

Shannon: In this play and in the *Henry IV* plays, Shakespeare does this side-by-side scene strategy brilliantly, like when he gives us that stunning revelation of the traitors in Act 1 of *Henry V* – how could they betray a friend like that! – sandwiched between the two Falstaff death scenes: oh right, Henry did that, too.

    Lisa: This is one reason why I use *Henry V* as my primer on reading Shakespeare in my second-year course. His use of juxtapositional commentary is so refined and beautiful in this play and is perfect for attuning students to its operations elsewhere.

Henry's most famous rhetorical performance comes on the eve of the battle at Agincourt. His army is exhausted, sick, and wildly outnumbered. Things do not look good for the English, and in the play Henry must summon every persuasive weapon in his rhetorical repertoire to urge them once more unto the breach. His *exordium* lays out two options: we are either destined to die, and thereby we are fulfilling God's will, *or* we are going to win, in which case, why do we need more troops?

Lisa: KICK HIM OUT OF THE REPUBLIC! Or, no, wait. KEEP HIM IN THE REPUBLIC! Shakespeare: simultaneously Plato's greatest nightmare *and* his greatest ally in the debate about the dangers of poetry to reason.

Lisa: … and thereby we are fulfilling God's will. God is clearly hedging his bets.

> If we are marked to die, we are enough
> To do our country loss; and if to live,
> The fewer men, the greater share of honor.
> God's will, I pray thee wish not one man more. (4.3.20–3)

He then invokes *ethos*, one of the three modes of persuasion alongside *logos* and *pathos*, in order to prove his credibility and by extension the credibility of his cause. A successful orator needs to persuade the audience that their character (*ethos* means "character" in Greek) is good, authentic, legitimate. Henry uses comparison, his favorite *topos* (a strategy of arguing a case or investigating a subject), in order to assure his men that he is in this war for the right reasons:

> By Jove, I am not covetous for gold,
> Nor care I who doth feed upon my cost;
> It ernes me not if men my garments wear;
> Such outward things dwell not in my desires.
> But if it be a sin to covet honor
> I am the most offending soul alive. (24–9)

Henry compares two different motivations (wealth and honor) and then throws in a reversal: if coveting honor is a sin, then I am guilty, emphasis on the word "if."[6] Once Henry has established the "facts" – first, that fewer men means greater honor and, second, that his motivations are for glory rather than gold – he uses language to create a future where they are all looking back on this day with nostalgia:

> This day is called the Feast of Crispian.
> He that outlives this day and comes safe home
> Will stand a-tiptoe when this day is named
> And rouse him at the name of Crispian.
> He that shall see this day and live t'old age
> Will yearly on the vigil feast his neighbours
> And say, "Tomorrow is Saint Crispian."
> Then will he strip his sleeve and show his scars
> And say, "These wounds I had on Crispin's day."
> Old men forget: yet all shall be forgot,
> But he'll remember, with advantages,
> What feats he did that day. Then shall our names,
> Familiar in his mouth as household words –
> Harry the King, Bedford and Exeter,
> Warwick and Talbot, Salisbury and Gloucester –
> Be in their flowing cups freshly remembered.
> This story shall the good man teach his son,
> And Crispin Crispian shall ne'er go by,
> From this day to the ending of the world
> But we in it shall be remembered,
> We few, we happy few, we band of brothers. (40–60)

Henry uses rhetoric to take his troops on an imaginative journey through time, where the men who stand before him now have already experienced the battle, the scars, victory, homecoming, and old age reminiscing. He projects us into the future to exercise critical empathy for our past (present) selves. It really is the most exquisite feat of persuasion and engages us in the imaginative and emotional work of remembrance of a time that has yet to pass.

To create this time-traveling nostalgia, Henry deploys a number of schemes focused on repetition: note his use of refrain, repeating "Crispian" every three lines for the first half of his

Shannon: For Henry, honor is like pie: more for me means less for you.

Lisa: Like France. He loves it so well, he'll have all of it. There's a neat underlying territorial mindset all over his language, isn't there? Which makes sense given that he's conquering a country and all, but I love to find these patterns woven in so beautifully.

Jessica: Unpopular opinion: bake more pies.

Shannon: Yes! And I suggested in my chapter that the audience already knows who wins, already knows that this clever bit of rhetorical prophecy will come true – because we DO remember Agincourt (if maybe mainly because Shakespeare wrote this play). Prophecy in the history plays is so fascinating and satisfying, telling us what we already know must happen.

Lisa: It's a right ouroboros, innit?

speech and then again in the closing remarks, perhaps suggesting a fireside song as yet unwritten. He uses "day" six times (four times in the first five lines!) to situate us in relation to time: this is just one day and yet it is *the* day that will be remembered until the end of days, even when all else is forgotten. This is classic hyperbole (exaggeration) and yet in that moment and in those dire conditions you *want it to be true*. In fact, Henry is gambling on it being so powerful that together they can *will it to be true*.

Henry needs every single one of his men to take an imaginative leap, invoking his now recurring trope that war is the great equalizer: "We few, we happy few, we band of brothers." This phrase is powerful because it uses *graditio* (Latin *gradationem*, which means ascent by steps, a climax) and *tricolon* (three parallel clauses, phrases, or words that happen in quick succession without any interruption) to build upon the idea that they are intimately bonded in this shared experience. Henry uses two words – "we few" – then three words – "we happy few" – and then reaches the apex of his speech with four powerful words – "we band of brothers." This takes him into the final section of his speech, where he makes explicit the transformation forged in war:

> For he today that sheds his blood with me
> Shall be my brother; be he ne'er so vile,
> This day shall gentle his condition.
> And gentlemen in England now abed
> Shall think themselves accursed they were not here,
> And hold their manhoods cheap whiles any speaks
> That fought with us upon Saint Crispin's day. (61–7)

This speech has everything and the rhetorical kitchen sink. Henry essentially promises everyone a knighthood and valorizes martial masculinity: blood is spilt, brotherly bonds are forged, and the rest of the guys back home are cursing their manhoods. It is no wonder this speech shows up on the (unintentionally hilarious) website "artofmanliness.com" where they present the St. Crispin Day speech as "manvotional" (presumably this neologism combines "man" and "motivational" – but seems etymologically closer to "man + emotional"). According to the Art of Manliness, "knowing how to inspire and lead others is an essential manly attribute." The website promises its twenty-first-century male readers that Henry's words "will stir you to focus on the legacy you are building and will pass on to your sons and to history" (McKay and McKay, para. 1).

I'm not even sure what to say about that. But I suspect Harry would smile wryly.

Shannon: Oh dear. Do they know what happened to Henry V's son? Or that Henry's own date with dysentery cut that legacy short? Context, people, context!

Lisa: The fact that they used "manvotional" instead of "manivational" suggests no. I wonder if folks rolled their eyes at Castiglione the way I roll my eyes at this website. And: what if people *did* roll their eyes at Castiglione and now he's in all the anthologies ... and the artofmanliness. com is the Castiglione of tomorrow and ... *we just put it in a book*?

Lisa: But Foucault isn't quite so bleak as all that, noting that there are all kinds of ways to work within networks of power. Others such as Judith Butler and John D. Caputo run with this idea, positing that refusing to accept the names and definitions imposed from "above" is power, too. The Boy, for example, has no political power at all, but his speech before Harfleur, in which he decides to go find better masters, leaves a bruise on the play's potentially jingoistic elevation of a national hero.

> **Jessica:** YES! In order to initiate change, we must deconstruct the narrative of a "monolithic institution" and understand that power – through a Foucauldian lens – is dispersed, local, "*embodied* and *enacted* rather than possessed, *discursive* rather than purely coercive, and constitutes *agents* rather than being deployed by them" (Gaventa 2003, 1, emphasis added).

Conclusion

The central question in this play is this: is Henry V an orator of hope or is he a rhetor gone rogue? The answer depends on your relationship to truth.

In *Institutio Oratoria*, Quintilian deals not only with the theory and practice of rhetoric but also with the foundational education and development of the orator. Quintilian's most arresting point about an orator-in-training is that they should be educated in morality above all else. To Quintilian, only a good person can be an orator. In *Nicomachean Ethics*, Aristotle argues that humans have an instinct for the truth and that truth and rationality are embedded in our very existence. However, post-Enlightenment philosophy leads to a suspicion of rational discourse whereby postmodern thinkers like Foucault (coming from Nietzsche) argue that only power organizes the world: those who win are stronger and more exuberant and can express their will through advantageous positioning in unbalanced networks of power. Plato's central question, *what is the nature of justice?* is replaced with the question of *who is able to exercise power?*

This shift in the status of truth in relation to power leads us to a conundrum: if everything is a will to power, how do you tell the difference between one axis of power and another? In other words, there is no way to measure the truthfulness of Donald J. Trump against Martin Luther King Jr. In some modern philosophical thinking, whomever wins the power struggle is the one who succeeds.

But that cannot be the only answer. Shakespeare gives us opportunities for critical hope that counter such a stark capitulation to power without values.

Classical philosophers believed that there is something that lies outside of power and that is reason. Living rationally in a world governed by reason enables humans to transcend the world of power and elevates us to a sphere of divine intelligence. In this formulation, rhetoric becomes the expression of human ability to live discursively in the world as rational beings. Rhetoric provides us with a path to living in a rational, contemplative space beyond the power struggles of coercion and seduction.

In this way, developing rhetorical literacy via Henry V and other orators has the potential to heal the deep divided differences of our time by training us to listen to one another with the intention of understanding and *transforming*. Rhetoric, then, becomes an exercise in empathy. Wayne C. Booth asserts:

> Rhetorology is where two sides join in a trusting dispute, determined to listen to their opponent while persuading the opponent to listen in exchange. Each side attempts to thoroughly consider the arguments presented by the other side, pursuing not just victory

but a new reality, a new agreement about what is real. Utilizing such tactics is meant not only to construct a stronger community but also to improve one's quest for knowledge. (*Rhetoric of Rhetoric* 46–7)

Let's come back to the orators of hope: Greta, Emma, David, Malala, and Autumn had to skip school to enact social change. Instead of getting in the way, how do we become integral to the process? In his 1993 Reith Lectures, Edward Said argues that higher education institutions must be places for advocacy and social justice. He argues that professors' jobs are to "publicly raise embarrassing questions, **Lisa:** In a world of Choruses, be the Boy. to confront orthodoxy and dogma (rather than to produce them), to be someone who cannot easily be co-opted by governments or corporations, and whose *raison d'être* is to represent all those people and issues that are routinely forgotten or swept under the rug" (*Representations* 9). This is where Shannon's distinction between "hope in" a set of values rather than merely "hope for" individuals calls upon us as educators and leaders to do this work of helping to tackle wicked problems.

NOTES

1 If reason – rational thought – is an access point to the divine in the classical sense, according to Aristotle in *Metaphysics Lambda*, Book XII, there is a substance which is eternal, intelligent, and, therefore, divine (300).
2 This moral ambiguity is unprecedented in Shakespeare's plays about kings. He is not an anti-hero like Macbeth or Richard III, doesn't have the poor judgment of kings like Lear or Leontes (or King John for that matter), and has a great deal more self-confidence than Hamlet. His only other close correlative is the duke from *Measure for Measure*.
3 There is some speculation that Shakespeare, bending to royal pressure or capitalizing on public appetite, gave this beloved character one final hurrah in a fan favorite, *Merry Wives of Windsor*.
4 "… this was a gesture that attacked the victim's honour, and that letting it pass unchallenged would mark them as cowards. Within the play the ruse is successful in starting a street fight. […] Here was a rude gesture, rude enough to provoke a fight, that Shakespeare could use upon the public stage without upsetting anyone except a few foreign diplomats and traders" (Goodman).
5 *Henry V*, n. "Tennis Balls" (TLN 408–16), 101. Edited by James D. Mardock, Broadview, 2014.
6 Richard Nixon used this strategy in his famous "Checkers speech" in 1952 when he responded to accusations of corruption and benefiting from campaign funds:

Now, was that wrong? And let me say that it was wrong. I'm saying, incidentally, that it was wrong, not just illegal, because it isn't a question of whether it was legal or illegal, that isn't enough. The question is, was it morally wrong? I say that it was morally wrong – if any of that 18,000 dollars went to Senator Nixon, for my personal use. I say that it was morally wrong if it was secretly given and secretly handled. And I say that it was morally wrong if any of the contributors got special favors for the contributions that they made.

And now to answer those questions let me say this: Not one cent of the 18,000 dollars or any other money of that type ever went to me for my personal use. (para. 4–5)

"We Should Just F**k around with Some Text": *Henry V* and the White Box Classroom

Lisa Dickson

Set in the fictional town of New Burbage, *Slings & Arrows* (2003–6) is an affectionate and irreverent spoof of the Stratford, Ontario, Shakespeare Festival. At the head of the ensemble cast, Paul Gross plays Geoffrey Tennant, the festival's once-rising star who has returned after a seven-year absence to become its reluctant and not-exactly-stable genius art director. As he is, in his own words, "not mentally equipped for the task at this time" ("Madness in Great Ones" 00:6:05), he takes up the job of conducting the corporate outreach workshop in which he is to teach best management practices by way of the Bard to the marketing department of a plastics company. After head-desking on the podium when faced with the absurdity of this proposition, he decides to throw away the curriculum and says: "I think we should just f**k around with some text" (00:22:48). In the next scene, Terry (Bob Martin) from accounting ("You da numbers guy!") listens to Geoffrey's instruction and then delivers a thoughtful and moving performance of Macbeth's "Tomorrow and tomorrow and tomorrow" speech. Accepting the accolades of his colleagues and an invitation to the theater bar for drinks, Terry sighs: "F**k, I love this!" (00:30:20).

This is my favorite moment in a series full of exemplary moments, not just because it is inherently beautiful but because it represents my highest aspiration as a teacher, the moment when the learner finds something remarkable in themselves, something that unlocks an experience of love – for themselves, for the art, for the community. The scene marks a moment of revelation and transformation when Terry "the numbers guy" discovers in himself a wonderful and complex multiplicity. And, although he is present and generous with his insight, Geoffrey mostly functions as the authority who gives up his authority and makes space for art and becoming.

When I set out to redesign my Shakespeare course, I had two things in the back of my mind: this scene from *Slings & Arrows*, and the Royal Shakespeare Company's 1970 *A Midsummer Night's Dream* directed by Peter Brook in a white box set designed by

Shannon: My experience as an undergrad was similar – thirty-five plays (Shakespeare and contemporaries) in twenty-eight weeks. When I started teaching, it was eight in one semester, now it's four or five and occasionally, like you, one.

Jessica: I was also trained under the "one play per week" model and so in my first teaching gig I just reproduced how I was taught. However, I discovered early on that a mad dash through the canon made any discussion of the plays superficial (and/or impossible) and I had to resort to "stand and deliver" lectures that were transactional rather than transformational. Coverage doesn't equal rigor, and yet we might need to say it louder for the people in the back.

Sally Jacobs. For this immensely popular production that ran five straight years in repertory and toured the world, Brook and Jacobs provided an open, mostly blank space featuring trapdoors, trapezes, and actors who bounced through the space like brightly colored balls. The credo for the production was: "It must be in [the audience's] imagination" (Bevington 50). When I took a Shakespeare course as an undergraduate back in the last century, we read thirteen plays in thirteen weeks. This time, with my Wyrd sisters as a distant but very present cheerleading squad, I assigned only one play: *Henry V*. I provided the students with a week-by-week schedule of activities, all of which were a fiction; indeed, while I had structured a number of assignments and provided a range of background materials, in terms of what happened in the classroom, my plan was to give the students two essential things: space and time. I built a white box and set them free inside it with Shakespeare to f**k around with some text.

This was my answer to the question *how does one design for critical hope and critical empathy?*

This is a particularly pressing question. When asked about the continuing relevance of *Macbeth* and its particularly dark look at power, director Gregory Doran responded with a question of his own: "What is the society we are creating in which there is this climate of fear which produces witches, or which needs witches?" (qtd. in Bogart et al. 157). I would narrow this question for the purposes of this discussion, to ask *what is the kind of education we are creating that produces witches and that, more importantly, needs witches to pry their bony fingers underneath the bedrock for the purposes of overturning foundations like a set syllabus, and a survey of great works, thirteen plays in thirteen weeks?* A standard syllabus, which lays out the required readings, assignments, activities, and policies for a course, seems to be a matter-of-fact, value-free document: just the facts, ma'am! We must remember, however, that each curriculum laid out in such a document "represents the *introduction to a particular form of life; it serves in part to prepare students for dominant or subordinate positions in the existing society*" (McLaren qtd. in Monchinski 25, italics McLaren's). By situating students within "an architecture of social power" (Shor 24), a syllabus can remind students that "Not all human beings bear equal weight in creating and assigning meaning and knowledge" (Apple qtd. in Monchinski 23) and that they, the students, are hardly ever the ones who get to assign anything. Demonstrating a great commitment to the principles of the democratic classroom, scholarly teacher Ira Shor argues that, under these circumstances, the traditional syllabus presents culture as nature: "That is, what has been socially and historically constructed by specific culture becomes presented to students as un-debatable and unchangeable, always there, timeless" (11). This version of the syllabus reflects what educational philosopher Paulo Freire calls the "banking system" of education, which identifies the authority figure as the creator and disseminator of knowledge and the student as passive recipient of that knowledge (*Pedagogy of the Oppressed* 72). In other words, the teacher "has" knowledge and "deposits" it in the students' brains to be "withdrawn" later, on tests and assignments. This model creates an environment for learning that is "linear and instrumental and to all intents and purposes, not meaningful learning at all. It is more concerned with assimilation of the young into an already established value system which has more to do with control than it has to do with liberation" (Dakers 113). Far from being social agents who recognize in themselves "the power to alter reality" (Shor 22), a condition necessary for the practice of critical hope, students become passive recipients of a fixed universe of knowledge, "*waiting for the professor to do education to them*" (10, my emphasis):

> [Students] have not had a dialogic curriculum where diverse, contending voices think out loud and discover meaning. Students rarely experience each other as sources of formal knowledge in an academic setting, so they lack habits of listening carefully to each other and of thinking together in class, where the words that count and the grade-giving power that matters have routinely belonged only to the teacher. (175)

In such a tightly controlled and disempowering framework, it is possible but far less likely that a student will discover transformative multiplicity in themselves or walk out of the classroom thinking, "F**k, I love this."

It is this institutional stolidity that the white box classroom attempts to disrupt by taking critical hope and critical empathy as its core values, values that demand that students be participants in the creation of knowledge, not mere observers. Once again, Shakespeare and his theater provide us with helpful structures and lessons that the Brook/Jacobs white box *Dream* epitomizes: a space was created for the imagination that had entrances all over, even in the walls and the ceiling, that allowed the actors to observe from many perspectives; all effects and props were created only by what the actors brought on stage with them; and while the action was shaped by the script,

Shannon: That's one of the reasons I love an assignment that my colleague Ann Braithwaite designed: her students end the course by writing a syllabus. That exploration insists on the constructed nature of the course outline!

Jessica: Why aren't we taking our cue from how meaning is created in theater and import this into our classrooms? In a Shakespeare play, a world unfolds over time (usually ~three hours) and space (many different staging options) through the co-design of meaning (via dialogue, gesture, action, clothing, tone, volume, etc.). Every single person in the three-dimensional space has a responsibility to contribute to the co-creation. Why is it then such a disconnect to think about that model in the university classroom (or, for that matter, the creation of a democratic society)?

Shannon: This is such a lovely model for a course. There can be some value in the "combination platter" course, with a little taste of a lot, but sometimes we just want to devour more of one thing.

> **Jessica:** How does the cumulative effect of this kind of work, which happens over an extended period of time (thirteen weeks), differ from the immersive "Hamlet Boot Camp" you discussed in the Hamlet essay? How does time work on transformation (and is *Henry V* better suited for a long, "slow burn" while *Hamlet* demands a "phoenix" approach)?

> **Lisa:** The difference is that the *Henry V* course is a second-year course and the *Hamlet* is a fourth-year course. I use *Henry V* to introduce students to techniques (all of those doors "in"), and, because the play is so much about how stories are made, it is exceptionally good as a primer for interpretive skills and complex evaluative mindsets so crucial to our discipline.

the form that the play took depended as much on the audience's imagination as on any preconceived structure. Likewise, in the revised Shakespeare course classroom, the space was not empty because it was informed not only by my overall philosophy of learning and by the text itself but by the limitations of space and time and the architecture of social power that was mitigated and flexed against but never entirely suspended or transcended. There are multiple ways to enter into *Henry V*, and we constructed trapdoors where we could do so, including structured exercises, traditional close reading, learning journals, group work performances, peer-to-peer learning, and so on. Our catchphrase was "This house has many doors," and students were encouraged to try as many doors as possible over the course of the term.

Shakespeare himself provides a model for critically hopeful and empathetic inquiry in *Henry V*. As we have argued elsewhere, Shakespeare's modus operandi is one of curiosity; he likes to throw a question or a problem into the middle of the room and then turn it and look at it from many angles, a method of exploration that is mapped onto the physical space of the Globe Theatre itself, where the audience surrounds the stage and no one sightline can claim absolute access to an immutable truth about what is going on there. The physical space of the theater and its stance regarding knowledge is reiterated within the play itself.

In Act 3, Henry's forces are laying siege to Harfleur, the first great test of the young king's military strength, personal grit, charisma, and ethical claims to France. In this series of scenes, Shakespeare asks us to consider what war makes of men and what men make of war. He gives us five perspectives on this question:

- The Chorus's description of "the well-appointed king" departing for France with his "fleet majestical" (3.0.4, 16)
- Henry's famous "Once more unto the breach" oration in which the English soldiers are elevated to paragons of valor and right and in which they are exhorted to "imitate the action of a tiger" (3.1.6)
- The Boy's insightful rumination on the hypocrisy and cowardliness of his Eastcheap "low" companions and his decision to find other masters
- The wrangling of the Irish, Scottish, Welsh, and English captains about the proper way to conduct war
- Henry's grotesque threats to the Governor of Harfleur in which his English soldiers are presented not as "noble English" but rather as vicious dogs ready to defile women and plunder the town

In the structure of Act 3, Shakespeare provides us with an opportunity and a method with which to conduct our own inquiry, one that is based on the principles of critical hope that mobilize students as producers rather than consumers of knowledge and asks them to pay attention to the ways that knowledge is made. They encounter *in* the play the very method they will use to *read* the play.

In the classroom, that method took the form of a "world café," a technique that allows large numbers of people to cover a range of material in a way that captures a multiplicity of perspectives. The class of forty-five students was divided into groups, each assigned to one of the moments described above and given time to muck away in it, asking questions and recording observations. Then the groups rotated to the next section, leaving one person behind to provide context and moderate the discussion with the new people. After a time, a new moderator was chosen to stay behind and the groups rotated again. They did not have to move as a unit, and each person could choose a new group, provided that by the end of the exercise they had visited all five groups. Then we did a last "gallery walk" and each student was instructed to add at least one observation to the record of another group and to bring back to their original group at least two insights from others. We reported out with an eye to making visible the connections and questions that arose from this overview. The method allows all students to weigh in, to use the work of their peers as a jumping-off point, and to "bring home" insights that shift their original readings. It's a method that allows us to cover a lot of ground without sacrificing detail or reducing students to passive "banks" for information. Rather, the café puts the students "in" the play, asking them to locate their perspective in multiple places and to compare those perspectives. In a way, the students are analogues of the play's Boy. The Boy is no "mere" observer; his authority as an observer comes from his active participation in the campaign of self-fashioning in which various stories about who he is, what England is, and who Henry is contest for his understanding and endorsement.

The five moments of Act 3 jostle one another uncomfortably, offering us an image of the English and their war effort that is alternately idealized and demystified, noble and depraved, merciful and vindictive, righteous and cynically self-interested. Shakespeare does not help us much in resolving these apparent contradictions. Likewise, his Henry can be reasonably viewed as naive and as well-educated and mature, an adolescent out of his depth and a cunning gamesman, a bluff, "honest" soldier and a spin-savvy manipulator, an agent of divine right and an ambitious conqueror seeking to stabilize a dodgy claim to

Shannon: Such a good way of thinking about him: which makes *The Hollow Crown* BBC version with Tom Hiddleston so appealing. In that production, the Boy lives and becomes the Chorus.

> **Lisa:** Yes, I did love that framing. It runs counter to those readings that posit the Chorus as an omniscient point of view, a reading that I find is not supported well by the text since the Chorus's declarations about the events are so often undercut by the action that follows them, as the students themselves noted. The BBC version really presses that idea of the embeddedness of our interpretations and challenges that omniscience by putting the Chorus's more jingoistic stance into play with the Boy's experiential, "boy's-eye" view.

Shannon: So true. I often think of that notion from Heraclitus when I read and reread Shakespeare: we never step into the same river twice, both because the river is transformed and because we are. My sixteen-year-old self (falling for *Henry V* for the first time) and my sixty-year-old self are wildly different, but so are the cultural moments in which we read or see him.

> **Jessica:** Ben Jonson, in the First Folio (1623), described Shakespeare as follows: "He was not of an age but for all time!" This is often interpreted as support for the universality of Shakespeare's plays, but I prefer to think of them as deeply particular in their adaptability to our cultural, historical, political, and personal moments. *Henry V* can be a stirring piece of pro-war propaganda (see Olivier 1944) or a damning condemnation of war (see Branagh 1989). The play remains (relatively) stable as we orbit around it.

Jessica: Historiography is a transformative concept; when you start to think about the history of history, and the act of situating narratives in the context of other historians' work – and even why ideas around history change over time – we move from "facts" and "truth" into fuzzier and more complex spheres like narratives and storytelling. This approach doesn't make something "less true" as much as it explodes the possibilities of truth via perspectives.

> **Lisa:** I wonder if theater itself – particularly Shakespeare's theater – is in some ways structurally historiographic in the ways that it incorporates the vast divergences of perspectives even in its performing spaces.

Shannon: Oh, and doesn't that fit perfectly with the repeated Chorus, who keeps telling us that we will co-create the play that the actors and theater are ill-equipped to create on their own.

> **Lisa:** It's a great thing to begin with when you build student performances into the syllabus. It lets them off the hook for production values and shifts the emphasis toward the evocativeness of good ideas. I love to pair this speech with the Players in the film version of *Rosencrantz and Guildenstern Are Dead* (1990), who stage Hamlet's pirate's battle with a rope and a dishcloth and it's utterly compelling.

the throne. What you see of Henry and his exploits very often depends on where you're standing.

As the students who were exploring the Chorus's opening encomium to the fleet noted, the ship of war looks great from "afar" but the closer we get to it, the less ideal it looks. Asked to "grapple your minds" (3.0.18) to the scene, to "play with your fancies" (7), the audience envisioning the progress of Henry's "brave fleet" (5) comes to see that it only "appears" (16) in the mind's eye to be majestic, that what awaits us as the Chorus brings us closer to the soldiers themselves are the "fatal mouths" (27) of artillery and, finally, a squabble over spoils, the "petty and unprofitable dukedoms" (31) that cannot buy peace. The group working on the Boy's speech noted that the Boy is an analogue for Henry himself, a youth in the company of Henry's old Eastcheap companions who has to decide who he is going to emulate: the inspiring Henry of the breach oration, the cowardly braggarts from Eastcheap, the fractious captains with their nationalist rivalries, or the Henry who will threaten virgins and old men to get what he wants. As Manheim argues with regard to Henry's multiplicity, "it is not that we cannot make a decision about him; we tend to make opposing decisions about him," for Henry is at once the "St. George who defeats the dragon of France" and "a ruthless murderer," a "juxtaposition that focuses on our eternal schizophrenia about wars and heroes" (qtd. in Davies and Wells 130). What the students concluded from their comparison of all of these options is that Shakespeare isn't so much interested in showing us a particular Henry or a particular England, but rather is dramatizing *how these narratives get made*, how they are granted authority, how they are deployed for particular ends. Shakespeare's not interested in showing us the truth, they concluded. Rather, he is interested in helping us see how we participate in making truths. In the context of a play about the rationalizations for war, the construction of truth and the role of interpretation become crucially important issues.

A particularly telling example of how this question is worked out dramatically arose from what appeared on its surface to be a very matter-of-fact, basic question about the staging of the siege that revealed itself to be inextricably connected to how we construct truths through perspective. This group was working on Henry's last, horrid threats in which he asks the Governor, "guilty in defence" (3.3.123) of Harfleur, to imagine consequences of resistance that include the defilement of "shrill-shrieking daughters" (115) and "naked infants spitted upon pikes" (118). The students asked me: "Which way is Henry facing?" Is he facing the back wall of the theater, the *frons scenae* with its musicians' gallery on the balcony where the Governor could stand on the "wall" of the town, or is he facing outward to the audience, imagining the galleries of the theater to be the "walls" and the yard to be the "trenches?" We wrangled with that question for some time. If Henry faces upstage to the Governor, does this align us in the audience with Henry's English soldiers ranged at his back? And if so, which soldiers are we? The noble English who "stand like greyhounds in the slips" (3.1.31) with "noble lustre" in our eyes (30)? Or are we the dogs of war with "conscience wide as hell" (3.3.93), "fleshed soldiers" (91) primed by blood for mayhem and brutality? Who are we asked to *be* in this war? Who *can* we be when faced with such a choice as a matter of survival? If, on the other hand, Henry faces *downstage* with his soldiers at his back, are we then the French – vulnerable virgins and babies – confronted with vicious English dogs who have lost their humanity to the horrors of "impious war / Arrayed in flames like to the prince of fiends" (95–6)? And is Henry, whom we cheered on in the "Once more unto the breach" oration, now transformed into – or, perhaps, revealed to be – that very "prince of fiends?"

How does the physical space of the theater, then, challenge our position as "passive observer?" Are there any "passive observers" in war? Is not, rather, every observer *located* in that moment, always in danger of losing life or sense of self in the face of brutality? Does not the act of observing ask us to choose what we believe in? Who we wish to be? Can one "imitate the action of the tiger" and not *become* one? Do "the disciplines / of the pristine wars of the Romans" (3.3.25–6) that Fluellen advocates survive contact with "these brave gallants, these hearts, these lads, this youth of England" who, it turns out, may well be "the dregs, sell your grandmother for a fire shovel" (Bogdanov 48) soldiers impressed against their will to be ground away to the tune of English glory? "And sword and shield / In bloody field / Doth win immortal fame," Pistol sings morosely (3.2.7–9). The Boy replies: "Would I were in an alehouse in London. I would give all my fame for a pot of ale, and safety" (10–11). The question of staging Henry's last-ditch act of intimidation of the French asks us to consider not what the truth of war is, but how we come to believe it and live it and, moreover, how *what* we believe depends on *where* we stand. Shakespeare educates us in critical empathy by giving us multiple places to stand. The world café method of inquiry likewise asks students to look "back" at all that they have seen from different places and to consider how those perspectives are shaping their understanding and commitments.

This attention to how knowledge and perceptions (which are not exactly the same thing) are constructed can elicit a question familiar to teachers of literature: "What's the *real* interpretation?" In the case of our study of *Henry V*, there was considerable debate and interpretational anxiety about the question of *who Henry really is* and whether his foreign wars are justified. The question is further complicated by the fact that even *Henry* doesn't know who he really is or whether his war is justified, as his soul-searching in the hours before the battle of Agincourt reveals. This interpretational uncertainty can often result in another response familiar to teachers of literature: "It's up to the reader to decide." This resorting to relativism actually represents a bit of progress on the road to critical thinking, since it acknowledges the reader's role in the creation of knowledge about a text and dislodges, to a certain extent, the idea that there is only one fixed reading that emanates from authority, either the author's or the teacher's. In the language of metacognition (thinking about thinking) and epistemology (the study of what we know and how we know what we know), the shift from "What is the *real* interpretation?" to "It's up to the reader to decide" represents a movement from "absolutist objectivism" grounded in a fixed, unambiguous universe of authoritative knowledge (Brownlee et al. 601) to a "subjectivist" stance that drifts in a universe of opinions (607). In the subjectivist state, a reader recognizes that knowledge might be unstable and evolving, but they see it in an individualistic way, as a matter of "opinion" that resists comparison and assessment. An absolutist objectivist might say that "the textbook says that Henry is a cynical manipulator"; a subjectivist might say, "I like Henry, especially played by Kenneth Branagh, so I think he's actually a good guy."

However, a reader looking at the issue from a "complex evaluativistic" (Brownlee et al. 606) stance might say, as one student did, that Henry plays a variety of "roles" and that "These roles must be used at different times for different purposes [...]. None of these interpretations need to be correct [...]. That is, his kingly person can be defined by his ability to diversely fashion himself and adapt his outward nature to suit his needs at different times" (Goudsward). What Shakespeare is asking students to adopt in Act 3 of his play is such an evaluativistic stance – one that is, in Brownlee et al.'s terms, evolving, context-bound, evidence-based, and connected to broader understanding of ideas and conditions (606) such as, in the case of *Henry V*, historical forces, theatrical convention, and so on. Leading us toward this complex evaluativistic stance, Shakespeare's *Henry V* asks us to compare and assess the differing perspectives of the Chorus and the Boy, the French and the English, in order to ask not *Who is the* real *Henry?* but *How are our war heroes made?* and *How does our sense of identity respond to changing conditions?*

And it is important to consider how the work happening in the play and in the classroom likewise shapes how the students perceive themselves within the context of the classroom environment. In an attempt to get a glimpse of this inner work, I asked them one question on the final exam: "What did you

Lisa: The final exam was also an optional assignment. Students were able to curate their own assessment models, with some guidance and scaffolding.

Shannon: I like that kind of choice, a menu of possibilities that not only acknowledges their agency but also allows them to make practical decisions based on what other demands their lives and courses make on them.

Jessica: Why don't we lead with this question in all the ways we assess learning? And not just in course evaluations but in key moments along our professional and personal journeys? It is a hard question to answer, and it compels us to think in deeper ways about how and why we've transformed (for better or worse).

learn?" I gave them no other guidance except to require them to talk about the play and about their own learning. One student, who made the observation quoted above about Henry's multiplicity, connected that understanding of Henry to a consideration of his own multiplicity:

> I could be seen as adaptable, uncertain, or unreliable, or even deceptive and fake. None of these interpretations needs to be correct [...]. But even the combination of these roles can only define my student self, not my human self. But within the institution of the university, a student is what I must be. But just as Henry the man is inseparable from Henry the King, Solomon the man is inseparable from Solomon the student. One piece of evidence for this is that I learned all this by being a student. (Goudsward)

This is the observation that launched me into this particular discussion of the Shakespeare course, and it was the lens through which I looked back on the way that semester developed. Here, the student acknowledges that the text tells him something about the fluidity and context-bound nature of identity, how Henry's ability to adapt to circumstances is as important to *who he is* as any particular statement about his "character." At the same time, the repeated "but" in the student's response points to a bit of nostalgia for a self, a "human" self that somehow escapes the confines of and reduction to the "institutional" definition of a "student," some actor who lives beyond the role he plays. As the student's discussion progresses, he breaks down that division through a comparison with Henry's similar struggle to find his "human" self within the constraints of sovereign responsibility, and the student realizes that his ability to fashion himself is something that speaks to his life as a whole. In this one discussion, I was able to watch a student move from absolute to subjectivist to complex evaluativist stances, and that one example prompted me to think about how that interaction of stances might be playing out in the class experience in general.

Many of my students thrived in the white box and relished the opportunity to "just f**k around with some text." They found it liberating. They found that they learned more and came to respect themselves and their fellow students as real sources of valuable insight. They enjoyed the opportunity to use "many doors," including their creativity, to get into Shakespeare's house. But some students foundered. While some of those who did will eventually find their feet again, once they recover from what Freire calls "fear of freedom" (*Pedagogy of Hope* 47) and get used to being knowledge producers, many were excluded by the structure we had built: the hard-of-hearing student who had difficulty with the noisy world café environment and the lack of subtitles on older film versions screened in class; the more introverted student for whom the classroom was space of insupportable din and chaos that produced paralyzing anxiety; the student who was completely on board with the classroom model but found the

Jessica: Is this a challenge Henry V has too? As he is someone used to being so comfortable moving between spaces (from London pubs to court, between languages, class identities, modes of masculinity, etc.), does he get to a point where, as king, he *cannot* see some truths or perspectives? I am thinking of his "little touch of Harry in the night" episode, so well-meaning in the Chorus's description but in reality backfiring to the point of deeply unsettling Williams and Bates (and Henry!). Is there a position one arrives at where you cannot see all?

> **Lisa:** And the flipside of that: does he get to the point where he can no longer be seen? My students staged that "little touch of Harry" scene in a rotunda gallery on campus where Henry began way up on the third floor of the circular staircase and worked his winding way down to meet Williams and then sadly retreated upward again as he lamented his state of royalty and prayed to God. It was such a great way of using space to explore his grappling with his many slippery and uniquely limiting personas.

tight space of the room too claustrophobic and hard to move through. In building a classroom grounded on the principle of critical empathy, I was hoping to make space for everyone, but there was still a great deal that I didn't "see" and was unable to respond to as I myself struggled to fit the freedom and productive chaos I'd enabled into the constraints of class time and grading rubrics.

The course experience reminded me that the empathetic space must itself evolve constantly, not just to "include" the so-called outliers within the borders of *my* brilliant system, but to be transformed by the particular knowledge those people bring to the space. This is the challenge I face next time 'round.

PART FOUR

Hamlet

Chasing Roosters on the Ramparts: Three Ways of Doing in *Hamlet*

Lisa Dickson

Facere veritatem: to do truth.

I am blocked.

Write about teaching *Hamlet*, they say. You know, that play that *literally changed the direction of your life*. The one you've been poring over ever since you were seventeen years old. The one that you've been teaching in wildly different circumstances to myriad students over the past twenty-five years or so. That one. No problem. Where to start? Blank page phobia.

I'm about to give up (again) when I look at my desk and see that a note card has floated up to the surface of the sea of notebooks and textbooks and tea cups and crumpled paper (that is, the detritus typical of "writer's block" montages in movies). The card says:

> Staring at a blank piece of paper, I can't think of anything original. I feel utterly uninspired and unreceptive. It's the familiar malaise of "artist's block" and in such circumstances there is only one thing to do:
>
> > Just start drawing.
>
> Shaun Tan (*The Bird King*, Introduction 1)

Okay, Shaun. I'm not UNinspired so much as overinspired, but point taken.

LISA sits down and draws. (See Figure 1.)

It is not a coincidence that thinking about *Hamlet* produces this image. I always experience exciting ideas as a tactile impression in the muscles of my back, right between my shoulder blades. Cultural theorist and feminist scholar Elaine Scarry identifies this tendency to elicit such a somatic connection to the abstract realm as one of the primary qualities of beauty:

Jessica: This is a beautiful image because it takes that process of reading – which is always so interior and silent even as the fireworks are going off in your brain and your spine is tingling – and gives it wings. And what does the picture look like of an audience member standing or sitting in the theater, eyes open and heart on fire?

Figure 1. Reading Angel

This crisscrossing of the senses may happen in any direction. Wittgenstein speaks not only about beautiful visual events prompting motions in the hand but, elsewhere, about heard music that later prompts a ghostly subanatomical event in his teeth and gums. So, too, an active touch may reproduce itself as an acoustical event or even an abstract idea, the way whenever Augustine touches something smooth, he begins to think of music and of God. (4)

When my mind touches *Hamlet*, I feel the folds of dark velvet over scales and spines and the heaving of contained fire. (Yes, Lisa, that is a helpful teaching tip: "Voilà! A velvet dragon. Class dismissed!") But Scarry is on to something here. In that notion of the "crisscrossing" of ideas, bodies and beauty, we have a model of embodied learning that links movement, particularity, and renewal, all qualities that define hopeful critical pedagogy. To talk about teaching *Hamlet*, for me, is to get to that space where ideas

Jessica: And yet how wonderful would it be to have spaces of learning where not only could you say that but that students would meet you there, in that space, with the trust to imagine different ways of knowing and of experiencing?

Lisa: This is what I'm trying to get to when I ask students what the play would look like if it were a room or how it would sound if it were a noise.

and the senses come together, the bodily experience of words in the mouth, in the physical playing space and in the breath.

Having broken my block with my initial sketch, I spend the next couple of weeks moving from computer to drawing desk, using the Sketchnotes to clarify the digressive spiderwebbing of my thoughts (there is *too much Hamlet*) and to lead me to unexpected places. I draw (draw from, as from a library; draw up, as from a well; draw on paper) past classroom experiences, concepts from critical reading – in this case, Scarry's ruminations on beauty and justice – and examples from the very well-worn pages of my copy of *Hamlet*, letting the colors and the spatial arrangement and the methodical retracing of words become its own kind of kinesthetic thinking. I'm encouraged as I go by Scarry's invocation of Richard Wollheim, a British philosopher who worked especially on the role of emotions in the visual arts: "one learns what one has been drawing only when the drawing is done" (qtd. in Scarry 116–17). I also turn to my favorite philosopher of radical theology, John D. Caputo, who reiterates the Augustinian mantra, *facere veritatem*: truth is something you *do*, not something you *have*. The Sketchnotes might look simplistic with their stick figures and stripped-down references, but I see them rather as a distillation, maps of a process that the linearity of text can't fully accommodate. They guide the observer but also allow for other paths. They are experiential for me, thinking in process, muscle and memory and shape and story.

Shannon: They are also beautiful and playful, and what a profound alternative to traditional formal essays for our students. Those essays suggest a closed conclusion, don't they, while the Sketchnotes focus on an open process and on possibilities.

Jessica: Incorporating the play as an embodied experience also leads to new forms of releasing meaning; by drawing, sketching, doodling, this decenters the authority or superiority of the WORD and makes room for other conduits of expression. Be right back – you've just given me permission to go make bad art.

Lisa: My work is done. ☺

To explore the relationships exposed or enabled by kinesthetic thinking means attending to the particularity of moments; carrying *Hamlet* in our bodies helps us both to follow worn interpretive paths of tradition and critical debate and to step off of those paths into the weeds of unexpected insight and delight that constitute the constant renewal of *Hamlet* in every encounter. Nineteenth-century French essayist Marcel Proust, Scarry tells us, identifies one of the errors we make about beauty: our tendency to generalize "life," because, in generalizing, "we have already excluded before the fact all beauty and happiness, which take place only in the particular" (18). The focus on the particular goes on to create in the observer a sense of capaciousness that expands beyond the immediate, a process that links the beautiful more than analogically to learning. Each encounter with beauty, Scarry argues, connects us to the new: "The beautiful thing seems – is – incomparable, unprecedented; and that sense of being without precedent conveys a sense of the "newness" or "newbornness" of the entire world" (22). Beauty, she goes on, "prompts the mind to move chronologically back in the search for precedents and parallels, to move forward into new acts of creation, to move conceptually over, to bring things into relation" (30). Thus, the very uniqueness of the beautiful object is an invitation to comparison, to relationship, to a lateral extension of care for other beautiful objects, for other beings with whom we wish to share our experience of it, for the world in which beauty is engendered. Here, then, I can see why both Shakespeare and my students elicit the tell-tale stirring of wings between my shoulder blades, since both the poetry and the classroom are sites of beauty that demand my attention to the immediate and open my mind to newness.

David G. Smith infuses the pedagogical moment with a mystery that chimes very well with both Scarry and Proust and our understanding of the qualities of hopeful pedagogy:

> Without an appreciation of the radical mystery which confronts us in the face of every other person, our theorizing must inexorably become stuck, for then we are no longer available for that which comes to meet us from beyond ourselves, having determined in advance the conditions under which any new thing will be acceptable, and thereby foreclosing on the possibility of our own transformation. (qtd. in Jardine and Seidel 3)

Paradoxically, attending to the particular requires an openness to the unscripted and unexpected, an act of hospitality toward, in Caputo's oft-repeated refrain, "we know not what." Transformation, agency, care for the difference of the Other, are all potentially implicated in particular moments of bodily engagement with beauty, with hope, with learning. These moments sprout wings from the middle of my back where motion and thinking "crisscross." They focus my attention on the unique encounter among people (these learners), the beautiful object (*Hamlet*) and these circumstances (this classroom space, this arrangement of learners within it). This unique intersection of forces prepares a way for the new, if I am willing to let it in.

I will walk us briefly through a few such encounters where ideas and bodies make each other: when we run up against the weird restrictions of stage space; when students gallop away after an offstage rooster; and when we discover that breathing with Hamlet connects us, like Augustine with music and God, to the heart of Hamlet's philosophical problem with words.

Shannon: Both here and in your *AYLI* chapter, Lisa, I am so inspired by your insistence that we feel the plays in our bodies. Aside from the occasional moving about of things in my classroom, I know I don't do that as much, but I am encouraged to try more explorations like these.

Jessica: My favourite teaching (and learning) moments are when we stand up, and by moving around we claim spaces as art-making venues: when we took over the steps of our oldest campus building and remapped it as the ship in the storm at the beginning of *The Tempest*; when we shuffled furniture in a room reserved for Senate and the Board of Governors and reframed it as a stage for *Henry V*.

Lisa: And these are the moments students remember, not my lectures and PowerPoint slides. And yet these moments are all but invisible in the metrics of "success" within which we operate: grading, orderly classrooms, and so on.

Encounter #1: Who's There?

Scene (Act 1, Scene 1): Enter Francisco, a sentinel, who stands on guard. Enter Barnardo, to relieve him (1.1.sd).

RUN-THROUGH #1: The classroom space is large, a typical amphitheater lecture hall with raked seats and an open lecturing area at the bottom. Francisco enters the open space and paces. Barnardo enters from the doorway at the back of the lecture theater. They shout at each other across the distance:

BARNARDO: Who's there?
FRANCISCO: Nay, answer me. Stand and unfold yourself. (1.1.1–2)

QUESTION: Why don't Barnardo and Francisco know who's there?

Answers accumulate: Francisco doesn't know which soldier is going to relieve him; it's dark or foggy; Francisco is far away, obscured by the ramparts or is wrapped up against the cold. These are all very logical ways of explaining the fact that Barnardo, who should know whom he is coming to relieve, clearly isn't sure who is out there on the ramparts, or that Francisco, who is supposed to be looking for *external* threats, is freaked out about someone (or some*thing*?) coming toward him from *inside the castle*. These answers, enabled by the vastness of the playing space that sets the two men far from one another, normalize Francisco's weird, seemingly misplaced suspicion to the point that it's easy for students to miss it. More work has to be done to bring his odd response into the light for critical exploration.

RUN-THROUGH #2: The seminar classroom is small and cramped and not at all ideal as a playing space. The "stage" is a narrow runway about six feet long between the chalkboard and the first row of desks. Francisco enters and stands watch. Barnardo enters and is literally about three feet from both Francisco and the audience when he says, nervously, "Who's there?" This is weird.

QUESTION: Why don't Barnardo and Francisco know who is there?

Answers accumulate: Francisco or Barnardo is old and blind, or drunk, or sleepy; Barnardo doesn't know all the soldiers in Elsinore; it's *really, really dark*, like freakishly dark; Francisco is *really, really wrapped up* against the cold or is facing away from Barnardo. (In the COVID-19 pandemic teaching space, where all the students are masked, the reason seems built in: they literally can't see each other's faces.) These are all very logical ways of explaining why Francisco and Barnardo can't see each other, even though they are standing there side by side under the bright fluorescent illumination of the seminar room. These answers go some way to resolving the weirdness of the staging.

> **Shannon:** I love the way the scene is played in Branagh's *A Midwinter's Tale,* the film about a motley crew of actors putting on *Hamlet* in a condemned church at Christmas. There is accidentally so much smoke on stage that they genuinely cannot see each other.
>
> **Lisa:** That movie is so good. "Oh Hamlet! Cast off thy colored nightie!" But especially the way that they fill up the empty seats with cardboard cutouts because the play doesn't exist without an audience.
>
> **Shannon:** Those cutouts imagine pandemic theatergoing pre-COVID.

Shannon: This idea is so important, I think, and vital to model for our students. Being okay with uncertainty – not in any lazy way – by playing through the possibilities and accepting that more than one might work, more than one might be true, is essential practice for critical empathy.

Jessica: Yes! the question is, how do we sit in the discomfort and really be present, and still, and open to what we have to learn from it. As Pema Chodron, my favourite Nova Scotian Buddhist, says, "if we commit ourselves to staying right where we are, then our experience becomes very vivid. Things become very clear when there is nowhere to escape" (2).

Jessica: I like this version the best because it embraces the weirdness of Elsinore and the inability to know anything for certain, even when you are looking right at it. "Who's there? Can you hear me? Is my mic on? Are you able to see me? I think you are muted? I just lost you. My wifi is unstable." These very postmodern questions underline the loneliness and alienation at stake in the attempt to establish connection.

Lisa: Yes, the play seems capable of absorbing the present moment so provocatively. Several of my students, in imagining a "COVID *Hamlet*," figured *the virus as the revenger*. Think on that for a whole new book.

Shannon: I really like your exploration of the one scene in two playing spaces, and such a nice way to demonstrate to students that our classroom spaces – however randomly assigned us – are never neutral.

Lisa: And the more neutral they seem, the less neutral they are.

But what if we don't? What if, instead of resolving the discomfort created by the smallness of the space and the nearness of the actors to each other and to the audience, we run at the weirdness? Now the students replay the scene and, instead of trying to normalize the weirdness of their circumstances by making Barnardo enter backward or Francisco hunch like an old man, they walk up to each other and shout, "Who's there?" and "Nay, answer me. Stand and unfold yourself" right into each other's faces. Suddenly the uncanny, out-of-joint nature of Elsinore becomes creepily clear: people who are looking right at each other can't *see*, name, or trust each other. Trapped in this confined space together, they can only look eye to eye and wrestle with questions of identity and suspicion. The Ghost, then, enters not so much as a freakish eruption into an otherwise normal space, but rather as a coalescence of an uncertainty that shapes all interactions in a state that isn't just rotten politically but epistemologically, too. Both the political situation and the means by which we are *to know anything about it* are distorted and obscured. O wretched state, indeed.

In the large, accommodating lecture hall, the space *aligns* the words and the actions in a more normalizing way, so that the weirdness of Elsinore has to creep into you and the weirdness of this moment becomes visible mostly in retrospect. We make the error of believing the space is neutral because we can easily use it to explain away the weirdness of the opening lines. But, as the play's pattern of oxymorons, Machiavellian double-dealing, madness, and dishonor develops, we begin to see how messed up and contradictory Elsinore is, through and through. We are with Hamlet, learning *along with him* how to behave in a world where words and actions *seem* aligned but aren't.

In the second instance, where the actors and audience are crammed into an unaccommodating playing area, the space *misaligns* the words and the actions in a way that makes the words absurd and starkly exposes the underlying misalignments of the world that Hamlet must navigate. We make the error of believing that the staging is incorrect because it produces this misalignment when in fact, we realize after exploring our less-than-ideal playing area, misalignment *is precisely the point*. Two responses of bodies in a particular space, two different ways to enter the rotten state of Denmark. What appears at first to be a "misfire" or bent reading opens the text like an invitation and emphasizes that the playing space, like the classroom space, is anything but neutral. (See Figure 2.)

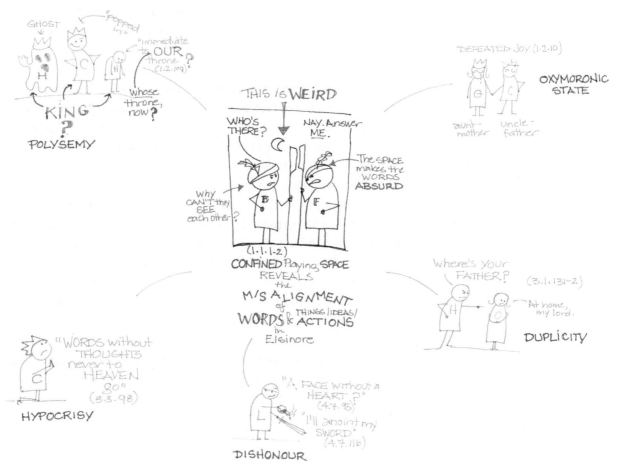

Figure 2. Sketchnote: *Hamlet* 1.1, Who's There? Misalignment of Words and Actions

Encounter #2: Chasing the Rooster

Scene: The ramparts of ELSINORE, night. MARCELLUS, BARNARDO, and HORATIO have encountered the GHOST of King Hamlet and, just as they are about to get it to speak, the cock crows and the Ghost flits about the stage, ready to disappear. Horatio calls to Marcellus to keep the Ghost from departing.

RUN-THROUGH:

The cock crows.

HORATIO: Stop it, Marcellus! (1.1.142)

MARCELLUS *runs around the stage chasing an imaginary rooster. He captures it, stuffs it under his arm and mimes closing its beak with his fingers.*

We sit on the floor and on chairs scattered amongst the disarranged tables of the classroom and there's a startled *beat … beat … beat* before the class, smacked hard by the wholly unexpected and cleverly apt interpretation of a not-quite-there stage direction, collapses into laughter. The "it" that Marcellus should be stopping has gone a-wandering in the student performer's wit and attached itself, not to the Ghost, which is its traditional home base, but to the cock, who until this moment had spent about 400 years quietly minding his own offstage business and is now, much to his imaginary surprise, on the run just for doing his job. An otherwise unexceptional character caught up, like the cock, in exceptional circumstances, Marcellus can't stop a ghost – he's not even sure there *is* a ghost – but he can darn well stop a rooster. And, honestly, is trying to stop the sunrise by silencing the messenger any weirder than trying to stop a ghost by striking at it with his partisan? The whole situation is bonkers. Besides, chasing fantasies puts him in good company; that young Hamlet *talks to himself all the time*. At least Marcellus has a rooster. At least he's *helping*.

The pronoun "it" in "Stop it, Marcellus" is meant to attach to the Ghost but here attaches like a bit of sticky lint to the rooster. The misalignment of the pronoun illuminates the characters' shared frustration when the Ghost, this slippery apparition, evades their attempts to pry some useful information out of it, leaving them instead to speculate, to grasp at old stories for explanations, citing Christmas when "The bird of dawning singeth all night long; / And then, they say, no spirit dare stir abroad" (165–6). The men are compatriots in a game of questions but can't keep the cock from crowing or dawn from breaking and driving away their only source of information. To have answers, it seems, they must dwell in infernal darkness, not the grace of day. As in the rest of the scene, in which they are shrouded in confusion and fearful of unseen and unrecognized enemies, they are left again without answers. The sun has risen too soon. Time is, indeed, out of joint.

We are prompted to ask what role the "general gender" plays in the affairs of state, in this congress between the worlds of war and occulted forces, masculine bravado and Machiavellian subversion, darkness and illumination. Who is Marcellus in all of this ("Who's there?")? Does he have any agency here? What underlies his presence on the ramparts: loyalty to the old king or obedience to the new one? Curiosity? More or less grudging duty? Is he just "comic relief?" If he is, in this weird rooster-chase, "merely" comic relief, then what, precisely, is he relief *from*? From this slightly bent, certainly unexpected embodiment of Marcellus, the

Shannon: That reference problem has never occurred to me before. At first glance, shouldn't Hamlet Senior's pronoun be "him"? But throughout the scene, the Ghost (also called "the spirit," "this sight," or "the apparition") is always "it," while the stories about Hamlet Senior when he was alive always refer to him as "he" or "him." It's such a small way to signify that they are unconvinced that the Ghost and the dead king are the same being.

Jessica: In my editing process (for myself and others) I always circle "it." More often than not, "it" represents fuzzy or underdeveloped thinking about the noun "it" is supposed to replace. The Ghost is itself (himself? themself?) a fuzzy and ambiguous concept, so the "it" slips and slides around any firm or locatable reference point. Shakespeare is so cool.

Shannon: So true. There are only about 180 lines between midnight and sunrise.

Jessica: Emerging thought: do you lose gender when you leave your body and shake off your mortal coil? Is Shakespeare an early adopter of gender-neutral pronouns?

Shannon: Maybe. Remember the gravedigger, who says that he digs neither for a man nor a woman but for one "that was a woman, but now she's dead." Are spirits, like angels, sexless?

Lisa: If so, maybe it's the Ghost's emphatic masculinity (in Hamlet Senior's armor) that makes him suspect.

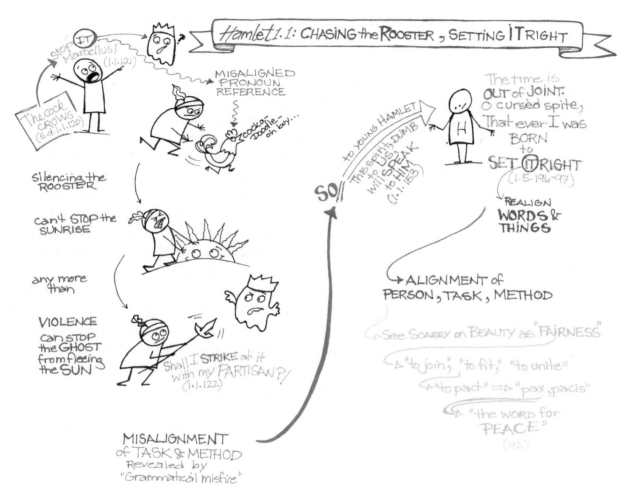

Figure 3. Sketchnote: *Hamlet* 1.1, Chasing Roosters, Setting *IT* Right

classroom discussion then gallops off in all directions, into questions about epistemology (must we embrace the infernal to achieve knowledge?), about fealty (does loyalty to a king persist after his death?), about our relationship to nature (are we mad to try to halt the sunrise or to raise a weapon against fate?), about social place (whose job is it, after all, to set the dislocated joint of the fair state?) and many more. (See Figure 3.)

What appears in the moment to be a comical misreading – the misalignment of the pronoun "it" with its proper referent – is in fact an invitation that reveals to us a more fundamental misalignment of words and things that torments Hamlet and complicates his attempts to "set" Elsinore "right." The task of

Shannon: Your sketch art is such a playful and profound way to explore an idea, Lisa – do you teach your students to work ideas through this way?

> **Lisa:** I demonstrate it when we are working through an idea and encourage them to do concept maps and Sketchnotes and remixes instead of traditional papers. I've not explicitly talked through the underlying epistemology of them, though.

re-setting the dislocated, misaligned epistemology of Elsinore brings us back to Scarry and the idea of beauty that she connects through a complex etymology with "fairness," a word with roots in concepts of joining, fitting together, uniting, and making pacts: "'Pact' in turn – the making of a covenant or treaty or agreement – is from the same root as "pax, pacis," the word for peace" (92). Trapped in a world where words and things have become unhinged, Hamlet's task is not merely to bring a murderer to justice, but, in so doing, to restore the beauty of the state.

What this incident in workshopping reveals is not a standardizable reading of *Hamlet*, but rather an example of what John D. Caputo calls "the suppleness by which thinking is able to pursue the matter at hand" (qtd. in Wain 245). The moment captures a kind of courage on the part of students, both the one who decided to chase the rooster on the stage, and the ones who agreed to chase it through the thicket of expectations that govern "serious" engagements with "serious" literature. From the standpoint of those expectations, the moment is at best a comic distraction, at worst a critical misfire. But from the standpoint of hopeful pedagogy, it's a success through and through, one that can be had only by being open to "that which comes to meet us from beyond ourselves" (Smith qtd. in Jardine and Seidel 3) and from beyond any *a priori* definition of either serious engagement or success.

> **Jessica:** When did we divorce delight from learning? When did the word "rigor" become the antithesis to "fun"? How did we move from play to policing, from being silly to surveillance? And how do we champion ludic pedagogy as a way forward?
>
> **Lisa:** Rigor ... mortis.
> I reiterate Rebecca Solnit's statement that, along with Shannon's "and, of course, pirates," is on the way to becoming a motto: "Joy is a fine initial act of insurrection."

These two examples of bent readings or productive misfires suggest that the purpose of the classroom encounter with *Hamlet* is to produce meaning from the unique circumstances of students' interactions with the text, with the space, and with each other, rather than to map student experience onto a preexisting set of expectations. The purpose of the teacher in this environment is not necessarily to "rein in" moments of rooster-chasing or weirdness, but to create an environment of safety and courage in which students can develop that "suppleness" of thinking required for critical engagement with the questions such moments elicit and enable.

Chasing roosters is not necessarily about anarchy, but is closer to what Scarry identifies as a sort of "pure procedural" aesthetic creation, an idea she extrapolates from John Rawls. A twentieth-century political philosopher who explored the idea of *justice as fairness*, Rawls described the concept of pure procedural justice in which "we have no picture of the best outcome, and we must trust wholly in the fairness of the procedures to ensure that the outcome itself is fair" (Scarry 116). In the analogous aesthetic realm, "one may have no prior vision and may simply trust oneself to the act of creating" (117). This yoking of the concepts of justice and beauty provides a framework for the creative acts of reading and experience that arise in a hopeful pedagogical space. Where the principles are in place – agency, transformation, and critical attentiveness to the embodied uniqueness of the circumstances – we need not commit to an *a priori* definition of success or specific "serious" reading in order to do serious critical work. Indeed, the serious critical work is enabled by this openness to "we know not what."

Encounter #3: Breathing with Hamlet

Richard Wollheim's assertion that we know what we're drawing by drawing suggests likewise that we know what we're saying by saying it, doing by doing it, and captures the particularity of hopeful critical engagement, providing me with a way to enter into my final example of embodied thinking: breathing with Hamlet in his long (and for me, life-changing) "rogue and peasant slave" speech (2.2.537–94). After a punishing and energy-draining series of verbal duels with people interested in tenting him to the quick, Hamlet finds himself, at last, alone. In this speech, Hamlet traces a conceptual circle from an envious admiration of "this player here" (536) through a disparaging assessment of his own "acting," and, after a cathartic explosion of passion, back to the Player, whose crafted and disciplined performance will be the path to "the conscience of the king" (592).

RUN-THROUGH: The class sits on the floor with their books in their laps. It's the end of a long second day of "*Hamlet* Camp," a one-week intensive course, eight hours a day, all *Hamlet*, all the time. We've been thinking hard for hours. Snacks and coffee mugs are scattered around us. We're tired when we turn our attention to Hamlet's first line: "Now I am alone" (534). Sprawled on the classroom carpet, we can relate to Hamlet's exhaustion here. Rallying for a last end-of-day push, we decide to forego the lecture I was going to give and instead read the speech aloud together a few times. We aren't thinking about the meaning of the words so much as paying attention to our breath, to our bodies' interaction with the lines, the long sentences where it's hard to catch a breath, the sudden stops and caesuras, the way that the consonants and vowels summon, shape, and direct our energy.

> **Shannon:** How wonderful to have that intensive experience. I sometimes think that the full emotional richness of this play is only possible if you are truly wrung out by the end of it: none of that cutting to two hours for me! I want the full four-hour exhaustive extravaganza!
>
> **Jessica:** Yes! Pema Chodron, in a continuation of the quotation I used earlier, reflects: "After a long retreat, I had what seemed to me the earth-shaking revelation that we cannot be in the present and run our story lines at the same time!" (2). *Hamlet* Camp is a kind of retreat, an immersive, in-the-present, transformative experience where the members of the class run the story lines in real time. Sign me UP.

The exercise attunes us to the link between words and action, thought and experience (the "crisscrossing" that makes Augustine think of God), something that Hamlet yearns for in his praise for the Player that opens the speech: unlike Hamlet, who "can say nothing" (555) and therefore can do nothing, the Player is able to bring words, body, and ideas into a state of unity, "his whole function suiting / With forms to his conceit" (541–2). The force of this desired unity is palpable in the way that the words of Hamlet's speech work in the body: the rising and falling of breath as Hamlet careens

Shannon: And maybe recrimination from others, if he is anticipating some response from the public theater audience. This speech has always struck me as neatly poised between the private and public: yes, he's alone, but then he seems to imagine himself as an actor being attacked by someone who disapproves of the way he plays his part.

> **Jessica:** I've never seen that extra dimension of self-consciousness before. Is this similar to the 3 AM rehashing of an unsettling conversation (or imagined conversation you did not have) where you come up with lines you wish you had used with an interlocutor that is, in real life, completely oblivious to your imaginative dialogue?

> **Lisa:** Also, Shakespeare casting an eye to a restless audience to say, "Hang on, hang on. I'm getting there!"

Lisa: Some editions of the play omit "O, vengeance!" The whole affair gives me a frisson, thinking about a parallel universe where, in 1986, Brent Carver used a different version of the play and instead of becoming an English professor, as I describe in our introduction, I became an oceanographer.

> **Jessica:** Every time we talk about *Hamlet* (or host virtual play readings, or I teach this scene) I hear your voice yelling "O, vengeance" with equal notes of lamentation and rage for the excised phrase. It is like you are a textual phantom pacing the margins of the text and haunting those misguided editors for their decisions to erase a life-changing line.

> **Lisa:** Avenge this foul and unnatural murder of my favorite line!

Shannon: I completely agree: when Olivier begins his film with "This is the tragedy of a man who could not make up his mind," I will only accept that premise if the "this" refers to "Olivier's film" and not "Shakespeare's *Hamlet*."

> **Lisa:** Olivier has a lot to answer for.

> **Jessica:** Since I spend my entire essay arguing that something is rotten in the state of Denmark, NOT HAMLET, and that the burden of being resilient should lie in the system and not in the individual, I will simply chime in here with an "amen."

through self-recrimination to accusation to the climactic demand for vengeance, where the violence of the words marks the spectacular lightning strike of justice made flesh in an act of retribution:

> … Am I a coward?
>
> Who calls me villain, breaks my pate across,
>
> Plucks off my beard and blows it in my face,
>
> Tweaks me by the nose, gives me the lie i'th' throat
>
> As deep as to the lungs – who does me this?
>
> Ha!
>
> 'Swounds, I should take it: for it cannot be
>
> But I am pigeon-liver'd and lack gall
>
> To make oppression bitter, or ere this
>
> I should ha' fatted all the region kites
>
> With this slave's offal. Bloody, bawdy villain!
>
> Remorseless, treacherous, lecherous, kindless villain!
>
> O, vengeance! (2.2.557–68)[1]

The students note how the string of words leading to that explosion – "Remorseless, treacherous, lecherous, kindless villain!" (568) – tightens the jaws, makes us spit through the chafing and hissing consonants, a pent energy that will not be released until "villain" opens our mouths for a breath and the "O" opens our chests so that the "v" in "vengeance!" can launch the word out of us like a geyser punching through stone.

For Hamlet, being, speaking, and acting should be aligned. "Seems, madam? Nay, it is. I know not 'seems'" (1.2.76), he tells Gertrude, and feels the misalignment as a physical pain: "But break, my heart, for I must hold my tongue" (159). Here, though, grinding through Hamlet's words, we *feel* the speech working in us, pulling that disjoint state to rights: it's very difficult to remain sprawled on the carpet when bellowing "O, VENGEANCE!" Hamlet's problem is not, as Laurence Olivier and others would have us believe, that he "thinks too much," but that he needs a space where words and actions are not misaligned. When he rises from the trough of "Am I a coward?" (2.2.557) to "who does me this? / Ha!" (561–2) he is not presenting to us his inaction, but the lack of overt, public opposition that would make his action honorable: no one steps up and "Plucks off [his] beard" (559) or "gives [him] the lie i'th' throat / As deep as to the lungs" (560–1). "Who does me this?" is an accusation hurled not at himself but at the empty room that for 500 lines has been full of indirections, false friends, ulterior motives, and lies. Like Marcellus, a mere man contending with a ghost, Hamlet has been striking at air with his partisan or trying to stop the sunrise by chasing a rooster. An honest man, Hamlet *would* act, if he could find someone to act against and a way to do it that would unify himself and the misaligned world of Elsinore.

Lisa: In our *Wyrd Words* podcast interview, Rodrigo Beilfuss recalls: "I found that when I was playing him, my toes were hurting because I was always ready for action ... but always stopping myself from taking the action" (Beilfuss). This is a brilliant instance of form, conceit, and body acting together.

Sitting down with my pencil and a piece of blank flip-chart paper, I think about this classroom experience. I read the speech aloud and let my pencil traverse the paper, rising and falling with the breath, the cadence, and the energy of Hamlet's rumination and recrimination. What I get is a roller-coaster line of steadily rising crests that breaks, explodes, and collapses as Hamlet struggles to contain his passions, to turn them in a productive direction. Successive drafts bring me at last to a circle: the Player. Everything begins and ends with the Player. Know what you are drawing by drawing. Act by acting. As my student, Kelsey Barendregt, astutely pointed out in her analysis of Hamlet's "consummation / Devoutly to be wish'd" (3.1.63–4) in his famous "To be or not to be" speech, "'Consummation' implies a union. Within this consummation, lying can lead to the truth. Through the duality of metaphor and paradox, greater understanding can be reached" (Barendregt). She continues: "Hamlet's 'to be or not to be' speech moves him from a way of being that values truth through authenticity to the 'undiscovered' way of being that values truth through duplicity and metaphor. This shift allows Hamlet to operate within a world where the lie can lead to the truth." The "play's the thing" (2.2.591) because here, and only here, is "acting" coextensive with speaking, lying with the truth.

As sixteenth-century philosopher and all-round Renaissance man Philip Sidney tells us in his *Defense of Poesy*, poetry never lies because it never claims to tell the truth, at least, not in any simplistic way (570–1). By marrying the precepts of philosophy to the matter of history (the general to the particular), poetry allows us to access another kind of truth, a "golden" world where words and things are united in the lie that is art (555). The play's the thing. And it is at this realization that Hamlet's roller-coaster of rising but thwarted energy and exhausted descent comes to an even track, in the steadying breath at "About, my brains" (2.2.575). In playing, he decides, form and conceit are connected. Acting is *acting*. A kind of beauty is restored. (See Figure 4.)

The circle I draw suggests a sort of infinite task for Hamlet and, I think, for us. The problem of restoring the beauty of the state (to join, to pact, to make peace) is one that we tackle often, with each new group of students, each unique constellation of bodies

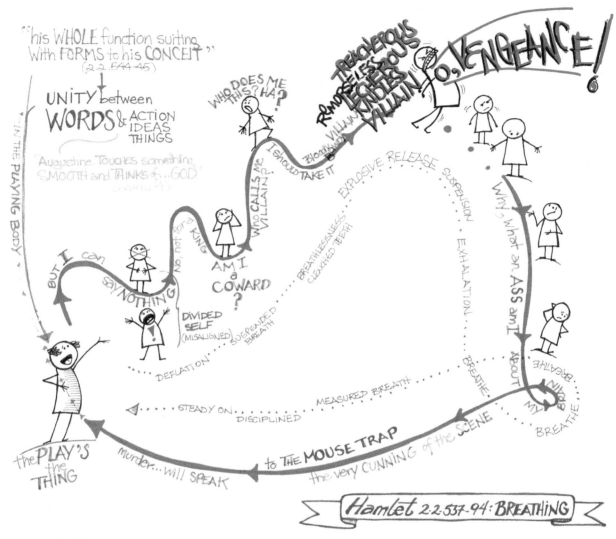

Figure 4. Sketchnote:
Hamlet 2.2.537–94,
Breathing

and minds that brings to us new demands, new conceptions of what is just, what "fits" here, now and perhaps to come. The critical insights traced in this chapter might not be new, but that's not the point. The point is to be attentive to the possibilities that arise from the unexpected, from "positive appreciation of the full polysemic possibility which can explode forth from within any occasion when adult and child [or group of learners] genuinely meet together" (Smith qtd. in Jardine and Seidel 3). The critically hopeful classroom is not one that fixes the world, pins it down, or delivers a truth about content; rather, it is one in which it is safe to *do the work* (both the text and the labor) of making the world new, again and again.

In his afterword to an essay collection with the best of all possible subtitles, *Experiments in a Curriculum for Miracles*, David W. Jardine turns to Hannah Arendt to capture this constant renewal of the call to make right. She says: "To preserve the world against the mortality of its creators and inhabitants it must be constantly set right anew. The problem is simply to educate in such way that a setting-right remains actually possible, even though it can, of course, never be assured" (Arendt qtd. in Jardine 189). Like Rawls's "procedural justice" or Scarry's "procedural beauty," this possibility exists not in the object or a predetermined outcome, but in the principle of renewal within which the work is done. For Jardine, it is the very particular and ephemeral quality of moments of connection within such a frame of possibility that gives them value: "it is only because these arrivals of insight and worthwhileness are impermanent, rare and finite that we can truly love them and dedicate ourselves, as best we can, again and again every September, to their arrival" (189). We attend to them the way we attend to beauty. Beauty demands that we be willing continually to revise our position in order to "place ourselves in its path," Scarry argues, calling this constant revision "a basic impulse underlying education" (7). In these encounters with one another, we hope to find ourselves "looking in the right direction when a comet makes its sweep through a certain patch of sky" (7).

Learning is a verb. *Facere veritatem.*

Shannon: And that makes it possible to return to the same texts again and again, too, thankfully for those of us who do reread and talk about the same poems and plays over and over again through a long career. If we had fixed the thing, like an insect with a pin, there would be no point: it would be done.

Jessica: In teaching Shakespeare's plays we have the privilege of rereading, revisiting, and rethinking the same texts with new people at different moments in diverse contexts. In *Think Again: The Power of Knowing What You Don't Know*, Adam Grant (2021) makes that case that while "intelligence is usually seen as the ability to think and learn" there is a "new set of cognitive skills that might matter more: the ability to rethink and unlearn" (1).

Lisa: And we also are working to *unlearn* our reflexive defaults to our own authority while trying to get the academy to *unlearn* so many unproductive and even harmful ways of *seeing learning*.

NOTE

1 In the Oxford edition of the play, the line "O, vengeance!" does not appear, but many other versions of the text, such as the one featured on *Open Source Shakespeare*, present this line.

Acknowledging the Complexity of Unknowing as an Act of Critical Hope in *Hamlet*

Jessica Riddell

I grew up on a quiet, dead-end street animated by a colorful cast of neighborhood dogs and cats who assumed larger-than-life personalities in our childhood imaginations. There was Jenny, the golden retriever who always wandered over for a visit but would steal our Halloween candy if we weren't looking (this happened not infrequently). There was Oliver, the overly friendly tomcat who would melodramatically throw himself in front of us on the sidewalk in the hopes of a belly rub. But most memorably, there was a miniature collie named Hamlet whose very presence tormented my twin brother and me. This small but vicious dog, untethered and unavoidable, guarded the corner of our dead-end street, making our daily walk to and from school a hair-raising experience. From afar this dog looked like a tiny version of Lassie, one of our childhood favorites, which made it all the more disorienting when Hamlet chased us, nipping our heels and barking with a tenacity that struck terror into our little twin hearts. Hamlet also lived a preternaturally long time, plaguing our regular commute from elementary school all the way up to high school without seeming to tire or age, kept young (in our minds) by his mission to ensure our daily disquiet.

> **Lisa:** I think this is the fictional Hamlet's purpose in our lives as well!

It was only in junior high school that I realized that Hamlet-the-Dog was named after Hamlet-the-Dane, and not until high school and beyond that I grasped the enormity of THE PLAY in stark contrast to the little dog that inspired our early childhood indignation. Until I sat down to write this chapter, I had never unpacked how this "DAMN DOG" (also, coincidentally, the inspiration for my earliest forays into swearing) mediated my earliest encounters with *Hamlet* or how I might trace my fear of the dog as part of a larger genealogy of fear I have teaching this play.

My formative memories of Hamlet-the-Dog form a rather fitting metaphor for my relationship with one of Shakespeare's most famous and difficult plays. Here is what these two Hamlets have in common:

- *Hamlet* **is unavoidable.** If one teaches and writes about Shakespeare, one cannot ignore this play. Even people who have not read or seen *Hamlet* know this play intimately and can quote lines and reference the plot. Almost no other literary text circulates in our Western cultural imaginary in this way. *Hamlet* would be a glaring omission on a Shakespeare syllabus, and its absence requires careful explanation. As a Shakespearean, you can't NOT teach this play unless you have a good reason.

- *Hamlet* **generates fear through anticipation.** When I design my course outlines (usually in the summer), I almost always talk myself into the idea that *this* will be the year we crack *Hamlet* wide open. As the term begins and we move closer to the allotted time on the syllabus that I've dedicated to THE PLAY, *Hamlet* renders me a Shakespearean caricature of the "whining schoolboy with his satchel / And shining morning face, creeping like snail / Unwillingly to school" (*As You Like It* 2.7.145–7). And yet the anticipation is always worse than the reality: once we begin, the play propels us forward, and this momentum allows us to act: to act out the scenes, to pull apart the language, to immerse ourselves in the three-dimensional life of the play.

- *Hamlet* **is larger than life.** Many people *say* they love *Hamlet*. It might, in some circles, even be gauche to claim otherwise. At the start of term, students will sometimes rhapsodize about their experience with the play; yet when we start to dig into the text, things can get downright disorienting. The daunting prospect of understanding *Hamlet*, and the social pressure to "get it," give the play an overdetermined weight that makes it difficult for students to see themselves in (and through) the play.

- *Hamlet* **doesn't get easier.** In my experience, the more exposure one has to *Hamlet*, the less one is guaranteed any definitive reading. Every time I read the play, or watch a production, a new line strikes me with fresh power, an encounter between two characters catches me by surprise, or the delivery of a familiar soliloquy haunts me in new ways. The more time I spend with *Hamlet*, the less I seem to have a solid grasp on the play.

My fear of the play is (thankfully) limited to when I try to *teach* the interpretive scope of the play. It is infinitely easier to

---

Shannon: Like the lady in the joke who complains after seeing *Hamlet* for the first time that it is just one cliche after another.

Lisa: >.< hee!

Shannon: I know what you mean! I designed my *Hamlet* seminar with the foolish notion that by the end of it I would finally "get" the whole of the play. This play always resists getting got.

Lisa: I think of Rodrigo Beilfuss in our *Wyrd Words* podcast, who, when asked the somewhat nutty question, "If Hamlet were a space, what would it be?" gamely answered that it is a "relentless jacuzzi." I was so delighted by this image – which itself resists fully getting got and captures, among other things, that sense of heat and constant motion that can't be fully escaped.

Lisa: I can hear the echoes of our nemesis "teacherly authority" here, that persistent belief that to be a teacher we must be "solid," that we must "grasp" things, subdue them, substantiate both the subject and *ourselves* through our mastery.

Shannon: Early on, I started to find a paradoxical pedagogy: the more I knew about a subject, the less satisfying I found the experience of a class. Getting thrown into teaching a Chaucer course was eye-opening: discovering the subject with them was much more exciting for all of us. While I don't want to ignore or denigrate professorial expertise at all, it can, if we aren't careful, close down rather than open out the play space for novices.

Jessica: How much have we internalized the need to have "the" answers – and what does that telegraph to others about mastery, expertise, and authority in relation to power? Can Hamlet and his messy journey model the impossibility of "right" answers – and even challenge us to think about why we are looking for that kind of meaning in the first place?

Shannon: Yes to all this! I feel like I collect productions, on film or on stage, in a way that makes the play less and not more fixed. Just one freshly delivered line can make me see a character or a moment completely differently.

watch a production because some of the interpretive difficulties can be resolved by witnessing and responding to a particular production. Since there is so much ambiguity and uncertainty about many key elements, *Hamlet* offers directors tremendous creative scope. Teaching the play, by contrast, comes with its own particular challenges because we must grapple with a multitude of decisions we cannot make, which significantly limits our ability to reconcile competing or conflicting interpretative systems. It is like reading a "choose your own adventure" book from start to finish rather than following the various pathways determined by a series of directorial or creative choices.

> **Jessica:** As a child I used to read all the possible endings at once to best determine the adventure I wanted to choose, which now seems like a rather fitting form of karma.

The challenge has been the following:

- How do I teach *Hamlet* hopefully rather than fearfully?
- How do we shape a pedagogical journey that makes space for (or, ideally, embraces) ambiguity, ambivalence, and instability?[1]
- And how do we embark on a guided reading that is coherent, rigorous, *and* (perhaps most importantly) delightful?

In the spirit of embracing messy learning journeys, I'd like to first outline a few failed attempts at teaching *Hamlet* and to speculate on why these approaches fell short; this gives us an entry point to explore how *Hamlet* teaches us how we might embrace the complexity of unknowing as an act of critical hope not just in our relationship to the play, but as a way to engage with adversity in the world more broadly.

Textual History and *Hamlet*

In our forays into the play, we might talk about how the interpretative complexity of *Hamlet* is compounded by the multiple versions of the play in circulation. While many of Shakespeare's plays were printed in a single edition in Shakespeare's lifetime (called a quarto[2]), almost all his plays are collected in the First Folio, a compendium of his works published in 1623 by his friends and business partners seven years after his death. There are three print versions of *Hamlet*: the First Quarto (Q1), published in 1603, is a highly suspicious text and has earned the moniker "the bad quarto." The Second Quarto (Q2), published in 1604/1605, is considered the "good quarto" and shares the same title but with the tantalizing addition: "Newly imprinted and enlarged to almost as much againe as it was, according to the true and perfect Coppie" ("*Hamlet*: An Introduction to This Text," para. 3). A version of *Hamlet* was printed for a third time in the 1623 Folio.

Shannon: I'm so glad I'm not the only one to have tried this – with disastrous results. I had mine try thinking through the two quartos with a "fish bowl" exercise, where a select group of students discusses a topic with others standing around them and listening. That is not a good use of a fish bowl, I now realize.

Lisa: I would argue, though, that the context in which you teach the play can make a difference and can still be inviting for students. In a course about the history of editing, the play becomes a masterclass in the crucial interpretive role played by editors who are often as invisible as ghost writers ("Who's there?").

Shannon: Maybe we're up against the truth that no one approach will grab all students. I'm in favor of the combination platter approach for undergraduates: a little taste of a lot of choices for ways to enter the play.

Jessica: Ha! Yes! I have started building "on-demand" digital resources (micro-lectures, podcasts, essays, OpEds) and I affectionately refer to them as "charcuterie platters." Students are encouraged to nibble and graze as their appetites and interests guide them: some are going to love the olives while others are heading straight for the brie. Choice, curiosity, and curation are important for both classes and charcuterie platters.

Lisa: Nobody truly loves olives.

Why This Didn't Work

This approach risks a SNOOZE fest. Personal disclaimer: I am fascinated with the colorful cast of characters vying for position through scribal and print publications of stage plays in the fraught political climate of late sixteenth century commercial and noncommercial drama. (Reading that sentence just put most of you to sleep.) With the exception of a few students interested in early modern print culture, the textual history of quartos (in my experience) leads to a lot of glazed-over eyes. This approach risks alienating students who are not titillated by the intrigue of a rogue player pirating the *Hamlet* text from memory to make a few bucks, or the tantalizing clues that Shakespeare and his business partners might have persuaded the printer to sell them the unauthorized Q1 copies and commissioned him to print the "authentic" Q2 directly from Shakespeare's authorial papers (and then advertised "the true and perfect Coppie" to gain traction in the book-selling market). Ultimately, while the circumstances of the pirated and authentic versions of *Hamlet* make for a riveting conspiracy theory, it doesn't help us get into the text itself and threatens to take us down rabbit holes without exits.

Genre Bending and Identity

In my early forays into teaching, one of my go-to moves was to introduce plays by discussing genre, the stylistic conventions in form, style, and subject matter, to help us understand where Shakespeare adheres to expectations (e.g., comedy, tragedy, history, romance) and when he violates or undermines them. A quick (and overly simplistic) definition of Shakespearean comedy, for example, starts with a discussion of how comedy is the symbolic resolution of social contradictions. Comedy presents us with individuals who challenge the social order, stages the conflict, and then usually reintegrates them into society, often through extraordinary plot devices like fairies or happenstance (not terribly useful if one is looking for practical solutions to restore an imbalanced social order). Many of the titles of Shakespeare's comedies specify social situations, either festive occasions (e.g., *A Midsummer Night's Dream* or *Twelfth Night*) or a genial attitude among the characters and between the play and its audience (e.g., *As You Like It* or *Much Ado About Nothing*).

In contrast, the titles of the tragedies focus on a single male hero (e.g., *Hamlet, Othello, Macbeth,* or *King Lear*) or a pair of lovers (e.g., *Antony and Cleopatra*). These titles suggest that the tragedies concern the individual, or more precisely, the failure or resistance of an individual to be reconciled to the society represented in the play. This is not to say, however, that tragedies aren't social in their concerns. *Othello* very clearly concerns the wider social significance of the hero's marriage, offering us much more a tragedy of social situation than of character. *Macbeth* is a tragedy that investigates power structures and legitimate authority. *King Lear* maps family relations onto the political sphere where heads, hearts, and kingdoms are at stake. Any tragic formula can be exposed as inadequate and essentializing; yet we might say that Shakespeare's tragedies represent the failure of social relations to offer a stable identity to the characters within a world of social disorder. That needs some unpacking.

Lisa: Rodrigo Beilfuss, who both played Hamlet and directed the play, notes how Shakespeare won't color inside the lines of genre or expectation: "the play itself plays with the genre: it's a revenge play using all the tropes of the revenge tragedy, but then it goes like, 'but not really, but not really,' right? Here is a revenge hero, but not really" (Beilfuss).

Shannon: And I love that about Shakespeare: he is a tireless experimenter with genre. That's why reading *Hamlet* AFTER *Titus Andronicus*, for example, is so revealing. Yes, he seems to say, I can do you a garden variety revenge tragedy, but I can then set revenge tragedy on its ear and make something really interesting.

Why This *Might* Work

The conversation on genre can still feel pretty abstract: while genre might help us think about *what the play does*, this approach doesn't get us closer to *who we are in relation to the play*. But there is a thread on genre worth pulling: tantalizingly, the genre of tragedy is a historical and social phenomenon that emerges only at very particular moments in time, whereas comedy and farce, morality and history have a more consistent cultural trajectory. In other words, dramatic tragedy is very old but seems to have appeared as a dominant form only intermittently in the history of Western literature:

- in Athens in the fifth century BCE
- in Rome in the century after the birth of Christ
- in England and Europe during the early modern period

Tragedy has tended to be compelling during periods of intense intellectual upheaval. The Athenian tragedies come out of the period that also saw the groundwork for Western philosophy being laid against the older polytheistic Greek religions. The birth of Christ and the emergence of Christianity is another significant sociocultural shift. Shakespeare's tragedies were written during the aftermath of the Protestant Reformation, which saw the rise of humanism, the European conquest of the Americas, the beginning of the scientific revolution, and a considerable expansion in world trade. What these periods have in common is the collision of two major ideological systems.

Shannon: I start with "*Hamlet* is the story of a university student with one clear idea about his own future: his parents have conflicting alternative plans for him: sound familiar?" My radical notion is that we should get our majors to read *Hamlet* once a year for four years and see where they are each time. The play is so fundamentally about the kinds of choices they have to make – and the ones that get made for them. .

Lisa: And Hamlet doesn't have any real guides as to how to negotiate these disruptions. The Ghost is surely not a good teacher. In some ways, his story shows that experience alone isn't enough; we also need someone to help us to frame those experiences in a way that gives us tools to grapple with them without locking us into one "tried and true," "father knows best" idea of what the best answer to those questions must be.

Jessica: Yes! Hamlet is a student without a [reliable] teacher. Is that why he takes such a shine to the Player, who teaches by mimesis? Compare with Lisa's discussion "that we know what we're drawing by drawing" remodeled as we know we are teaching/learning by representing?

The clash between the old system and the new one creates tremendous pressure on individuals, institutions, and society more generally. The results are deeply unsettling and often violent. These conditions make for good tragedy.

Hamlet, both the play and the titular character, dramatize the tension of living between two ways of knowing and all the messiness that accompanies transformation. The opening line in the play shouted out into a fog – "Who's there?" (1.1.1) – introduces a key problem in the world of the play: clear perception is impossible. The use of in-between spaces and disorientation is not a Shakespearean invention but rather a fundamental component of Classical tragedy. In Aristotle's *Poetics* (the first extant philosophical treatise on dramatic and literary theory), *hamartia* is usually translated as "fatal flaw" (*Poetics* 27). However, this term can also be literally translated as "unknowing" (96). If *hamartia* represents radical unknowingness, tragedy shows us a person confronting a situation that is systemically or structurally unstable rather than a central character who has an inherent weakness or flaw. This insight gives us an entry point into the play through a conversation about two competing frameworks: one that focuses on the individual versus a systems-focused approach to resilience.

Stripped down to its studs, the story is a very human one that our students can recognize. Hamlet is studying at university and abruptly leaves school and all of his friends in the middle of term when his dad dies unexpectedly. He arrives home in his grief and disorientation to find that everyone he loves is gaslighting him with toxic positivity. He is alone and lonely; with the exception of Horatio (who is equally confused), his friends and confidantes (Rosencrantz, Guildenstern, Ophelia) no longer tell him the truth. He's been at university long enough to start questioning older ideological frameworks but he's still a bit fuzzy on new ways of understanding the world.

Literary critic and children's author C.S. Lewis characterizes Hamlet as a "haunted man – man with his mind on the frontier of two worlds, man unable either quite to reject or quite to admit the supernatural, man struggling to get something done as man has struggled from the beginning, yet incapable of achievement because of his inability to understand either himself or his fellows or the real quality of the universe which has produced him" (102). While the struggle is real, Lewis places too much responsibility on the shoulders of an individual and not enough on the system built upon structural and systemic inequalities. This play isn't about Hamlet's failure to act, or his inability to make up his mind: he isn't some whiny, spotted teenager in the midst of a self-indulgent existential crisis (although I have been there and it is a MOOD). Hamlet doesn't lack resilience or grit when faced with a changing world. The world is flawed. The system is rigged. He never stood a chance because something is rotten in the state of Denmark.

So what do we do with this knowledge? This play teaches us three fundamental lessons: beware of toxic positivity, acknowledge the messiness of transformation, and reframe resilience as a systems approach rather than as an individual responsibility.

Combating Toxic Positivity

The way we tell stories about our situation matters for Shakespeare and no less for us. Narratives help us to make sense of the world, especially when the world feels radically disorienting. One just has to look at Lear's defensive claims, "I am a man / More sinned against than sinning" (*King Lear* 3.2.59–60), or Hamlet's final instructions to Horatio, "And in this harsh world draw thy breath in pain, / To tell my story" (*Hamlet* 5.2.341–2), for examples of how we use words to make meaning from chaos, and how acts of storytelling shape our own and oftentimes others' perceptions of reality.

Lisa: It seems to me that what you're getting at with these examples of "failed" approaches is not so much that the approaches are not good, but that they don't align with your idea of what your classroom should do, which is to validate student imaginative engagement with complexity and to disrupt the foreclosures of that engagement that these approaches can represent. In these examples I see you tacking closer and closer to the centre of your teaching philosophy.

Shannon: Othello's "Speak of me as I am; nothing extenuate, / Nor set down aught in malice. Then must you speak / Of one that lov'd not wisely but too well" (5.2.342–5) is an especially problematic example. Tell my story fairly, with balance, he says, in which case you will have to say THIS about me.

Lisa: "[T]hese words are not mine," quoth Claudius. "No, nor mine now," Hamlet replies (3.2.89–91). If you're gonna say, "tell my story," you are making a leap of faith, because stories, once told, don't belong to you, an idea that students grapple with when confronted with the instability of the text.

Jessica: In Lin-Manuel Miranda's *Hamilton* (2015), the final song explores who gets to be part of the narrative. George Washington reflects, "Let me tell you what I wish I'd known / When I was young and dreamed of glory / You have no control / Who lives, who dies, who tells your story?" (*Hamilton*). How does this link to the now ubiquitous call to "speak your truth" – as if your truth is both incontestable and authentic?

In the midst of trauma, two narratives can emerge that imagine very different futures, which in turn exposes invisible power structures: 1. toxic positivity and 2. critical hope. Exemplifying the former, from the moment we first encounter him, Claudius reeks of toxic positivity. His first words draw attention to the inversion of the social order just as he deploys rhetoric promising us that everything is going to be fine:

Though yet of Hamlet our dear brother's death

The memory be green, and that it us befitted

To bear our hearts in grief, and our whole kingdom

To be contracted in one brow of woe,

Yet so far hath discretion fought with nature

That we with wisest sorrow think on him,

Together with remembrance of ourselves. (1.2.1–7)

Shannon: A little of the "Make Denmark Great Again"? I always wish I could reconstruct the feeling of watching this for the first time, NOT knowing that Claudius is a murderer and a usurper. If we are naive readers (or his court), this might just look like keeping calm and carrying on. Once we know, we can see his toxic positivity as one of the ways he means to cover up his crimes. Nothing to see here!

Lisa: This is why I love the idea of looking at the play as unfolding in time, rather than looking at it from a "bird's-eye view": we can map the ways that accumulating information and growing understanding of context change our beliefs – about Hamlet, about Claudius – emphasizing that, from a human perspective, there is no "fixed" reality but rather a constant dance with change and revelation. I find that this perspective makes me more patient with characters and less likely to issue "judgments." It's a formative, rather than summative, way of seeing things.

Jessica: I ask my students to imagine being at the Globe on opening afternoon for the world premiere of Hamlet: what happens to you when you come to this with a totally clean slate?

Lisa: He is by statute meant to be transformed into a king but is unable to assume that role. That, I think, is the "thwarted action" of the play, not Hamlet's inability to "make up his mind." It happens at the level of the state, not necessarily or solely in the state of his own mind, although it has severe repercussions for the latter.

Shannon: He is literally disappointed, "removed from an appointment or position" according to the OED (n. 1). (Fun fact: this is the only play in which Shakespeare uses that word, and it is the Ghost who calls himself "disappointed" because he is cut off before his time.)

Lisa: Hmm, that shifts our modern idea of disappointment (the loss of something you expected – future-oriented) to a more historical idea (the loss of something you already had – past-oriented). It seems like Hamlet is caught in an eddy between past and future.

He reassures us that, despite the death of the king, life will be back to normal in no time because he has orchestrated a smooth succession of power:

> Therefore our sometime sister, now our queen,
>
> Th'imperial jointress to this warlike state,
>
> Have we, as 'twere with a defeated joy,
>
> With an auspicious and a dropping eye,
>
> With mirth in funeral and with dirge in marriage,
>
> In equal scale weighing delight and dole,
>
> Taken to wife. Nor have we herein barr'd
>
> Your better wisdoms, which have freely gone
>
> With this affair along. For all, our thanks. (8–16)

Claudius suggests that we just have to stick together ("contracted in one brow of woe") and look for the silver linings (like "mirth at a funeral"). Claudius's brand of toxic positivity effaces conflict and does not permit room for disagreement or discontent. In fact, he reminds the court that they have been complicit, having "freely gone / With this affair along." Claudius's narrative denies that Denmark, and by extension Hamlet, are in the midst of radical transformation precipitated by the king's death; instead, he advocates for a return to normality ASAP. There is no room for critical hope in Claudius's brand of leadership, no understanding of complexity and discomfort as a necessary process of transformation, and certainly no candid and uncomfortable conversations as a way forward into the unknown.

Toxic positivity threatens to break Hamlet apart because it denies the fact of his transformation. Hamlet tries to deploy critical hope, most notably in his engagement with theater: play-acting and performance offer Hamlet a way to be broken open, to occupy the position of learner, and to embrace empathy. He is perhaps most at ease when he meets the traveling theater troupe and finds room to breathe when he puts on an antic disposition. However, his forays into critical hope are short-lived and the pervasiveness of toxic positivity as expressed by his mother and those closest to him denies Hamlet the opportunity to find meaning in uncertainty or distill purpose to make the world anew. Hamlet has no one to show him the path of critical hope, with tragic consequences.

Acknowledging the Messiness of Transformation

Sadly, the one person who might've been able to help Hamlet is now the cause of his deep disorientation. Hamlet Senior, dead and undead, is one of the most interesting and "unknowable" elements of the play. Marcellus offers an interpretation of the Ghost based on a mixture of religious belief and folklore:

> It faded on the crowing of the cock.
> Some say that ever 'gainst that season comes
> Wherein our Saviour's birth is celebrated,
> The bird of dawning singeth all night long;
> And then, they say, no spirit can walk abroad,
> The nights are wholesome, then no planets strike,
> No fairy takes, nor witch hath power to charm,
> So hallow'd and so gracious is the time. (1.1.162–9)

Horatio's reply, "So I have heard and do in part believe it" (170), calls attention to his inability either to embrace these old forms of belief or to abandon them entirely. The Ghost represents the intersection between systems of meaning. Marcellus urges Horatio, "Thou art a scholar, speak to it, Horatio," (45) suggesting that the Ghost is a kind of intellectual problem that only a scholar can unpack. However, there is the discontinuity between the Ghost and the early modern academic world that Horatio and Hamlet inhabit. Significantly, Hamlet and Horatio were both students at the University of Wittenberg, a center of new humanist learning (and not coincidentally, where Martin Luther began the Protestant Reformation). Hamlet points to the limits of their learning when he tells Horatio: "There are more things in heaven and earth, Horatio, / than are dreamt of in your philosophy" (1.5.174–5).

The Ghost is one of the famous interpretive quandaries for actors and directors, audiences and readers. In the first scenes of the play, it seems to be there, as it were, in the flesh. Everybody who occupies the spaces it enters can see it. However, by the time we get to Gertrude's bedchamber in 3.4, only Hamlet can see the Ghost. Why? Is it that Gertrude can't see it because of her guilt? Does the Ghost make a point of only appearing to men? How does he control who sees him and who doesn't? The play simply gives us no tools with which to interpret the discrepancy in the Ghost's visibility – a discrepancy that actually radically changes the kind of play we are watching depending on how you stage the Ghost. If there is a visible ghost, it proves

Lisa: Or that it might speak Latin.

Shannon: So much in this scene seems pulled from Ludwig Lavater's *Of Ghosts and Spirits Walking by Night* that it's pleasing to imagine they might think the Ghost just knew it in the original Latin, not in the 1572 English translation (which Shakespeare probably read).

Lisa: ☺ What a dang hipster.

Shannon: A tempting interpretation in a National Theatre production (2010) made it clear that Gertrude DID see, but either she couldn't admit it to herself or she was gaslighting poor Hamlet.

Lisa: And, in an added metatheatrical turn of the screw, so much depends on how actors see what is *not* written, responding to ghosts between the lines.

the existence of a supernatural and archaic world. A ghost that everyone can see tells us that we are in an archaic imaginative space, a world where the supernatural and the natural are tightly integrated. It also classifies the play generically as a revenge tragedy. But a play where the hero is dogged by a ghost only he can see is a psychological drama, a more modern form concerned with the inner life and revealing the isolation of an individual. The complexity of unknowing that surrounds the Ghost (is he good? bad? evil? benevolent? in limbo? hell?) is never fully resolved. Shakespeare positions the Ghost as a kind of Schrödinger's cat of possibilities, and in the interstitial spaces we can find critical hope (I *want* to believe the Ghost is Hamlet's dead dad reaching beyond the boundaries of death to help Hamlet navigate the systems he as king created, but I cannot be *sure*).

Challenging Resilience

This acknowledgment that transformation takes us into unknown and contested territory brings us to our final and perhaps most important lesson from the play: resilience. We hear a lot about resilience and its saccharine sibling, "self-care." There are countless memes and self-help books, tips and checklists. Get gritty. Bounce back. Lean in. Organizations and institutions have started sending out weekly "wellness" emails: one of our colleagues noted that in addition to the standard self-care tips (sleep, exercise, breathe – and repeat!), her university has added advertisements for mental health courses accompanied by a substantial registration fee. "Why is it," she lamented, "that the very institution that is making me unwell is charging me for the cure?"

Ay, there's the rub.

Resilience is a strength worthy of cultivating; however, when systems of power use "resilience" as a means to avoid making systemic changes to better support people, something *is* rotten in the state of Denmark. Andrew Zolli puts it another way: "Where sustainability aims to put the world back into balance, resilience looks for ways to manage in an imbalanced world" (para. 3). When it places responsibility on the individual, resilience asks us to continue to cope in deteriorating conditions rather than do the work necessary to change the systems that make us unwell. If a system is built around the need to endure, whereby individuals are asked to absorb more change and disturbance in order to maintain a normal level of productivity as members of this system, there is no relief. There is no room for critical hope.

> **Shannon:** Yep, that was me. And I know it's not the same voice that is making me unwell who is offering help, but still …
>> **Lisa:** Different heads, same dragon?

> **Lisa:** And that right there is a description of two paths toward "resolution" in the tragic genre: change the world or change yourself. Make the world more accommodating or, in the words of U2: "become a monster / So the monster will not break you" ("Peace on Earth").

> **Shannon:** In this framework, Hamlet's thoughts of suicide make all the sense in world. Like Cordelia's "nothing," it's a way of saying "Not playing that game today."
>> **Lisa:** Hamlet's thoughts of suicide and Ophelia's ultimate death show us that "not playing the game" means not being at all. It seems like the tragic crux here is that the only options are to be deformed by the system or to leave it, both of which leave the abusive system intact.

If the system is making us unwell, what is the cure? For Lear, the best medicine for leaders is to "Expose thyself to feel what wretches feel" (*King Lear* 3.4.34): those in power must work harder to understand how the poor and disenfranchised are weathering the storm. Lear's revelation, that marginalized voices must be given permission to speak uncomfortable truths and we *must* listen, comes too late for him to heal the Body Politic. But it isn't too late for us to exercise critical empathy and choose the path of critical hope.

The question becomes: how do we put the world back into balance when we are in a state of constant disequilibrium? How do we, in Ira Shor's formulation, challenge the actual in the name of the possible? *Hamlet* provides us with an example of what happens when we continue to ask individuals to take on more stress without dismantling the systemic causes. And yet this play is not without critical hope. "Unknowing" and loss of meaning can become an object of aesthetic representation so that, by dramatizing anxiety, we can finally master it. Incoherence is mastered by making it finally into an object of representation. In other words, making art that engages us in the work of critical hope and critical empathy are ways to expose and even begin to dismantle systems of oppression.

> **Lisa:** As a way of maybe poking at this assertion, which I am myself very invested in, I recall again Amelia Sargisson's searching questions in our *Wyrd Words* podcast about how we can come to truths and epiphanies without so much "carnage" on stage ("Fizzy Rebels: Part 1"). Ophelia's death – or Desdemona's in Amelia's example – is a great critique of the system, but she's still dead, and her use as commentary does dick-all for her and has consequences both for people who have to play those roles night after night and for people who are asked to take that in for the purposes of a lesson. Amelia asks whether we should keep staging this destruction of women in the name of exposing truths. I don't know what to do with this yet, but it has caused something seismic to happen in by brain.

Moving from Fear to Critical Hope

Failure – and therefore also success – is NOT merely an individual responsibility shorn of context or outside the systems within which the individual exists. Context matters. I recently shared a self-help post about hope with Lisa and Shannon that made me really cranky, but I couldn't initially explain why. The narrator talked about how their therapist was holding a hope balloon for them: the speech bubble proclaimed, "sometimes it happens that you can't hold [the hope balloon] yourself along with everything else you are carrying." The therapist goes on to say: "I'll remind you every week that it's here. I'll show it to you as often as you need to see it" (Revelatori). The pastel colors and simplistic font grated on my last nerve, but it wasn't until Lisa growled, "Take the bricks off my back so I can hold my own damn hope balloon," that it clicked. Instead of holding other people's hope balloons, why don't we start with the bricks?

Returning to our opening conversation around fear – of the dog, the Dane, the play – I have been able to forge a clear pathway from fear to hope only when I acknowledged my own discomfort. Parker Palmer reminds us that "we cannot see the fear in our students until we see the fear in ourselves" (*Courage to Teach* 48). Until I wrote

Shannon: And, as Duke Senior says, "Sweet are the uses of adversity." We've been talking about teaching for critical hope as, among other things, offering a series of openings in which students can see themselves contributing to the interpretive conversation, as co-creators of the knowledge of the classroom. An open text like *Hamlet* gives us so many opportunities for those hopeful openings.

this chapter, I had been flailing around this play with a series of false starts because I wasn't able to articulate the context and therefore boundaries of my fear. Palmer goes on to say: "Whatever the cost in embarrassment, I will know myself better, and thus be a better teacher, when I acknowledge the forces at play within me instead of allowing them to wreak witless havoc on my work" (30). Alas, *Hamlet* (and, concomitantly, teaching *Hamlet* as an act of becoming, as a process rather than a product) asks us to embrace the complexity of unknowing as an act of critical hope, not just in our relationship to the play but as a way to engage with adversity in the world more broadly.

NOTES

1 Joseph McDonald (1988) argues that "teaching is not properly depicted as the deliberate application of means to technocratic ends. Teaching requires wilder images [that encapsulate] three of our culture's villains: ambiguity, ambivalence and instability" (McDonald 482).

2 "The term 'quarto' denotes a specific size of book – and in this case indicates that it was made of sheets of paper which had each been folded twice to produce a book of a similar size to a modern paperback. Playscripts of this type were relatively cheap to buy, unlike the larger and grander folio size" ("Bad Quarto of *Hamlet*," para. 2).

Wonder and Dust in a Hopeful *Hamlet*

Shannon Murray

If you hold a healthy awareness of your own mortality, your eyes will be opened to the grandeur and glory of life.

> – Rainer Maria Rilke (qtd. in Palmer, Naropa University Address)

I want to talk about the possibility that a meditation on death can be a hopeful practice. The Rule of St. Benedict urges followers to "Keep death daily before your eyes," which might at first glance seem a pessimistic, even hopeless way to live (Benedict 4.47). But it may help if you know that I find Shakespeare's tragedies to be very hopeful creatures, certainly more hopeful than most of his comedies. I remember a student, Conor Dever, arguing that real hope doesn't result from living in a pleasant, happy world. Instead, the most profound experience of hope comes when things seem darkest, when all the evils of Pandora's box are free, but you can still see a spot of light – or a spot where light might appear, at some moment, in some imaginable future (Dever). Shakespeare's great tragedies train us to look for that spot. They create worlds of pain, cruelty, loss, chaos, and disappointment but insist that we look to the promise of light. As another student, Rose Henbest, taught me, the act of hope involves deciding, consciously, to look for and to that light (Henbest).[1]

Through this play, especially in Hamlet's meditations on human life and the inevitability of death, I see the active practice of both hope and empathy. In extreme age, in illness, in infancy, and in death, we are perhaps at our most vulnerable, and those states ought to kindle in us compassion and fellow feeling. They

Lisa: "To hope is to give yourself to the future, and that commitment to the future makes the present inhabitable" (Solnit 4). I need to think a bit more about how looking at the HORIZON of death can jibe with "commitment to the future." Help!?

Jessica: Pema Chodron says, "What we are talking about is getting to know fear, becoming familiar with fear, looking it right in the eye. [...] The kinds of discoveries that are made through this practice have nothing to do with believing in anything. They have much more to do with having the courage to die, the courage to die continually" (2–3).

Lisa: I really dig this logical connection between vulnerability and empathy. In *Precarious Life: The Powers of Mourning and Violence*, Judith Butler posits that vulnerability is at the heart of sociality and ethics: being attached to others makes us vulnerable to loss and even violence, but it also instantiates a "collective responsibility for the physical lives of one another" (30). She suggests that to deny vulnerability and grief and the ties that they reveal is to lose our bearings in the world.

Jessica: Does vulnerability render the distinction between self and the Other more permeable and less impervious, which then allows us to do the work of empathy (while maintaining the element of the "critical" to keep us from collapsing into the Other)?

Lisa: Yes. I think so. Basically, Butler suggests that, if we deny difference – that there is someone outside of me, who is different from me, whom I might lose or who might hurt me – we cannot understand how "a political community is wrought from such ties" (25).

are reminders that the greatest of us has weak moments, and if we are observing weakness in others, we may remember that this weakened soul may have been strong once or once had the potential for strength and goodness and joy. As the play points out, Alexander may come to dust, but just reverse the syntax, and that lowly dust was once Alexander the Great: how wonderful, wonderful, and again wonderful that is. These can seem like opposing notions – life is wonderful; life is vanity – but "Sometimes, the opposite is also true" (qtd. in Johnson, "Discovery Day").

That last phrase is Beethoven's (though here, of course, in translation), something he scrawled in the margins of a musical manuscript.[2] The phrase is enigmatic in its context; what exactly he meant or why he wrote it at that point in the score is unclear. It echoes the idea John Keats sketches – also enigmatically – in his letter on "negative capability": the way some artists can hold two opposite notions in the mind at the same time (41). (I touch on this idea a little in my chapter on *Lear*.) Both address something about the ability to feel contradiction and to hold onto both sides of it without attempting (I interpolate here) an oversimplified decision or conclusion or resolution. It is to see life as neither all this nor all that. It is a step, I believe, to empathy and to hope, and it is something Shakespeare accomplishes in his best work.

Lisa: As an example of this idea, Rebecca Solnit uses F. Scott Fitzgerald, who says, "One should … be able to see that things are hopeless and yet be determined to make them otherwise" (qtd. in Solnit 11), which is, ironically, a certain definition of hope itself.

Let me start with Hamlet's lines, so often quoted out of context, about what an extraordinary thing humans are. He is in a cagey conversation with Rosencrantz and Guildenstern, who are trying to find out why Hamlet is behaving strangely. This comes as part of his answer: "What a piece of work is a man, how noble in reason, how infinite in faculties, in form and moving how express and admirable, in action how like an angel, in apprehension how like a god: the beauty of the world, the paragon of animals" (2.2.299–303). These lines read like the Renaissance European idea of itself in a nutshell, and I hear echoes of Pico della Mirandola's *Oration on the Dignity of Man* (1496), that rousing argument for humans as the most admirable of all beings. We are so admired, Pico writes, exactly because, of all creatures in the Great Chain, we have the choice to imitate the angelic or the bestial, to look up or down, to create a place for ourselves in that hierarchy, depending on our thoughts and actions. He imagines God saying:

We have made thee a creature neither of heaven nor of earth, neither mortal nor immortal, so that with freedom, honour, and pride, as maker and moulder of thyself, thou mayst fashion thyself in whatsoever form thou dost prefer.

It shall be in thy power to descend to the lower, brutish forms of life; thou shalt be able, by thy soul's judgement, to rise again to the superior orders, which are divine. (Pico della Mirandola 20)

How aspirational! All other creatures simply are what they are, what they are created to be, but we to some extent make ourselves. Pico's argument is so triumphant, so delighted with our place in the universe: "Who would not admire, this our chameleon? Or who look with greater admiration on any other being?" (21). Hamlet's lines, taken from their context, read like Pico's. How truly wonderful humans are, admired in the world, almost angels or gods.

But these lines are embedded in a speech that asserts the opposite at least as convincingly. (Because, sometimes, the opposite is also true.) Hamlet has already listed some of the greatest attributes of the world only to suggest that, in his present state, their beauty is lost on him: "this goodly frame the earth seems to me a sterile promontory, this most excellent canopy the air, look you, this brave o'erhanging firmament, this majestical roof fretted with golden fire, why, it appeareth no other thing to me than a foul and pestilent congregation of vapours" (2.2.293–8). The earth is both goodly and sterile; the "majestical roof" of "golden fire" is also "foul and pestilent." Yes, it is a statement about the shift in perception that happens in a depression – and Hamlet is characteristically self-aware in recognizing it – and it's also a statement about how the world is both glorious and blighted at the same time, depending on where or how you choose to look.

It helps me to remember two things here. First, Shakespeare was not writing just for the page or for just any theater: he was writing for a very particular and peculiar space, probably the Globe, so Hamlet's "majestical roof" is literally the painted ceiling above the stage and below the tiring house, and the "foul and pestilent congregation of vapours" then becomes yet another of the play's jabs at the early modern audience, in this case an olfactory one. This is so very *Hamlet*: transcendent optimism followed by undermining pessimism, tagged with a joke. And second, Hamlet is talking to Rosencrantz and Guildenstern, whom he knows to be untrustworthy, so his speech may be calculated to control his uncle's spies.

> **Lisa:** It reminds me of Gerard Manley Hopkins in "The Windhover": "No wonder of it: shéer plód makes plough down sillion / Shine, and blue-bleak embers, ah my dear, / Fall, gall themselves, and gash gold-vermilion" (ll.12–14). "Gash gold-vermillion" in the turned soil of a field. He seems to hold those two states in his hands at once by positing that, rather than being opposed, the broken and the beautiful are co-dependent.
>
> > **Jessica:** I love that. And reminds me of kintsugi, the Japanese art of putting broken pottery pieces back together with gold. The flaws are the beauty, and the cracks are the place to where art happens.

Hamlet ends this mini-lecture on the way of the world with this extraordinary line: "And yet, to me, what is this quintessence of dust?" (303–4). That's an exquisite summary of humanity: we are the very best ... of dirt. The *Oxford English Dictionary* includes this exact line in its definition of the figurative meaning of "quintessence" – "the purest or most perfect form or manifestation of some quality, idea, etc." (OED n. 1a) – and that certainly works. How appealing, though, is its first definition, which relies on the literal meaning of the word: "a fifth essence existing in addition to the four elements, supposed to be the substance of which the celestial bodies were composed and to be latent in all things" (n. 3a). So, humans are perhaps both the purest form of the thing and some extraordinary fifth element, beyond the four, that raises them

Lisa: This whole discussion: mind blown emoji. I love it with such a passion.

> **Jessica:** Oh yes! What makes us human is almost ineffable; in cooking terms, there is umami (the fifth taste, in addition to sweet, sour, salty, and bitter), which is translated as "essence of deliciousness" in Japanese and is more of a deepening of taste than a something we can locate in the taste receptors on the tongue.

Lisa: Endless heart emojis. Each one of these options would produce a different kind of play in production. This question would be an excellent prompt for students to use as architecture for their own *Hamlet* performances.

> **Jessica:** These combinations produce such different pathways. I am trying to figure out which version is the most critically hopeful.
>
> **Shannon:** I'm not sure, but I tend to the last as the most critically hopeful, emphasis on the "critical." That alternative recognizes both the way things are and the way they could be. But I could disagree with myself at another moment.

Jessica: This is an awesome flex. We get a glimpse of you looking at Holbein writing to us about Hamlet, bending the space-time continuum of looking, seeing, and writing. This detail transports us into an eternal present, suspended in time in order to sit with you on a bench looking at an almost 500-year-old painting that asks us to contemplate our lives as ephemeral and fleeting.

> **Lisa:** An eternal present, but also a particularity of embodied experience, in a place in a time that shapes the writing.

Jessica: Ah, Castiglione's *sprezzatura*!

---

above the rest of creation. Still, what are we the quint-essence of? Insensate dirt, lint, earth, loam, grit, grime, soil, sand, soot.

This whole passage, from the opening comments about the earth to the final ones about human existence, balances the sense that we are both wonderful AND dust. Not that we are wonderful BUT we are mere dust. Both are true, though they seem contradictions, because sometimes the opposite is also true. Hamlet is explaining his state of mind as one in which he can see both sides of this opposition, though in his affliction, he is capable of *feeling* only the unpleasant one. A disinterested audience member (a Horatio, for example) might feel both at once. There is the ultimate wicked problem: what is human life – great *or* pointless, great *but* pointless, or great *and* pointless?

To illustrate this hopeful balance of wonder and dust, I want to bring in one of my very favorite paintings: Hans Holbein's *The Ambassadors*. (I write this sitting in front of it now, in Room 4 of London's National Gallery.) If you don't know it, look it up and stare for a while. The National Gallery has it online here: www .nationalgallery.org.uk/paintings/hans-holbein-the-younger -the-ambassadors. It might not look extraordinary at first: a full-scale double portrait of two French ambassadors to the court of Henry VIII, Georges de Selve and Jean de Dinteville, one secular and one a cleric, with a two-tiered table between them covered in books, globes, and musical and scientific instruments. Each object rewards careful analysis, each leading to another branch of knowledge or idea or problem. Literary critic and professor Stephen Greenblatt calls the arrangement of objects "carefully casual," and that is just the way to put it (*Renaissance* 79). There is intention, tangled and esoteric, in the scattering of these human constructs on that Turkish tapestry. Those objects represent a kind of serious game, a puzzle with seemingly endless threads and meanings, what Greenblatt calls "the elegant play of distinguished and serious men" (85). It is a celebration of a Renaissance humanist ideal. What a piece of work is a man!

And yet.

There is a lute, but one string is broken; and a brace of flutes, but one is missing. There are little errors in the instruments and on the globes, so something feels unfinished, imperfect, off. Most strange of all in this strikingly lifelike portrait is an indistinguishable slash of paint suspended in the air between the feet of the two men. Perhaps the most famous element of the painting, it is an anamorphic skull, executed by a clever geometrical elongation of an image and visible only from the extreme right side of the painting. People in Room 4 crowd along the back wall, craning to see what appears when that slash of paint is looked at from another angle. Only from a new perspective can you see this other view of the world. (There's a metaphor in that.) So, we are immersed in two things at once here: a feat of clever technical skill and a new take on the old traditions of the *vanitas* and *memento mori* painting. In those works of art, objects – often including a skull – are arranged to suggest the vanity of worldly things and the inevitability of death.

At its simplest, the painting might read something like this: yes, when you look at it from one perspective, this human life is extraordinary, varied, high-minded, searching, even beautiful – but just shift your position and you'll see it is also fleeting, mutable, short-lived, vain. The most beautiful hymn or piece of music, the most intricate of calculations or explorations or inventions, and the most accomplished and vigorous of young men will all pass away, all fade, all wither and die. What a piece of work is a man – and sometimes the opposite is also true.

But here's why I wanted to bring in Holbein as a foil to set *Hamlet* off: I don't believe the skull gets the last word. As virtuosic an artistic performance as it is – and positioned so that we look for it *after* surveying everything else – the skull might seem to offer the strongest argument. And if that were the painting's final word, its true conclusion, the painting would indeed be a straight *memento mori*, a reminder that all is vanity and everyone dies. But two things, I think, undermine the skull's dread voice. For one thing, it doesn't exist on the same plane as the rest of the image. As Greenblatt writes in *Renaissance Self-Fashioning*, "It is only when one takes leave of this world – quite literally takes leave by walking away from the front of the canvas – that one can see the single alien object, the skull" (82). Just as the two young men and their treasures might be obscured when we move to see the skull, the skull recedes into that unintelligible slash of paint when we (inevitably) return to the front of painting. So rather than "this may seem true BUT the opposite is really the truth," the painting suggests that "this is true, AND that is true, AND when you return to your first position, the first is true again." Because human life may be wondrous *and* it is also brief *and* it is admirable *and* it will come to dust. Sometimes, the opposite is always also true.

The second thing is barely visible and is often cropped in reproductions. At the very top left corner of this massive panel, the heavy green arras is held back just enough to reveal part of a crucifix. Not at the center, not in an artistic tour de force like the anamorphic skull but simply peeking out, it is another part of that conversation: a promise that although all that lives must

Jessica: Is this where we locate critical hope: in the "and"?

> **Lisa:** It makes me think of the "yes, and" of improv, which, I think, has many things to say about teaching and learning, too.

Lisa: One more iteration suggested by art: *while* becoming dust, we continue to make beauty, or we make beauty *because* we come to dust.

> **Jessica:** The relationship between beauty, art, and (im)mortality is something Shakespeare explores in his sonnets 1–18. The poet persona initially urges the young man to procreate to carry on his beauty, but then changes course in order to assert that art is the only true vehicle for immortality. We make art because we must die.
>
> **Shannon:** When we read the sonnets, I ask my students, "So, if the young man is immortalized in this art, what's his name? What does he look like?" So, who exactly is getting the immortality treatment?

die, there is still a life hereafter. Itself an image of an image of a death, the crucifix reminds us that after life and death comes life again, all carefully and casually offered in this most serious of humanist games. Taken as a whole, the painting offers a beautiful and ultimately compassionate vision of human life, its wonder, its futility, its final hope.

So far you have indulged me as I talk about my favorite painting, so now I reward you by getting back to what I am supposed to be talking about: wonder and dust in *Hamlet*. (Maybe you've already figured out the connection.) Holbein's masterpiece, like Shakespeare's, makes us feel the wonder of the world and know at the same time its futility, all while persisting still in wonder and admiration and hope. Both works of art also do lots of other things: they are both in their way encyclopedic. Just as Holbein crams theology, cosmology, hymnody, music, textiles, geography, mathematics, tapestry, shepherd's dials, quadrants, the Virgin Mary, the crucifixion, and more into his work, in *Hamlet* we need to untangle early modern medicine, psychology, family relationships, love, flowers, friendship, university, bad poetry, reformation, cosmology, doubt, burial rites, Caesar, Alexander, purgatory, Denmark, Poland, Sweden, England, theater, acting, fencing, and, of course, pirates. Any thread we pull leads to others, and that's why it's such a maddening, engaging, shifting, and endless play.[3]

Which brings me to that most recognizable of all Shakespeare scenes, rivaled only by Juliet at the balcony or the Wyrd Sisters on the heath: Act 5, Scene 1, in the graveyard. What "to be or not to be" is to language, Hamlet holding Yorick's skull in his hands is to image. (Rare is the performance T-shirt or poster that doesn't feature it.) It is, like the famous soliloquy and like the "What a piece of work is a man" moment, deeply concerned with life, death, and the space between, but unlike them, it is uncomfortably physical, visceral, concrete, even foul-smelling. Here we have real bones, real skulls, knocked about by someone whose daily job it is to handle human remains – literally what remains when our life is over.[4] It's such a wonderful example of one of Shakespeare's most effective structural strategies. He moves us (and Hamlet) from stories, ghostly apparitions, and abstract reasonings about death, through a play enacting a death (twice), an accidental murder, and finally to the physical aftermath of dying. Poet T.S. Eliot wrote in "Whispers of Immortality" that John Webster, one of Shakespeare's gorier contemporaries, was able to "see the skull beneath the skin" (1–2). Such a great phrase! It applies equally well to Hamlet, who has been able to see living humans and imagine them dead

Lisa: This is how I am going to end every list from now on. It is my new "etc."

Shannon: "Pirates could happen to anyone."

Lisa: Imagine a production that wafted the stench into the audience so that it lingered throughout the rest of the play. Oh right, that's the Darren Nichols "rotten Denmark" version from *Slings & Arrows*.

Jessica: The early modern theatergoers would have a better frame of reference for the smell of mortality in the streets of London, with its public scaffolds and recurring plagues, not to mention the open sewers and the smell of the Thames on a hot windless day. Death lived amongst them, assaulting their five senses. I wonder if our postmodern world would be better served with *memento mori* since we've gone to such lengths to distance ourselves from death.

Lisa: This makes me think of something Amelia Sargisson (actor, playwright) said in a *Wyrd Words* podcast episode about the OED definition of love: "cannot bear to see dead." She wondered what the world would be like if we took that to heart in a general way ("Fizzy Rebels: Part 2"). I wonder: what are the consequences for Hamlet and his early modern contemporaries of this ability to imagine living humans as dead?

Jessica: Is this a morbid version of critical empathy? To imagine the Other as sans everything? To imagine oneself too in that other state?

and then in someplace after death. No wonder he is so fascinated here, first with nameless skulls that are made to stand in as examples of one profession or other, and then with the bones of someone he knew ("I knew him, Horatio") and loved (5.1.169).[5]

When we get to this scene in class, I ask my students to take a little time to contemplate their own hands, to see how they move, to mark their lineaments and follow the blue of their veins, to catalog details, colors, bumps, hairs, and lines. Now imagine that, someday, that hand will stop moving. It is inevitable, it is obvious, and yet it is a devastating thought. Thank heavens most of us cannot hang onto it for long before we mercifully forget. (The older I get, the longer that forgetting takes.) I then share with them an extraordinary little poem from the century after *Hamlet*, by eighteenth-century poet Philip Pain:

> Scarce do I pass a day but that I hear
> Some one or other's dead, and to my ear
> Methinks it is no news. But oh! did I
> Think deeply on it, what it is to die,
> My pulses all would beat, I should not be
> Drowned in this deluge of security. (71)

The poem does at least two things hinted at in *Hamlet*'s graveyard scene. For one, it insists on the difference between the *common* unthinking acceptance of death and the *particular* realization of the full meaning and force of that truth. Yes, people die every day, and that is not news. But if we think deeply on that fact, or stare at our moving hand, or see the skull of a friend from childhood, we risk drowning in the heart-pounding realization that life ends: our life will end. Of course, like my students and like Pain's speaker, most of us duck into that realization and resurface quickly; we tread water and try to ignore what lies beneath us. Someone like Hamlet lives in those waters and risks any moment going under.

The whole episode between the gravediggers, between Hamlet and Horatio, and then between Hamlet and the first gravedigger takes what was already a well-worn tradition and makes it new, so that it feels both familiar and fresh, an uncliché cliché. Like the *anamorphosis* in *The Ambassadors*, the image of a young man holding a skull is visual shorthand for the fleeting nature of life, for the vanity of worldly things, for the inescapable truth that all eventually turns to dust. It works so well on the page, but on the stage, how much more startling, especially for the first viewers, to witness a man tossing pates about in what was the first early modern scene set in a graveyard and

> Lisa: What an image! I suppose this is what every atavistic fear of the deeps is based on, in a way.
>
> Jessica: And Ophelia shows us what happens when one forgets to tread water and succumbs to the pull of the current. I wonder if she was drowned in a deluge of security?
>
> Lisa: "deluge of security." Love that.

Lisa: Consider that anatomies and displays of human bodies were very much linked to criminality in the early modern period and this "tossing about" of "respectable" bones becomes all the more shocking.

> **Jessica:** And yet there are a lot of body parts on the early modern stage. In Ford's *Tis Pity She's a Whore* (1626), Giovanni enters a room filled with people brandishing his sister's heart on the end of his dagger. Bones seem a little less messy in comparison to all the body parts flying around the early modern stage.

> **Lisa:** Severed heads and fleshiness are about death, while skulls are about mortality, which are slightly different concepts. The former is about time and the latter about eternity.

Lisa: Now, the "cannot bear to see dead" that Amelia pointed to in the definitions of love becomes so much more insistent than in the general philosophical rumination on mortality. Judith Butler notes that "one mourns when one accepts that by the loss one undergoes one will be changed possibly forever" (21), that we find ourselves "submitting to transformation … the full result of which we cannot know in advance" (21). And, weirdly, I find some shocking resonances with my definition of learning, which is also, ideally, a willing submission to the idea of one's own transformation.

> **Jessica:** The comparison of mourning and learning made me initially recoil (how could that be?) but I've returned again to the idea that in both states we must sit in a prolonged state of discomfort. To learn and to grieve are two processes that ask us to navigate interstitial spaces, cross thresholds, and undergo journeys where we cannot see the final destination.

the first use of a skull as a stage prop (Sofer 91). We, like Hamlet, are right to be both appalled and amused by the rough handling of sacred dust.

Let me point out the clever movement of the scene from a general experience of death to a particular one. As Hamlet and Horatio watch the gravediggers do their work – we assume they haven't heard the conversation about a high-born woman's suicide that starts the scene – they chat about various types such as lawyers and land sellers and gentlewomen who will all come to that same end. Everyone dies, yes, and turns to clay, but the specific skull that comes next isn't just anyone's. The gravedigger knows the identity (how, we aren't told) of one of them: Yorick, a man Hamlet had loved as a child and played with in joyful and physical ways. The scene insists that while it may be helpful to remember that everyone dies, there is something insufficient about the generalization: once we are reminded of the real human to whom this skull belonged, the scene changes. That is where the wonder comes into this scene. That skull had a tongue once and could speak – and how marvelous that is. It may be true that death is the common end of humans, and we should feel it as common, but the opposite is also true: death is common and it is also particular, and I dare say we feel it more easily in the particular.

I keep using that idea of the common and the particular, so it is worth mentioning that Gertrude is the one who first raises the dichotomy in her response to Hamlet's excessive (she thinks) mourning for his father in Act I. Now, I think she is wrong in this instance. It does not seem to me unreasonable to feel the death of a father for two months. And her question to Hamlet is of the "why can't you just get over it" variety, which we all recognize now is an unhelpful response to any kind of depression. She tells Hamlet that "tis common: all that lives must die, / passing through nature to eternity" (1.2.72–3), and when he acknowledges the truth of her statement, she responds: "if it be, / Why seems it so particular with thee?" (74–5). What a question! Of course it is particular: that is the whole point. We know pain happens to everyone. Other people suffer as we do – that fact is at the core of our ability to empathize – and if we live long enough, all of us will feel the loss of someone we love. But although it may be some small consolation that our suffering is shared, that consolation is surely unsatisfying. When we feel loss, we feel it in all its particulars, as an individual and not-to-be-replicated experience all our own. That in itself is wonderful. Individual humans matter to us in ways that we may struggle to feel about the general run of humanity. So of course the death of fathers is common, but when it is my own particular father, the truth that lots of other fathers have already died will not help me. How can the newly widowed Gertrude not see that, I wonder?[6]

With these two words, though – the common and the particular – she catches at a basic truth about human life. We can know that bad things happen in the world, that people sicken, feel loss, die, or even triumph, love, and feel joy, but having it happen to you makes it different. The common and the particular seem like opposites, but they are, to invoke Beethoven again, both true. And holding those two opposites in your mind at the same time is surely a step toward empathy, knowing that, though we can think about the general experience of life with a disinterested eye or with philosophical distance, the particular experience – even of something as small as a toothache – is different. Thinking that through is a step toward critical empathy.

And that is something that theater (and imaginative literature generally) does so well. It tends to give us not just a generalized world or experience but a person or people living through that experience: a particular within the general. *Hamlet* matters because it is about a *someone*, a particular human, one who we see is loved and admired by those around him, especially by Horatio and Ophelia. Ophelia may be torn in her loyalties and affections, but in this play, Horatio is concerned only for Hamlet's welfare; he is one who suffers all in suffering nothing, and when Hamlet lies dying, he stoically tries to join him. If critical hope means the possibility of seeing a better future, the world not just as it is but as it might be at its best, then a focus on the wonderful in human life is essentially hopeful: to train the eye to see what is glorious and grace-filled in life and in other humans. That is easier when all goes well, when your father's ghost hasn't asked you to murder your uncle, for example. To insist on seeing the world as wonderful, as full of wonder, and to wonder at it, to see it with awe, that takes an exercise of critical hope.

So, *Hamlet* gives us a world for the main character in which he will be tempted to see the futility of human life, but there is also so much in this play to excite wonder. Just think of Hamlet's reaction to the arrival of the players and to the impromptu recitation of the speech about Hecuba. Yes, the players can be useful to him in his quest for the truth about his uncle, but that doesn't completely explain how excited he is to see them. He clearly *loves* theater: the poor prince has trouble containing himself as he requests a speech of the Player and then proceeds to speak it himself. There is real joy in his

Jessica: Is it possible that Gertrude's particular loss erases Hamlet's particular grief in a moment where empathy cannot exist? Regardless, Gertrude's response to her grieving child is really toxic.

Lisa: I agree that this is toxic for Hamlet. But I feel some empathy for Gertrude since she herself is swept up in fast-paced political change. She hasn't been afforded the time to mourn, perhaps, and the health of the state depends on her ability to suture the old realm into the new. Hamlet is grief-struck, ill-served as a son, but also politically dangerous to the peace.

Lisa: I have to say that this essay has been very helpful to me, as I lost my father a few weeks ago. I hate it when villains like Claudius say helpful things, but his observation that "your father lost a father; / That father lost, lost his" (1.2.89–90) has been rolling around in my head for months. The notion of the "common" experience is a bit of a rope to follow along the treacherous path through that experience of death and love and the vulnerability that reveals our connections to each other. Poor Hamlet, who, melancholic and alone in his grief, is neither kith nor kin.

response, I think, a joy that takes him temporarily outside his own troubles, and what a lovely illustration of the power of art and theater there! That speech about Hecuba witnessing her husband's death, in the larger context of the fall of Troy, might be the epitome of the *vanitas* idea that underscores the play. This is not just about war and death; it is a reminder long before Denmark is taken over by the Norwegian Fortinbras that great kings may fall but so, eventually, do all great kingdoms. All is vanity, yes. But Hamlet's full human response to it – and to the ability of the actor to summon tears for someone he doesn't even know (the professional empathy of the actor) – is fully wonderful. It acknowledges the power of art, the power, in this case, of humans to create great and powerful and moving theater. What amazing things humans can do!

We get a sense that Hamlet himself is part of that wonder as well. Ophelia's lament for his (possibly) lost wits and lost potential makes him sounds like the perfect Renaissance man:

The courtier's, soldier's, scholar's, eye, tongue, sword,
Th'expectancy and rose of the fair state,
The glass of fashion and the mould of form,
Th'observ'd of all observers […] (3.1.151–4)

His peculiar and particular brand of greatness, even when it seems hidden or thwarted or unfulfilled, still insists on wonder: we wonder at him, his full humanity. So even when my heart breaks each time I experience his death in a good performance, when I think back on the play as a whole it is Hamlet's broad humanity, his life, that I think of, not the promised end. I think "Wasn't Hamlet wonderful," not "Isn't Hamlet really dead." So that's the balance I'm arguing for here, in a play that spends so much time forcing us to look, with Hamlet, at death and skulls and self-slaughter and the afterlife, it manages nevertheless to celebrate the opposite – not the vanity but the variety and value of human life.

I started this chapter in January of 2020 and am finishing it in June. The world has changed. But this strange and terrible moment in human history – the COVID-19 pandemic – is a good moment to be reading and watching and thinking about *Hamlet* and other great tragedies. Comic and light distractions might seem the better choice when we or the world is already suffering, but thoughtful models of hope in difficult times are surely more valuable. They give us ways of thinking past the darkness. Many of us have been forced to realize the

Lisa: I remember a professor of mine telling me about taking her pre-teen daughter to see *Hamlet*. The girl turned to her toward the end of the play and said, shocked, "Mum, does Hamlet *die*?" I envy that moment so much. I wish I could get back to the moment when I didn't know that Hamlet would die. But then again, don't we all wish a little bit to find that place in our past when we didn't know that we would die? What was the world like, to us, then? If a definition of love is "cannot bear to see dead," what was the nature of love, then? Were love and death born together?

Jessica: And yet the shocking callousness of tiny humans about death (and their almost matter-of-factness about inevitability) blows my hair back every time. The other day my six-year-old asked me very gravely, "Where do mommies go when they die?" I spent fifteen minutes talking about various kinds of spiritual beliefs about the afterlife. After he sat there patiently listening, he shrugged and said, "I thought mummies went to Egypt." And then I realized we should spend more time talking about homophones.

Lisa: Oh, wow. Ha! He's been infected by the puns!

precariousness of our lives, to feel the particularity of our mortality, our dusty destiny. But just shift our perspective, like moving around *The Ambassadors*, and how hopeful human life is. Keats and Beethoven are both surely right: we have to hold both opposing notions in our minds at the same time, because opposites may also be true. Human life comes to dust, and human life is full of wonder. To stop at the first is pure pessimism: to think just the second might be hollow, not seeing the way things are, what Jessica calls "toxic positivity." The genius of a work like *Hamlet* is to give us a narrative of critical hope, one that sees life as it is but glimpses at the same time its potential for wonder.

> **Jessica:** I love this very much. When we peer over the edge of the unknown – in our particular griefs and in the common experience of a global pandemic – there is a sense of groundlessness; we find ourselves in a radical vulnerability that is both terrifying and tender, beautiful and awe-full. And it is there – in the "and's" between places – where we find hope.

NOTES

1 And even when they are full of cruelty, selfish ambition, bad choices, and casual slaughter, I see profound empathy in the tragedies, too, though that is sometimes more demanded of the audience than modeled in the characters.

2 I heard it first in a lecture by Steven Johnson on music history, a wonderful "Discovery Day" for the London Symphony Orchestra's celebration of Beethoven's 250th birthday.

3 I believe that if Shakespeare had known the form, this would have been his Tolstoy-length novel. I teach a seminar on the play – billed as "all Hamlet, all the time" – and after thirteen concentrated weeks, we are far from exhausting it. I am sometimes tempted to focus the seminar JUST on the gravedigger's scene.

4 Did you know that some performances actually use a real skull in their performances? The Royal Shakespeare Company, for instance, has a skull donated by a pianist, Andre Tchaikowsky, for just that use. I'm not even sure how to talk about that level of literalness, of having an actor contemplate a real human skull and not a plaster prop.

5 I wonder whether the familiarity of the scene erases some of its real power. The temptation could be to stop at the recognition and lose the shock of seeing a man surprised to find he is holding the remains of someone he knew. When my younger sister died and we took her ashes to be scattered in the ocean, I was briefly overwhelmed by the rawness of that moment: that this was all that was physically left of a particular human life. And though I can quickly shift to remembering the person who was or to knowing that memories matter, not ash, it is still shocking, almost unfathomable. That it should come to this. How is that possible? What little remains. These are all Hamlet's conclusions, brought on by Yorick's skull.

6 A lack of empathy on her part? Public embarrassment that her son is behaving badly? She doesn't feel the loss, so why should others? Her grief is in proportion, maybe, so she expects proportion (or at least decorous expediency) of others.

Epilogue: The Value of the Edges

In this epilogue, we wanted to extend, mimic, and mirror the conversation we are having with Shakespeare in the book. Like Shakespeare's theater and his plays, our book experiments with conversation in its many forms, from the introduction where we speak in a unified voice to the prologue with our three individual journeys, the monologic chapters and the dialogic margins, and now a transcript of a conversation in the epilogue. In modeling messiness, we have tried to unlearn habitual practices and move away from overly polished, impervious spaces to make the processes visible. In preparation for the epilogue, we asked ourselves some guiding questions: How has this process transformed us? What are the contradictions that we continue to struggle with as we think about teaching Shakespeare for critical hope and critical empathy? But we began with the edges: What is the value of the margins?

SHANNON: The margins brought an immediacy to what we were doing. We found ourselves bringing into that whatever we happened to be reading or seeing or thinking at the particular moment. That spontaneity mirrors the kinds of conversations we have in our classrooms, as we connect the course material to the particulars of our lives or to the general state of the world. It's how a 400-year-old play can be new each time we encounter it as a community: it changes because we have.

JESSICA: I was struck by Philip Auslander's writing about the ways in which "liveness" has been mediatized or captured in digital artifacts – like recorded rock concerts or filmed theater events. How can you (re)create liveness and capture the energy of an otherwise ephemeral moment? His work made me think about our marginalia as a kind of mediatized live chat. There is a quality of dialogue, a lively banter, in the margins that differs from our chapters.

LISA: It models conversation so that it keeps the open-endedness of the text, so it's not the final word; it's part of a word. One of the things that we noted when we were writing the marginalia is that from each comment in the margins, we could have had another margin that would have launched another conversation. My ideal version of the printed book would be to have big margins so that people can write in them, modeled perhaps on interactive online experiences, where the text just keeps propagating. People could come back and rewrite the essays, over-write them, turning them around or turning them inside out. That would be awesome.

SHANNON: Lisa, I love that you imagine our marginalia engendering more marginalia and on and on! I treasure secondhand books that come with scribbles in the margins, because then I'm a witness to a conversation someone has had with the author. I'm so excited by the recent argument by Claire M.L. Bourne and Jason Scott-Warren about the Shakespeare First Folio that might actually show John Milton's marginalia in it (see Hurdle and Schuessler). What a conversation to be able to eavesdrop on! We're intentionally doing something that happens accidentally in the world.

JESSICA: We are so postmodern we have become early modern. Renaissance books were so precious that they were passed down by different readers (and libraries); readers would write in the margins, circle things, doodle, and even respond to other marginalia. I like to think about our margins as rabbit holes. They're places where an idea in the main chapter sparks a new connection or way of thinking and we go, "Oh, and did you know this?" And "Oh, I never thought about it that way!" We go down rabbit holes together and pop up at a different place. It's a dynamic way of reading, interpreting, and commenting. Speaking of rabbit holes, could we think through margins as a place on the edges (outside of the center). The Wyrd Sisters in *Macbeth* exist outside of centrally located authority. How do our margins work through that lens?

LISA: Well, I was thinking vocational margins. I am not marginalized. I'm writing from an institution where I have tenure, I'm a full professor, and I'm a white, middle-aged, middle-class woman. I have a lot of privilege as a writer. We have a lot of privilege. We've been able to work on this book for five years. We've had the resources to do it. We have MS Teams and Zoom to enable collaboration, along with the ability to travel across this huge country to work in person together. I see this whole project as an opportunity to leverage that privilege, to create some space for other people down the road. So, here's the wyrd book! Maybe that makes a little gap in the wall for someone else's, different kind of wyrd book to sneak in, and that makes room for another and then: so much wyrdness everywhere!

JESSICA: Inviting privilege into conversations about margins is really important. Context matters. You're the center of somebody else's margin, and you're on the margin of somebody else's center. And the centers and margins are not fixed, and they're not always locatable; they're changing, fluid, dynamic, and contextual. As we wrote this book, we shifted our perspective from looking to the center to looking over the edge. By shifting our perspective and peering over the edge into the possibility of the unknown, we invited others into a new center of wonder and curiosity. I think that was the most powerful shift for me in this process, which has fundamentally shaped my understanding of my place in the world.

SHANNON: I love, love, love that metaphor. And we're already moving into that second large question we want to tackle, which is *how are we transformed by this experience?* But I want to say one last thing about the margins; it struck me that, early in this process, we identified what we found joyful in our teaching and scholarship, what gave us the greatest excitement and engagement, and it was conversation. It can feel chaotic or tentative at times, but by deciding we would hang onto the joy in the messiness, we preserved rather than erased the process, the fluidity of academic conversation.

LISA: Yes, and that's one of the shifts that we hope our students will make, right? The shift from product to process, because that's the engine of inquiry. I generally get very frustrated with traditional structures of publishing and learning grounded in a finalized, authoritative presence or statement. You know, those practices that sort of crush the joy out of this work. Thinking more about process is like being on the *platea*, the edges of the stage where the clowns talk directly with the audience and comment on the pageants going on around them.

SHANNON: That's right. We wanted to create a kind of collaboration that maintained rather than melded our separate voices. The chapters – each of us taking on the same play from a different angle – do some of that work, but the marginalia goes further, preserving even our disagreements. And capturing that process models something valuable for our students; it's important to show them that even scholars who usually agree can have and hang onto significant (and sometimes not so significant) differences of opinion. Modeling evidence-based disagreements is essential to creating "wicked students," as Paul Hanstedt says – students able to embrace complexity and ambiguity.

LISA: Yes, embracing the wicked! Once I asked myself, "Well, what does a hopeful classroom look like?" I found it harder and harder to continue within the structure of assumptions about the classroom that I inherited as a student and novice teacher. That question has really asked me to be way more courageous than I think I actually am, but I keep trying, because it has gotten to a point where I can't talk the talk and not walk the walk anymore. I can live no more by thinking, as Orlando says.

JESSICA: The "talking the talk and then walking the walk" conundrum poses a fundamental challenge: how do you articulate a pedagogical philosophy and then anchor it in practice? Are you *doing* what you *say* you are doing? But even before that, I had to able to speak and write in my voice, in a voice that *sounds like me* (messy, complex, silly, and playful), while also navigating power and its relationship to authority (disciplinary expertise and "mastery"). This has been the most revolutionary for me. To be able to write something where I'm not pretending to sound "like" a Shakespearean scholar or a social scientist, where a close friend can read this and say, "I can *hear* your voice when I read this," fundamentally changed how I understand my role as a scholar and teacher – and a public intellectual.

SHANNON: I love everything you just said. We joked early on that we would take the Nova Scotia College of Art and Design's motto, which is "we will do no more boring art," and change it for ourselves, so ours would be "we will do no more boring scholarship." I think our response, though that's a wonderful rallying cry, is more complicated. It's that we will do no more scholarship that that doesn't sound like us.

JESSICA: I suspect for many years I sounded more like the Shakespearean scholars who trained me than my self. I had to (re)learn how to authentically show up as an "undivided self," as Parker Palmer talks about in *The Courage to Teach*. Can we, as humans, as academics, show up in a vulnerable space and invite all of our experiences, perceptions, and selves into the conversation? Can we show up in an authentic way? How do we model that for ourselves and others, even though it takes tremendous courage and vulnerability? Can you step away from the podium, sit in a circle, sound like yourself, while also making space for others to sound like themselves?

SHANNON: You're so right about the vulnerability it takes to "sound like yourself." I know how prone I am to mimicry, which is especially a temptation for me when I work with you two, because I love your voices so much. We referred many times in our chapters to Stephen Greenblatt's idea of Renaissance "self-fashioning," and that's what it feels like I've been doing over this last three or five years: not so much uncovering a hidden voice, but working to construct one that is wholehearted and true to my principles.

JESSICA: I have to relearn and reinforce the value of the vulnerable act of showing up, of being authentic – even as I worry I'm "too much" or "too noisy" or "too loud" or "too [insert adjective]." I worry about that all the time. Even though I have to relearn those acts of vulnerability, there is some progress in the transformative journey because once you see it, you can't unsee it. I'm irrevocably changed through that process.

LISA: You know, life has intervened in emphatic kinds of ways in this process, and because the process has been so iterative and collaborative, it has been slow because messy things tend to be slow and inefficient, which I think is interesting in and of itself.

JESSICA: Over the last five years, we had so many personal as well as professional transformations. There was never a moment where the three of us were free from health crises, caregiving, parenting, or COVID. From the personal to the global pressures, the stars never aligned with a perfect moment where we could sit down and write this book uninterrupted. We wrote this book in the margins of our days, in grief, joy, childcare, menopause, cancer, death – in all of those spaces. It would have been really easy for us to say, "I can't do this: I'm sorry but X in personal life or Y in my professional life made this untenable." Instead, we harnessed X and Y by naming, claiming, and aiming these experiences to make us better as thinkers, as scholars, as teachers, as parents, as partners, as friends, as citizens of this world. Life is full of messy complexity; and in those spaces of the messiness and hardness is where beauty is found.

SHANNON: That's lovely.

LISA: I wonder if we could talk about limitations, or things that we have really had to push hard up against, things we'd do differently. What kinds of complicities or complications have been revealed in this process? "I fail a lot and I try hard" is what I have scribbled in the margins of many nightstand books about pedagogy right now. For instance, I have struggled in our discussions about hope and empathy, and the willingness to hear someone else, to make a hospitable space for difference, when the world around me is so fractious and polarized and in some cases cruel. I've found myself deeply tested in my capacity for tolerance and listening.

SHANNON: Yes, and there's the pesky gap between our aspirational values and the practice of those values. I've been nervous to tell people I'm working on a book on hope and empathy, because then I better bloody well be hopeful and empathetic. This past pandemic year, for all kinds of particular and global reasons, tested my hope especially, but the very fact that we were having this academic conversation about critical hope helped. Lisa always reminds us that hope is a verb, and I think it's also a muscle: we need to work it in easy times so that it can do the heavy lifting when things get hard.

JESSICA: We finished the chapters right before COVID hit. We had, I imagined, completed the bulk of the work. We had theorized critical hope, critical empathy, and critical love. We found our philosophical lenses and literary guides. I thought we were awfully clever. And then in March 2020, schools shut down, universities shut down, and – in a strange twist of fate – my husband was diagnosed with cancer. Almost overnight I had small children at home, my partner was facing a significant health crisis, and we had to grapple with a global pandemic to boot. I imagined the universe testing me: can I live these theoretical principles in extreme circumstances? On the darkest days, I would read our book, which became my road map in the midst of a world that didn't make any sense. If I hadn't had this book, these design principles, and my wyrdos, I would not have been able to deploy hope in navigating the universal and particular complexities over the past few years.

SHANNON: Exactly. If we hadn't been thinking about Shakespeare and hope and empathy over this last year, I'm convinced I would have struggled even more than

I did, because we were actively engaged in conversations about ways those plays (and our favorite theorists like Freire, hooks, and Palmer) offer a framework for understanding hope and empathy. It wasn't easy – the pandemic has tested so many of us in so many ways – but Shakespeare is an excellent though challenging teacher.

LISA: I keep thinking about something that Shelby Richardson, artistic director of Method Contemporary Dance Society, says in our *Wyrd Words* podcast. In talking about the difficulty of starting a dance company in a pandemic, she notes that the negotiation of limitations *is the work*. In that light, I can see that the upheavals of the past years weren't *distractions* from the work, they *were* the work. So, we asked what it would be like to live and teach as though hope is a verb, and then, to use Shelby's words, the universe answered.

SHANNON: Right, and that makes me think of the phrase we keep coming back to from Parker Palmer: when your heart breaks, you can allow it either to break apart or to break open.

JESSICA: Parker Palmer's distinction between broken apart and broken open was almost a daily mantra for me. There is a moment where you have a choice and you can break apart: you can get hard, you can get impervious, you can get mad, you can get rigid. But to break open is to take that leap of faith and to say that I'm going to be vulnerable in this openness, even as it's easier for me to cut someone out, cancel-culture style, put up walls, and get the f**k outta there. I think that Shannon's invitation and Lisa's hospitality get to the heart of the invitation to messiness.

SHANNON: And I keep being reminded of what Lisa was saying a little while ago about the importance of intervention. We three can allow ourselves to be vulnerable and open in our work with some security: we are all full professors in fairly stable institutions, so if we're making this an intervention, an invitation for our junior colleagues or our students to do the same, then we had better show up to support them, because for so many people, vulnerable is dangerous.

JESSICA: I think that's really important to understand when hope is courageous and when it's dangerous: our job is not just to be there for students and junior colleagues but for us to tackle the systems within the structures and the policies, the perceptions, and the mindsets. As Lisa always says, "are you gonna blame the salmon or you gonna blame the dam?" That concept is elegant in its simplicity. The formulation asks us to exercise critical empathy: the salmon are merely using the pathways and the structures that have been created for them. By extension, the dams are the structural spaces that have created the conditions where they gather. You can either blame the salmon or you can blame the dam. OR you have to dismantle the dam and/or build some salmon ladders. We've been banging our heads up against various dams for many years, individually and collectively. But we have also learned how to build ladders as we strive to dismantle those big structures.

LISA: When you break something open, something unexpected emerges. Maybe critical hope is about being able to respond generatively to whatever is born.

Thank you, wyrdos. Thank you, reader.

By the pricking of my thumbs,
Something wicked this way comes.
Open, locks,
Whoever knocks! (Macbeth)

Works Cited

Ahmad, Jibran, and Asif Shahzad. "Nobel Winner Malala Visits Hometown in Pakistan for First Time Since Shooting." *Reuters*, 31 March 2018, www.reuters.com/article/us-pakistan-malala-swat/nobel-winner-malala-visits-hometown-in-pakistan-for-first-time-since-shooting-idUSKBN1H7052?il=0. Accessed June 2020.

Albright, Ann Cooper. "Tracing the Past: Writing History Through the Body." *The Routledge Dance Studies Reader*. 2nd ed., edited by Alexandra Carter and Janet O'Shea, New York, Routledge, 2010, pp. 101–10.

Aristotle. *Aristotle's Metaphysics Lambda*. Oxford, Oxford UP, 2019.

———. *Nicomachean Ethics*. Indianapolis, Hackett Publishing, 2014.

———. *Poetics*. Translated by George Whalley, Montreal, McGill-Queen's UP, 1997.

Armstrong, Katherine, and Graham Atkin. *Studying Shakespeare: A Practical Introduction*. London, Routledge, 1998.

Arnold, Matthew. "The Function of Criticism at the Present Time." *The Norton Anthology of Theory and Criticism*. 2nd ed., edited by Vincent B. Leitch et al., New York, W. W. Norton & Company, 2010, pp. 695–713.

Auden, W. H. "Under Which Lyre." *Collected Poems,* edited by Edward Mendelson, New York, Random House, 1976, p. 335.

Auslander, Philip. *Liveness: Performance in a Mediatized Culture*. Hove, Psychology Press, 1999.

Austin, J. L. *How to Do Things with Words*. Cambridge, Harvard UP, 1975.

"Bad Quarto of *Hamlet*, 1603, Also Known As the First Quarto of *Hamlet*." *British Library,* www.bl.uk/collection-items/bad-quarto-of-hamlet-1603. Accessed June 2020.

Barendregt, Kelsey. "Reading Journal: *Hamlet*." ENGL 499: Independent Study, Renaissance Literature (*Hamlet* and Pedagogy), University of Northern British Columbia, 2019.

Barton, John. "Using the Verse." *Playing Shakespeare*. Royal Shakespeare Company, 1984.

Beilfuss, Rodrigo. "Interview with Rodrigo Beilfuss, Part 2: Playing Hamlet." *Wyrd Words* [podcast], Season 1, Episode 5, 2021, open.spotify.com/episode/0J0aylunN0k8m1QpuLlInQ.

Benedict, Saint, Abbot of Monte Cassino. *The Rule of St. Benedict*. Translated by Anthony C. Meisel and M. L. del Mastro, New York, Image Books, 1975.

Bevington, David. *This Wide and Universal Theatre: Shakespeare in Performance, Then and Now*. Chicago, University of Chicago Press, 2009.

Bible: King James Version with the Apocrypha, edited by David Norton. London, Penguin Classics, 2006.

Boerhaave, Herman. *Boerhaave's Orations*. Leiden, Brill Archive, 1983.

Bogart, Anne, et al. *Shakespeare, Language and the Stage: The Fifth Wall Only*, edited by Lynette Hunter and Peter Lichtenfels, Andover, Cengage Learning EMEA, 2005, pp. 138–60.

Bogdanov, Michael. "Bogdanov: The Henrys." *The English Shakespeare Company: The Story of "The War of the Roses" 1986–1989*. Shepherd's Bush, Nick Hern Books, 1990. p. 48.

Booth, Stephen. "On the Value of *Hamlet*." *Reinterpretations of Elizabethan Drama: Selected Papers from the English Institute*, edited by Norman Rabkin, New York, Columbia UP, 1969, pp. 137–76.

Booth, Wayne C. *The Rhetoric of RHETORIC: The Quest of Effective Communication*. Hoboken, John Wiley & Sons, 2009.

Booty, John E. *The Book of Common Prayer, 1559: The Elizabethan Prayer Book*. Charlottesville, University of Virginia Press, 2005.

Branagh, Kenneth, director. *Henry V*. BBC, 1989.

——. *A Midwinter's Tale (In the Bleak Midwinter)*. Castle Rock Entertainment, 1995.

Brownlee, Jo, et al. "The First-Year University Experience: Using Personal Epistemology to Understand Effective Learning and Teaching in Higher Education." *Higher Education,* vol. 58, no. 5, 2009, pp. 599–618.

Butler, Judith. *Precarious Life: The Powers of Mourning and Violence*. New York, Verso Books, 2006.

Caputo, John D. *More Radical Hermeneutics: On Not Knowing Who We Are*. Bloomington, Indiana UP, 2000.

——. *On Religion*. Hove, Psychology Press, 2001.

——. *The Insistence of God: A Theology of Perhaps*. Bloomington, Indiana UP, 2013.

——. *Truth: Philosophy in Transit*. London, Penguin Books, 2013.

Carroll, Lewis. *Alice's Adventures in Wonderland and Through the Looking-Glass*. Oxford, Oxford UP, 2009.

Castiglione, Baldassare. "From Castiglione's *The Courtier*." *The Norton Anthology of English Literature*. 10th ed., vol. B, edited by Stephen Greenblatt, New York, W. W. Norton & Company, 2012, pp. 176–92.

Caxton, William. Preface. *Le Morte d'Arthur, Volume 1*, by Sir Thomas Malory, edited by Janet Cowen, London, Penguin Classics, 1970, pp. 3–8.

Chodron, Pema. *When Things Fall Apart: Heart Advice for Difficult Times*. Boulder, Shambhala Publications, 2016.

Coleridge, Samuel Taylor. *Lectures 1808–1819: On Literature, Volume 2*. London, Routledge & Kegan Paul, 1987.

——. "Table Talk." *Coleridge's Writings on Shakespeare*. New York, Capricorn, 1959.

Collier, John Payne. *The History of English Dramatic Poetry to the Time of Shakespeare and Annals of the Stage to the Restoration. A New Edition, Volume 2*. London, George Bell and Sons, 1879.

Congreve, William. *The Way of the World*. Sligo, HardPress Publishing, 2006.

Craig, Charmaine. "The Problem with Only Liking Things We Find Relatable." *PBS*, 25 August 2017, www.pbs.org/newshour/show/problem-liking-things-find-relatable. Accessed 21 January 2020.

Cunningham, J. V. *The Collected Essays of J. V. Cunningham*. Chicago, Swallow Press, 1976.

Cunningham, Sally. "*King Lear*, Critically Beloved: The Ontological Guidance of Critical Love," ENG112: English Literary Tradition, the Middle Ages and the Renaissance, Bishop's University, 28 November 2017.

Dakers, John R. "The Hegemonic Behaviorist Cycle." *International Journal of Technology and Design Education*, vol. 15, no. 2, 2005, p. 113.

Dakin, Mary Ellen. *Reading Shakespeare with Young Adults*. Urbana, National Council of Teachers, 2009.

Davidson, Cathy N. *The New Education: How to Revolutionize the University to Prepare Students for a World in Flux*. New York, Basic Books, 2017.

Davies, Anthony, and Stanley Wells. *Shakespeare and the Moving Image: The Plays on Film and Television*. Cambridge UK, Cambridge UP, 1994.

Dekker, Thomas, and Thomas Middleton. *The Roaring Girl*, edited by Kelly Stage, Peterborough, Broadview Press, 2019.

Dever, Conor. Personal interview. January 2019.

Dickson, Lisa, Shannon Murray, and Jessica Riddell. *The Wyrd House*, 2021, www.thewyrdhouse.com/.

"disappoint, v." *Oxford English Dictionary Online*, December 2017, www.oed.com/view/Entry /53508?rskey=ArbIlw&result=1#eid. Accessed 21 January 2020.

Dweck, Carol S. *Mindset: The New Psychology of Success*. New York, Penguin Random House, 2006.

Eagleton, Terry. *William Shakespeare*. Malden, Blackwell Publishing, 1986.

Egan, Gabriel. *Shakespeare and Ecocritical Theory*. London, Bloomsbury, 2015.

Eliot, T. S. "Whispers of Immortality." *Poems*. New York, A. A. Knopf, 1920.

Elyot, Thomas. *The Book of the Governor*, edited by Henry Herbert Stephen Croft, Whitefish, Kessinger Publishing, 2010.

Ericsson, K. Anders. *Peak: How All of Us Can Achieve Extraordinary Things*. New York, Penguin Random House, 2017.

Fitzgerald, F. Scott. "The Crack-Up." *Esquire*, 6 October 2017, www.esquire.com/lifestyle/a4310 /the-crack-up/. Accessed 21 January 2020.

Foucault, Michel. *The Use of Pleasure, Volume 2 of the History of Sexuality*. Translated by Robert Hurley, New York, Vintage Books, 1990.

Freire, Paulo. *Pedagogy of Hope: Reliving Pedagogy of the Oppressed*. London, Bloomsbury Academic, 2014.

———. *The Pedagogy of the Oppressed*. 30th Anniversary Edition. Translated by Myra Borgsman Ramos, New York, Continuum, 2010.

Gaventa, Jonathan. *Power after Lukes: An Overview of Theories of Power Since Lukes and Their Application to Development*. Brighton, Participation Group Institute of Development Studies, 2003.

Gibson, Rex. *Teaching Shakespeare: A Handbook for Teachers*. Cambridge UK, Cambridge UP, 1998.

Gonzalez, Emma. "Emma Gonzalez's Powerful March for Our Lives Speech in Full." *YouTube*, uploaded by *Guardian News*, 24 March 2018, www.youtube.com/watch?v=u46HzTGVQhg. Accessed 17 January 2019

Goodman, Ruth. "Excerpt – 'How to Behave Badly in Elizabethan England' by Ruth Goodman." *Folger Shakespeare Library*, 18 December 2018, shakespeareandbeyond.folger.edu/2018/12 /18/excerpt-how-to-behave-badly-in-elizabethan-england-by-ruth-goodman/. Accessed 17 January 2019.

Gosson, Stephen. "Plays Confuted in Five Actions." *Shakespeare's Theater: A Sourcebook*, edited by Tanya Pollard, Oxford, Blackwell Publishing, 2004, pp. 85–114.

———. *The School of Abuse*. Southport, Franklin Classics Trade Press, 2018.

Gorgias. *The Encomium of Helen*. Translated by Brian R. Donovan. 1999, faculty.bemidjistate .edu/bdonovan/helen.html. Accessed 4 June 2021.

Goudsward, Solomon. "Final Exam Essay: What Did You Learn This Semester?" ENGL 280: Shakespeare, University of Northern British Columbia, 2019.

Grant, Adam. *Think Again: The Power of Knowing What You Don't Know.* New York, Viking Books, 2021.

Greenblatt, Stephen. *Renaissance Self-Fashioning: From More to Shakespeare.* Chicago, University of Chicago Press, 2012.

———. *Tyrant: Shakespeare on Politics.* London, W. W. Norton & Company, 2018.

Gurney, Kyra. "Last Fall, They Debated Gun Control in Class. Now, They Debate Lawmakers on TV." *Miami Herald*, 25 February 2018, www.miamiherald.com/news/local/education /article201678544.html. Accessed 17 January 2019.

Hamilton: An American Musical. Performances by Lin-Manuel Miranda, Leslie Odom Jr., Phillipa Soo, and Jonathan Groff, Atlantic Records, 2015.

Hamlet. Directed by Nicholas Hytner, performances by Major Rory Kinnear, Patrick Malahide, and Clare Higgins, September 2010–January 2011, National Theatre, London.

"*Hamlet*: An Introduction to This Text." *The Folger Shakespeare*, shakespeare.folger.edu /shakespeares-works/hamlet/an-introduction-to-this-text/. Accessed June 2020.

"*Hamlet* (Quarto 1, 1603)." *Internet Shakespeare*, internetshakespeare.uvic.ca/doc/Ham_Q1 /complete/index.html. Accessed June 2020.

"*Hamlet*: The Facts." *Hedgerow Theatre*, hedgerowtheatre.org/hamlet-the-facts/. Accessed June 2020.

Hanstedt, Paul. *Creating Wicked Students: Designing Courses for a Wicked World.* Sterling, Stylus Publishing, 2018.

Harvey. Directed by Henry Koster, performances by James Stewart and Josephine Hull, Universal Pictures, 1950.

Hazlitt, William. *The Miscellaneous Works of William Hazlitt, Volume 2.* Philadelphia, Henry Carey Baird, 1854.

Henbest, Rose. Personal interview. November 2019.

"Henry V." *The Hollow Crown*, directed by Thea Sharrock, performances by Tom Hiddleston, Julie Walters, and Geraldine Chaplin, BBC Two, 2012.

Hill, Janet. "My dear Jess." Received by Jessica Riddell. 15 October 2017.

Holbein, Hans. *The Ambassadors.* The National Gallery, London, 1533.

Holinshed, Raphael. *Holinshed's Chronicles of England, Scotland, and Ireland.* London, Routledge, 2013.

hooks, bell. *Teaching Community: A Pedagogy of Hope.* London, Routledge, 2003.

Hopkins, Gerard Manley. "The Windhover." *Gerard Manley Hopkins: The Major Works*, edited by Catherine Philipps, Oxford, Oxford UP, 2009, p. 132.

Hurdle, Jon, and Jennifer Schuessler. "Milton's Shakespeare Was Just a Trans-Atlantic Tweet Away." *New York Times*, 19 September 2019, https://www.nytimes.com/2019/09/19/theater/milton -shakespeare-notes-first-folio.html. Accessed 18 July 2022.

Jacobs, Dale. "What's Hope Got to Do with It? Theorizing Hope in Education." *JAC: A Journal of Composition Theory*, vol. 15, no. 4, 2005, pp. 783–802.

James, William. *Varieties of Religious Experience: A Study in Human Nature.* Hove, Psychology Press, 2002.

Jardine, David W. "An Open Letter After a Tough Class and An Afterword to Readers." *Counterpoints,* vol. 452, 2014, pp. 185–9.

Jardine, David W., and Jackie Seidel. "We Are Here, We Are Here." *Counterpoints,* vol. 452, 2014, pp. 1–6.

Johnson, Samuel. *Notes to Shakespeare, Volume III: The Tragedies*, edited by Arthur Sherbo. Charleston, BiblioBazaar, 2007.

Johnson, Steven. "Discovery Day: Beethoven." LSO Discovery Day Series, 19 January 2020, St. Luke's Church, London, UK. Lecture.

Jonson, Ben. *Timber, or Discoveries*, edited by Ralph Spence Walker, Westport, Greenwood Press, 1976.

Joseph, Miriam. *Shakespeare's Use of the Arts of Language*. Philadelphia, Paul Dry Books, 2008.

Keats, John. *Selected Letters*. Oxford, Oxford UP, 2002.

King, Martin Luther, Jr. "I See the Promised Land." *A Testament of Hope: Essential Writings and Speeches of Martin Luther King Jr.*, edited by James M. Washington, New York, HarperCollins, 1991, pp. 268–78.

King, Ros. "Reading Beyond Words: Sound and Gesture in *The Winter's Tale*." *Pedagogy: Critical Approaches to Teaching Literature, Language, Composition, and Culture*, vol. 7, no. 3, 2007, pp. 385–400.

Knight, Will. "Google and Others Are Building AI Systems That Doubt Themselves." *MIT Technology Review*, 9 January 2018, www.technologyreview.com/2018/01/09/146337/google-and -others-are-building-ai-systems-that-doubt-themselves/. Accessed 21 January 2018.

Lavater, Ludwig. *Of Ghosts and Spirits Walking by Night*, edited by May Yardley and J. Dover Wilson, Whitefish, Kessinger Publishing, 2003.

Lewis, C. S. *Selected Literary Essays*. New York, HarperCollins, 2013.

Lewis, John. "We Are the Beloved Community." Interview by Krista Tippett. *On Being*, 5 July 2016, onbeing.org/programs/beloved-community-john-lewis-2. Accessed 21 January 2020.

Lucia, Brent. "A Hybrid Discourse: Confucius Meets Booth in the Rhetorical Borderlands." *Enculturation*, 26 January 2017, enculturation.net/a-hybrid-discourse. Accessed 21 January 2018.

MacDonald, Ann-Marie. *Goodnight Desdemona (Good Morning Juliet)*. Toronto, Vintage Canada, 1998.

Machiavelli, Niccolo. *The Prince*. Translated by Rufus Goodwin, Dallas, Dante UP, 2014.

"Madness in Great Ones." *Slings & Arrows*, written by Susan Coyne, Bob Martin, and Mark McKinney, directed by Peter Wellington, TMN, 2003.

Maguire, Laurie E. *Studying Shakespeare: A Guide to the Plays*. Malden, Blackwell Publishing, 2004.

McDonald, Joseph. "The Emergence of the Teachers' Voice: Implications for the New Reform." *Harvard Educational Review*, vol. 89, no. 4, 1988, pp. 482–3.

McKay, Brett, and Kate McKay. "Manvotional: We Few, We Happy Few, We Band of Brothers." *Art of Manliness*, 13 September 2008, www.artofmanliness.com/articles/manvotional-we-few-we-happy -few-we-band-of-brothers/. Accessed 17 January 2020.

Milton, John. "Lycidas." *The Norton Anthology of English Literature*. 10th ed., vol. B, edited by Stephen Greenblatt, New York, W. W. Norton & Company, 2012, pp. 1468–73.

———. *Of Education. Bartleby*, www.bartleby.com/3/4/1.html. Accessed June 2021.

———. *Paradise Lost*. Norton Critical Edition, edited by Gordon Teskey, New York, W. W. Norton & Company, 2004.

"mock, n." *Oxford English Dictionary Online*, December 2019, www.oed.com/view/Entry/120525 ?result=1&rskey=LKnKEs&. Accessed 21 January 2020.

"mock, v." *Oxford English Dictionary Online*, December 2019, www.oed.com/view/Entry/120530 ?rskey=LKnKEs&result=8#eid. Accessed 21 January 2020.

Monchinski, Tony. *Education in Hope: Critical Pedagogies and the Ethics of Care*. Berne, Peter Lang, 2010.

"Nothing." "Rabbit." Concordance of Shakespeare's complete works. *Open Source Shakespeare*, www .opensourceshakespeare.org/concordance/. Accessed 5 December 2017.

Nixon, Richard. "Address of Senator Nixon to the American People: The 'Checkers Speech.'" *The American Presidency Project*, www.presidency.ucsb.edu/node/270215. Accessed 17 January 2019.

Olivier, Laurence, director. *Hamlet*. Two Cities Films, 1948.

———. *Henry V (The Chronicle History of King Henry the Fift with His Battell Fought at Agincourt in France)*. Two Cities Films, 1944.

Onion, Rebecca. "The Awful Emptiness of 'Relatable.'" *Slate Magazine*, 11 April 2014, www.slate
.com/blogs/lexicon_valley/2014/04/11/relatable_the_adjective_is_everywhere_in_high_scchool
_and_college_discussions.html. Accessed 17 January 2020.

Palmer, Parker J. "Naropa University Presents Parker Palmer & 'Living from Inside Out.'" *YouTube*,
uploaded by Naropa University, 4 June 2014, www.youtube.com/watch?v=OWRDKNXPq3Y.

———. *The Courage to Teach: Exploring the Inner Landscape of a Teacher's Life*. San Francisco,
Jossey-Bass, 2007.

———. "The Soul of Depression." Interview by Krista Tippett. *On Being*, 17 January 2003, onbeing
.org/programs/the-soul-in-depression/. Accessed June 2021.

Pain, Philip. "Meditation 8." *Quest for Reality*, edited by Yvor Winters and Kenneth Fields, Chicago,
Swallow Press, 1969, p. 71.

Pico della Mirandola, Giovanni. *Oration on the Dignity of Man*, edited by Sebastian Michael, based
on the translation by Charles Glenn Wallis, Optimist Creations, 2018.

Pizzolato, Jane Elizabeth. "Meaning Making Inside and Outside the Academic Arena: Investigating
the Contextuality of Epistemological Development in College Students." *Journal of General
Education*, vol. 56, no. 3/4, 2008, pp. 228–51.

Popova, Maria. "Hope, Cynicism, and the Stories We Tell Ourselves." *Brain Pickings*,
www.brainpickings.org/2015/02/09/hope-cynicism/. Accessed 17 June 2018.

Prynne, William. *Histriomastix*. London, Forgotten Books, 2017.

Puttenham, George. *The Art of English Poesy: A Critical Edition*. Ithaca, Cornell UP, 2016.

"quintessence, n." *Oxford English Dictionary Online*, December 2019, www.oed.com
/viewdictionaryentry/Entry/156701?rskey=GetxcI&result=1#eid. Accessed 21 January 2020.

Quintilian. *Institutio Oratoria, Volume 1*. Cambridge, Harvard UP, 1989.

R.E.M. "Losing My Religion." *Out of Time*, 1993.

Revelatori. *Facebook*, 1 October 2020, www.facebook.com/revelatori/photos/pcb.275845416440151
2/2758454037734858/. Accessed June 2021.

Richardson, Shelby. "The World Answered Me: Conversation with Shelby Richardson,
Part 1." *Wyrd Words* [podcast], Season 2, Episode 3, 2021, open.spotify.com/episode
/2nIRlUprY3A79SipGI7kVh.

Riddell, Jessica. "Helping Our Students to Develop Rhetorical Literacy." *University Affairs*,
7 January 2020, www.universityaffairs.ca/opinion/adventures-in-academe/the-power-of
-rhetoric/. Accessed June 2020.

Rohde, Mike. *The Sketchnote Handbook*. Berkeley, Peachpit Press, 2013.

Said, Edward W. *Orientalism*. New York, Vintage Books, 1979.

———. *Representations of the Intellectual: The 1993 Reith Lectures*. New York, Vintage Books, 1994.

Sargisson, Amelia. "Fizzy Rebels: Conversation with Amelia Sargisson, Part 1." *Wyrd Words*
[podcast], Season 2, Episode 9, 2021, open.spotify.com/episode/5sWzUHqkgwK9l7lIv411yD.

———. "Fizzy Rebels: Conversation with Amelia Sargisson, Part 2." *Wyrd Words* [podcast], Season
2, Episode 10, 2021, open.spotify.com/episode/1OTAyTrCSVy6OpKELJaU35.

Scarry, Elaine. *On Beauty and Being Just*. Princeton, Princeton UP, 1999.

Schulz, Kathryn. "The Rabbit-Hole Rabbit Hole." *New Yorker*, 5 June 2015, www.newyorker.com
/culture/cultural-comment/the-rabbit-hole-rabbit-hole. Accessed 16 November 2017.

Shakespeare, William. *As You Like It*, edited by Alan Brissenden, Oxford, Oxford UP, 2008.

———. *Hamlet*, edited by Roma Gill, Oxford, Oxford UP, 2007.

———. *Henry V*, edited by Gary Taylor, Oxford, Oxford UP, 2008.

———. *Julius Caesar*, edited by Arthur Humphreys, Oxford, Oxford UP, 2009.

———. *King Lear*, edited by Roma Gill, Oxford, Oxford UP, 2012.

———. *Othello*, edited by Michael Neill, Oxford, Oxford UP, 2008.

———. *Romeo and Juliet*, edited by Jill L. Levenson, Oxford, Oxford UP, 2008.

———. *The Merry Wives of Windsor*, edited by T. W. Craik, Oxford, Oxford UP, 2008.

———. *Twelfth Night*, edited by Roger Warren and Stanley Wells, Oxford, Oxford UP, 2008.

Shields, Erin. "Stories in the Water: Conversation with Erin Shields, Part 1" *Wyrd Words* [podcast], Season 2, Episode 7, 2021, open.spotify.com/episode/2QL2HNxnKUDIvrQXO3KcLp.

Shor, Ira. *When Students Have Power: Negotiating Authority in a Critical Pedagogy*. Chicago, University of Chicago Press, 1992.

Sidney, Philip. "Defense of Poesy." *Norton Anthology of English Literature*. 10th ed., vol. B, edited by Stephen Greenblatt, New York, W. W. Norton & Company, 2012, pp. 547–85.

Sofer, Andrew. *The Stage Life of Props*. Ann Arbor, University of Michigan Press, 2003.

Solnit, Rebecca. *Hope in the Dark: Untold Histories, Wild Possibilities*. 3rd ed., Chicago, Haymarket Books, 2016.

Something Wicked This Way Comes. Directed by Jack Clayton, Disney, 1983.

Stetka, Bret. "Steven Pinker: This Is History's Most Peaceful Time – New Study: 'Not So Fast.'" *Scientific American*, 9 November 2017, www.scientificamerican.com/article/steven-pinker-this-is-historys-most-peaceful-time-new-study-not-so-fast/. Accessed June 2021.

Stevens, Athena. "Directing Theatre in the 21st Century." Women and Power Festival. Shakespeare's Globe Theatre, 14 May 2019, London, UK. Lecture.

Stoppard, Tom. *Rosencrantz & Guildenstern Are Dead: A Play in Three Acts*. New York, Samuel French Inc., 1967.

Stubbes, Philip. *Phillip Stubbes's Anatomy of the Abuses in England in Shakspere's Youth: Collated with Other Editions in 1583, 1585, and 1595, Volume 1*. London, Trübner, 1877.

"Svante Thunberg." *Dramaten*, www.dramaten.se/medverkande/rollboken/Person/5200. Accessed June 2020.

Talking Heads. "Heaven." *Stop Making Sense*, 1984.

Tan, Shaun. *The Bird King: An Artist's Notebook*. New York, Scholastic Inc., 2010.

Thompson, Ayanna, and Laura Turchi. *Teaching Shakespeare with Purpose: A Student-Centred Approach*. New York, Bloomsbury, 2016.

Thunberg, Greta. "Greta Thunberg to World Leaders: 'How Dare You? You Have Stolen My Dreams and My Childhood.'" *YouTube*, uploaded by Guardian News, 23 September 2019, www.youtube.com/watch?v=TMrtLsQbaok.

U2. "Peace on Earth." *All That You Can't Leave Behind*, 2000.

Uyehara, Mari. "The Sliming of David Hogg and Emma Gonzalez." *GQ*, 30 March 2018, www.gq.com/story/the-sliming-of-david-hogg-and-emma-gonzalez. Accessed June 2020.

Wain, Kenneth. "Chapter Six: The Politics of Hope." *Counterpoints*, vol. 260, 2004, pp. 229–75.

Water Docs editors. "She Walked the Talk: Farewell to Water Warrior Grandmother Josephine Mandamin." *Water Docs*, 22 February 2019, www.waterdocs.ca/news/2019/2/22/she-walked-the-talk-farewell-to-water-warrior-grandmother-josephine-mandamin. Accessed June 2020.

Weiner, Gail. "Ultra-Independence Is a Trauma Response." *Gail Weiner*, 14 August 2020, www.gailweiner.com/post/ultra-independence-is-a-trauma-response. Accessed June 2021.

"What People Are Still Willing to Pay For." *Forbes*, 15 January 2009, www.forbes.com/2009/01/15/self-help-industry-ent-sales-cx_ml_0115selfhelp.html#1a635b026758. Accessed 17 January 2019.

Worthen, W. B. *Shakespeare and the Force of Modern Performance*. Cambridge UK, Cambridge UP, 2002.

Young, Iris Marion. "Chapter II. Asymmetrical Reciprocity: On Moral Respect, Wonder, and Enlarged Thought." *Intersecting Voices: Dilemmas of Gender, Political Philosophy, and Policy*, Princeton, Princeton UP, 1997.

Zolli, Andrew. "Forget Sustainability, It's About Resilience." *New York Times*, 2 November 2012, www.nytimes.com/2012/11/03/opinion/forget-sustainability-its-about-resilience.html. Accessed June 2020.

Index